PRAISE FOR *Nuestra América*

"Lomnitz...adds to the burgeoning literature on immigration, ethnic identity, and racial hatred with this introspective memoir tracing the odyssey of his Ashkenazi Jewish ancestors...poignant."

—*Foreign Affairs*

"[Lomnitz] takes his rich family history and builds a narrative of universal significance...There is no end of intriguing anecdotes in these pages...A masterpiece of historical and personal investigation."

—*Kirkus Reviews* (starred review)

"An intelligent book about a family's struggle to find a home they could call 'our America.'...a timely reminder of the humanity of immigrants...riveting."

—*Foreword Reviews*

"An extraordinary journey—vital, absorbing, elegiac, and so finely honed."

—PHILIPPE SANDS, author of *The Ratline* and *East West Street*

"Lomnitz's riveting family memoir is an account of trauma and displacement, but also one of resilience, passion, and even joy. From Romania to Peru to Colombia to Israel to California to Mexico and beyond, his forebears, vividly portrayed, lived lives of profound political and intellectual engagement and were intimate with important historical actors."

—CLAIRE MESSUD, author of *The Burning Girl*

"Profound, riveting, and moving. Claudio Lomnitz reconstructs his family's history vividly, and brilliantly weaves the lives and fates of German and Romanian Jews who fled to South America into the complex web of Latin American culture, history, and politics…Lomnitz illuminates a poorly understood chapter in twentieth-century Jewish history and sheds light on the human condition and the quest for meaning amidst dark times." —LEON BOTSTEIN, President of Bard College

"A beautiful, poetic book in the voice of a wise, erudite, and insightful narrator. Like a great novel, it illuminates the souls of its protagonists and the times in which they lived. Like a great ethnography, it is world-making. I have read many memoirs, and this one is among the most captivating." —THOMAS W. LAQUEUR, Professor Emeritus, UC Berkeley, and author of *The Work of the Dead: A Cultural History of Mortal Remains*

"Lomnitz provides a poignant, finely wrought meditation on displacement, loss, and linguistic genealogies. *Nuestra América* invites us to think hard about what we can recognize, what we can know, and what we can protect when it comes to those we call kin." —STÉPHANE GERSON, Professor of French Studies, French, and History, New York University

"In *Nuestra América* Claudio Lomnitz reveals his strengths as a historian, as well as his disarming vulnerabilities in a process of self-discovery, while unearthing a family saga worthy of a great Latin American novel." —EFRAÍN KRISTAL, Distinguished Professor of Comparative Literature, UCLA

"This extraordinary book illuminates the agency of people in dark times, through transatlantic, multilingual, and pluricultural stories. *Nuestra América* interweaves the archive of the history of the Jewish diaspora with that of Lomnitz's own family. Against the tragic background of global twentieth-century events, we learn the workings of individual lives and how these individuals deal with decision-making at the most critical moments of social and political experience."

—GRACIELA MONTALDO,
Columbia University, co-editor of
The Argentina Reader

"A brilliant and beautifully written book…Lomnitz brings new meaning to *Nuestra América* as a necessary place for active *new beginnings*, which he has inherited." —ARCADIO DÍAZ-QUIÑONES,
Princeton University,
author of *La memoria rota*

Our America,

Nuestra América,

Unsere Amerika

OUR AMERICA,

NUESTRA AMÉRICA,

UNSERE AMERIKA

My Family in the Vertigo of Translation

Claudio Lomnitz

Other Press | New York

First softcover edition 2022
ISBN 978-1-63542-220-7

An earlier version of this book was published in Spanish in 2018
by Fondo de Cultura Económica, Mexico City, Mexico.

Lyrics on page 406 from "Forever Young" by Bob Dylan.
Copyright © 1973 by Ram's Horn Music; renewed 2001 by Ram's Horn Music.
All rights reserved. International copyright secured. Reprinted by permission.

Production editor: Yvonne E. Cárdenas
Text designer: Julie Fry
This book was set in Espinosa Nova.

10 9 8 7 6 5 4 3 2 1

Library of Congress Cataloging-in-Publication Data
Names: Lomnitz-Adler, Claudio, author.
Title: Nuestra América : my family in the vertigo of translation /
    Claudio Lomnitz.
Description: New York : Other Press, [2021] | Includes bibliographic references.
Identifiers: LCCN 2020022227 (print) | LCCN 2020022228 (ebook) |
    ISBN 9781635420708 (hardcover) | ISBN 9781635420715 (ebook)
Subjects: LCSH: Lomnitz-Adler, Claudio — Family. | Lomnitz-Adler, Claudio. |
    Jews — South America — History. | Jews, German — South America —
    Biography. | Jews — Migrations. | Jewish diaspora. | South America —
    Social conditions — 20th century.
Classification: LCC F2239.J5 L66 2021 (print) | LCC F2239.J5 (ebook) |
    DDC 980/.004924 — dc23
LC record available at https://lccn.loc.gov/2020022227
LC ebook record available at https://lccn.loc.gov/2020022228

Contents

"Thus, for instance, after the earthly family is discovered to be the secret of the holy family, the former must then itself be destroyed in theory and in practice."

— KARL MARX, *Theses on Feuerbach*

The Language of Paradise

Family history, for what?

This is an account that speaks of how strangers help shape everything that we call ours. It begins in exile, like the Odyssey, and it bends and strains toward reunion. It is my family's story, and it is also my story.

The collapse of Europe triggered a dizzying cycle of displacement. So much so that this account appears to have an unpredictable quality, skipping between countries and provinces that were only remotely connected. In many of those places — Peru, Colombia, Romania, France, Israel, Chile, Mexico — my family has had the kind of role that in Hollywood is known as a cameo: fleeting apparitions, minor parts, testimonials. There is something very Jewish in this.

In the Christian kingdoms of medieval Iberia, for example, the Jews were the property of the king, who referred to them as "our Jews." They lived in Jewish quarters (*juderías*) and moved about the cities dressed in peculiar clothing that was both a mark and a seal. Nevertheless, marginal though they were, those "Jews of the king" had an important role in the spiritual life of the community: they were condemned to be eternal witnesses of Christian happiness, to that to which they had turned their backs when they denied that Jesus was the Messiah. According to the logic of the Christian monarchs, Jews must be confined, identified, and punished, true, but they must also be protected so that they could carry out the theological role of the condemned witness: always present but never invited to the banquet. Someone is always required to envy whatever is deemed to be normal, because normality can scarcely justify itself on its own.

Of course there was also a material function for these people. Christian law prohibited usury. Jewish law also prohibited it, but only within the religious community. That is, Jews could freely charge Christians interest. For this reason, Christian monarchs made sure that "their Jews" were moneylenders and that they charged interest. This marked them as usurers and thus all but ensured that Christians would reject them as sinners. Afterward, the king would levy taxes against these same Jews, making himself the ultimate beneficiary of the greatest part of the income earned through usury, though without himself ever having violated Christian law. To use a rather unpleasant Jewish concept, the Jewish userer was something like the Christian king's version of a *Shabbas goy*. The Jew did what was religiously forbidden to the Christian, but he did it for the Christian's benefit, even more than for his own.

The point is that Jewish marginality was in fact crucial for the Christian order. The Jew's place as forced witness served to highlight the blessings of that order, a dramatic role akin to that of hired mourners, whose loud wailing lent gravity to the funerals of great personages. On the other hand, the supposed fiscal immorality of the Jews was in fact indispensable for the proper functioning of the Christian economy, and their marginalization was nothing if not a formula to separate capitalism both from society and from the person of the king without the crown losing any of its earnings. Jewish marginalization was a useful fiction; costly for Jews, of course, but convenient for those in power.

Something similar happens to those who are relegated to immigrant status in national societies: they are a shadow, like the Jews in medieval Iberian towns, and they are also a witness that reminds the citizen of the nation's real or imagined blessings. The myth of the American Dream would not hold if there were not migrants who were perceived to desire a life in the United States. And then again, migrants perform indispensable work that people from "good families" prefer not to do, even while national society prefers to imagine that it can get by without them. Like the medieval Jew, today's migrant is at once a demeaned witness and a key economic player. Necessary, but always made to feel dispensable.

Just plain Kartoffel

My father, Cinna Lomnitz, was born in Cologne in 1925, but he left that city with his parents when he was eight years old. They first went to Brussels, where they stayed for only five years before making their way to Santiago de Chile in 1938. German Jews were then called *yeques*. Looking for the origin of this term, I find disagreement and speculation; but the theory that most convinces me is that *yeque* comes from a Yiddish term that signifies "jacket" or perhaps "suit jacket" (from the German *Jake*). Eastern European Jews referred to German Jews as "jackets" because they seemed to them very modern and assimilated: the *yeques* no longer dressed in the garb that was worn in the villages and ghettos of Russia or Poland, and which set those villagers apart as Jews; on the contrary, they dressed in the same manner as other German city folk.

Among Ashkenazi Jews, the *yeque* stereotype underscores a certain rigidity of character, associated with the assimilation of bourgeois values, a high level of education, secularization, and, frequently enough, pretentiousness. The superiority of the *yeque* with respect to the Jews of Eastern Europe — from Poland, Lithuania, Galicia, Ukraine, Russia, or Romania — was obvious to many: German Jews were civilized. They had enjoyed full citizenship since the first third of the nineteenth century, while in Russia this was not granted until the Russian Revolution. *Yeques* had come to have expert knowledge in worldly affairs — science and white-collar professions, medicine, and law — rather than closing themselves off to study the Torah and the Talmud. Following this trend, my grandfather Kurt ("Ricardo") was a lawyer, and his brothers, Walther and Günther, were doctors. None of them was immune to nationalist passion, either, and they fought on the German side in the First World War. My grandfather was in fact awarded the Iron Cross for his courage driving ambulances at the front.

My great-uncle Walter Lomnitz, medical military officer
in World War I, was a pacifist who loved his horse.

My grandmother Bronislawa (Bronis), for her part, was
an opera singer, and a passionate fan of the music of Gustav
Mahler. Bruno Walter himself had visited her parents to ask
that they let her sing professionally. This was necessary because
her father, a wealthy textile wholesaler, was against the idea: he
considered a stage career to be something akin to singing in a
cabaret. My grandmother's professional singing career was cut
short because of Germany's rising anti-Semitism in the 1920s,
but Bronis later gave singing classes in Santiago de Chile, and
she attended concerts and operas devotedly during the many
years that she lived in New York City and London.

With all this, my father had everything he needed to be a
perfect *yeque*; however, and for reasons that I only half understand, Cinna never developed "*yeque* pride." As a young boy
in Brussels, he quickly learned that having a German identity

was a disadvantage. Belgium had suffered a cruel German invasion during the First World War, and the country was at that time anxious about a second invasion under Hitler, which took place soon enough. My father and his brother preferred to speak French between them so as not to be classified as *Boches* (a derogatory term for Germans). Beyond their ardent desire for camouflage and to lose themselves in their surroundings, I believe that my father was irritated by German/*yeque* rigidity and an almost universal lack of any sense of humor. Above all, he was averse to what the Greeks called hubris: a sense of pride that ends up challenging the gods.

Perhaps all of this explains why, when on a certain occasion I asked my father to teach me German, he turned to the back seat of the car where I was sitting and told me that there was really no point. As he saw it, knowing how to pronounce correctly the words *ja*, *nein*, and *Kartoffel* was more than enough. Cinna then asked me to pronounce the word *ja* a number of times, then *nein*, and finally *Kartoffel*. Before long, I was able to pronounce them perfectly. This would be the first and final German language lesson my father would offer me.

Comme c'est curieux

Many years later, I had the opportunity to learn more German. I was invited to spend a year in Berlin, at the Wissenschaftskolleg, a prestigious institution that was built to allow professors such as myself the time and mental stimulus in which we might best develop our work. While there, I lived in Grunewald, a neighborhood in the midst of lakes and forests on the western edge of the city, the name of which means "green forest." Grunewald was an upper-middle-class suburb at the end of the nineteenth century, and there were once a good number of Jews living there. Walter Benjamin, for example, lived at 23 Delbruckstrasse, just a few blocks from the castle at the Koenigsallee, where I was staying.

My stance on German had not changed from the time my father gave me my first lesson. I enjoyed the sound of the language, and I pronounced it with pleasure and never without emphasis; nonetheless, I refused to make much effort to learn it. If the language of Goethe entered freely into my unconscious, it would be most welcome, but I would make no effort to take control of it.

The Wissenschaftskolleg offered three free weeks of German lessons. I took them in order to be able to move freely through the city. Beyond this stimulus, I also found it pleasurable for once to take a class instead of always teaching them, and above all on something that wouldn't be of any lasting use to me. My plan was just to follow my curiosity into the impractical; and after all, it would only be for three weeks.

The classes were offered in a mansion that the institute owned on the Wallotstrasse. At the entrance, embedded in the sidewalk, were two small squares of bronze with the names of the members of the Jewish family who had lived there. They had been murdered by the Nazis, sent to a concentration camp the name of which I don't recall. The murder of Jews was ever the companion of theft, and the large house soon became a retreat for Joseph Goebbels's hunting club. Now I would study German in this same house, and I had even been invited to do so (with all expenses paid) by a public institution under the auspices of the German republic.

What does one say to an experience like this? Just *ja?* Of course not. But *nein?* One cannot deny that the situation is now different. Then it hit me. In the end, the answer had long been given to me by my father: *Kartoffel!* I remembered Cinna's enthusiasm for the theater of the absurd, his love for Eugène Ionesco, who will appear in another part of this story.

Wo wohnt der Mörder?

My father wasn't very involved in my education. He never corrected my homework, for example, and I remember only a few occasions when he helped me with a class. The first of these was in Berkeley. I was perhaps eight or nine years old, and I needed to recite a poem from memory. I had been asked to choose it myself, and I had no idea where to begin. To help me, my father opened up an edition of *Through the Looking-Glass* and read "Jabberwocky" to me out loud, with a good deal of meaningful emphasis:

> *'Twas brillig, and the slithy toves*
> *Did gire and gimble in the wabe:*
> *All mimsy were the borogoves,*
> *And the mome raths outgrabe.*

How fascinating to grasp the drift of a poem so well and yet not understand a word! This was the first poem I ever memorized, apart from children's songs. My father had a finely tuned ear for the displacement of language, and at nine years old I also had some understanding of this. Why build a bridge of understanding to the senselessness that was for us Germany? It was, in fact, precisely for this senselessness that I so enjoyed the sound of German, which is at once so emphatic and improbable. "Excuse me, sir" is said in a sneeze: *Entschuldigen Sie!* How could I not love such a singular language even a little? My father arrived in Santiago de Chile when he was thirteen years old. His schoolmates used to beg him to say, "Where does the murderer live?" in German, and Cinna did not understand why the answer — *Wo wohnt der Mörder?* — caused such hilarity, until he finally figured out that for his friends, the phrase sounded very much like the extremely Chilean expression *huevón de mierda* (roughly translatable into English as "fucking jerk"), only pronounced with a pompous and very sonorous German accent.

Where does the murderer live? That autumn of 1938, the murderer lived in Berlin, and his name was Adolf Hitler. But in Santiago, all that German madness seemed very far away, *pus huevón*. Apparently, at least. While I was at the Wissenschaftskolleg, some colleagues insisted that with or without the language, I was German, because in my house we listened to the music of Mozart and Mahler when I was a boy. They believed that I understood everything even while comprehending nothing. Maybe they were right, who knows?

Panglossia

What language was spoken before Babel? What was the language of Paradise? This is a question that has enjoyed various moments of splendor since the eleventh century, including recently, at the dawn of European unification, as Umberto Eco has pointed out.[1] At the end of the nineteenth century, the desire to transcend Babel was reborn, yet again, among Eastern European Jews. In Russia, Poland, Lithuania, and Romania, Jews suffered intense discrimination, and at the same time they were denied any form of political autonomy. In the nearby Austro-Hungarian Empire, Jews had enjoyed citizenship since 1867; however, Yiddish was not recognized as a language (it was seen as a *Mauscheln* — a Jewish slang or accent — a failed attempt at German), and anti-Semitism informally took root in the universities and in the government bureaucracy. It is no coincidence, then, that the idea of a linguistic union had resurfaced among Eastern European Jews.

Historically, the obsession with panglossia has taken two forms: [1] a search for the perfect language (the language of Paradise); and [2] a search for a universal, common language, built on shared features. Among Eastern European Jews, the language debate followed three paths: Hebraism, Yiddishism, and Universalism, the latter propped up by the invention of Esperanto.

The goal of the Hebraists, to which my grandfather Misha belonged, was to unify the Jewish people through a return to their original language (i.e., Hebrew), which had the not incidental advantage of also being the language of Paradise. It is well known, for example, that students of Kabbalah consider each (Hebrew) letter of each (Hebrew) word of the Torah to have an encoded divine meaning, and so the language is for them irreplaceable. In addition, Hebrew is both the language of the Torah and of the Promised Land; for this reason, it would serve well as the language of the future for a Jewish people that was then scattered and oppressed. It is no stretch to say that the Hebraists saw Hebrew as the language of redemption for the people of Israel.

The second tendency, less messianic, was to choose Yiddish. This reflected a political orientation less concerned with uniting the remote past with a projected national future than with recognizing the culture of Ashkenazi Jews as a historical formation imbued with the value of every great popular form of expression. Before he was forced to emigrate due to the implacable anti-Semitism of the Romanian academy, the philologist Lazăr Şăineanu wrote one of the earliest studies of Yiddish. In this study, he showed that Yiddish had existed for centuries in the Roman province of Dacia, and that it had taken elements from all the languages around it, just as Romanian had done. In this way, Şăineanu showed his colleagues that Yiddish was a vernacular language as rich and "traditional" as any of the supposedly "national" languages of the region.

Yiddishism was for Eastern Jews a form of nationalism rooted in the recognition of historico-popular traditions. Its advocates were not especially interested in finding the Jewish language spoken before Babel — prior to the destruction of the Second Temple and the diaspora — but rather in reclaiming the dignity of popular speech, a goal that implied working to transform Yiddish into a printed language and to create with it a literature, a theater, a learned poetry, and so on. My grandparents were also interested in this path, and it is worth noting that the Hebrew option did not always conflict with its Yiddish counterpart. There were between them common interests and passions.

The third tendency was even more ambitious and radical. In 1873, Ludwik Zamenhof, a Jewish philologist from Bialistok who had gained notoriety through his work on Yiddish, finished developing Esperanto. He meant this language to be universal, or at least to transcend the ethnic antagonism that divided people in the very heart of Europe. Zamenhof invented Esperanto using a mix of the language families that seemed then to be the most relevant: Latinate, Germanic, and Slavic. He proposed in this way a kind of "Proto-Indo-European" that was entirely new.

Zamenhof's universalist radicalism led to Esperanto becoming a target for the Nazis, who systematically murdered any speaker of the language. The communists, for their part, adopted Esperanto with enthusiasm, since their internationalism went well with the idea of universal language. Only later, during the dark years of Stalin's regime, would its speakers find themselves persecuted.

The search for linguistic union was nothing short of a passion of Eastern European Jews from the end of the nineteenth century to well into the first half of the twentieth century. Their goals included the standardization and dissemination of Yiddish, as well as the revival of Hebrew (a process that involved rescuing it from its liturgical use in order to transform it into a modern language). They were also open, as it happens, to inventing a new universal language that might transcend national horizons.

All of this happened long before I was born.

Alingualism

My mother arrived in Tuluá, Colombia, from Europe in 1936. She was four years old then, and at that point she stopped speaking altogether. Larissa had spent her first two years in Paris, and the following two in Nova Sulitza, Bessarabia, which was then part of Romania. During her early childhood, she had regularly heard Yiddish, French, Russian, and Romanian. I imagine that she spoke some mix of all of these languages, maybe with some predominance of Yiddish. When her family brought her to a new place that filled her ears with yet another language (Spanish), she gave up trying to find any consistency between all of those languages, and just stopped talking altogether. She remained mute for an entire year, but afterward she quickly came to find herself in the Spanish language as if America had always been her destiny.

My mother effectively distanced herself from Yiddish and Russian before even fully learning them, and it is for that reason that she did not teach these languages to her children. I don't blame her for this, yet it is undeniable that I failed to learn two of the languages more or less indispensable for writing this book: Russian and Yiddish. The loss of Yiddish, especially, was simultaneously the symptom and the effect of the dismantling of the Jewish community — how could my mother have retained it while growing up in the Colombian provinces? In all of Colombia there were then fewer than four thousand Jews, and in some of the towns in which she lived — Sogamaso, for example, or Manizales — hers was practically the only Jewish family for miles.

My father, for his part, had adopted something of a chameleon's strategy. He was a natural linguist. Even so, it was Cinna who denied me German, the third of the four key languages that I lack for this book. In effect, he refused to extend a bridge to the terror and ingratitude that he and his parents had left behind. I imagine there was a sensibility at work that resembled one of the rules of kashrut: "You will not cook a calf in the milk of its mother." That is, if you're going to eat the calf, you must at least allow it some dignity and not cook it in the milk of the one who loved it most. My father observed a kind of inverted corollary of this rule, which might be expressed in the following way: You will separate your son from the language of those who wished to exterminate him. It was in this way that I lost three languages before I even learned them: I lost Yiddish and Russian because of their new status as excessive and unassimilable, and I lost German because of an inclination to avoid cruel or unholy mixtures.

Finally, unlike my grandfather Misha and my parents, I failed to study Hebrew. In the end, my parents did not send us to Jewish schools, and I have never lived in Israel. I did manage to learn the beautiful letters of Hebrew when I studied for my bar mitzvah. I know the form of the language, but I do not understand it.

Born in a sea of linguistic dispossession, I retained a bit of my father's imitative facility. I also have his enthusiasm for phonetics and a certain semantic intuition. I learned, also, the exemplary capacity of forgetting that was practiced by my mother, her pragmatism. For me, linguistic displacement is a mark of origin.

When I was five years old, I learned French at the Alliance

Française in Santiago; at seven years old, when we moved to California, I learned English and forgot my French. From that moment forward, I have remained sandwiched between Spanish and English, feeling comfortable to a certain point in each of these languages, but also insecure in both. Spanish is my Yiddish, and English is my Esperanto, but I have always lacked the perfect language: the one that names things without distorting them. For me there is not, nor can there be, a language of Paradise such as those possessed by the truly great writers, who make their homes in their language. My mother tongue is a linguistic shipwreck; and it is from there that I write the story of my grandparents.

America

My father knew a lot about geology, and, according to his point of view, South America is an immature continent. The Andes were to him dizzyingly dramatic. "Mother of stone, foam of condors," as Pablo Neruda put it. As a geophysicist, he did not find peace amidst such deep stirrings.

When I was four years old, we took a family trip to Peru. Among my memories of the journey is a stop in Arica, as well as a nauseating plane ride to Pisco. I preserve in my mind an image of the red-chalice desert of Atacama and of the Morro de Arica, the site where the Peruvian colonel Alfonso Ugarte threw himself into the abyss rather than surrender to the Chilean army. And the taking of the frigate *El Huáscar* in that same War of the Pacific (1879–83), when the Chilean military beat Peru and Bolivia and appropriated their southernmost provinces…In those days, we boys still played with lacquered lead soldiers, and as a proud Chilean all of this fascinated me.

The immolation of Alfonso Ugarte,
painted by Agustín Marazzani (1905).

I remember also an afternoon among the cliffs of the Antofagasta coast, walking with my brothers, looking for anemones and starfish. The sun-filled and freezing Pacific snorted up between the slender tongues of perforated rock. An octopus hid itself in the whirlpool.

Later, in Lima's Chorrillos neighborhood, I read a plaque commemorating the struggle of the valiant Peruvian people "against Chilean barbarism." I was four then and read rather slowly, so that when I finally came to the part on the Chilean invaders, I cried out in disbelief, "Mami, it says here '*Chilean barbarians*'!" (We, good-hearted Chileans, were barbarians?)

In Lima, we also visited an archaeological dig. My grandfather Misha was there, though I don't recall how he got there or why. He knew the archaeologists, or at least he knew how to approach them, because they allowed us to touch the cloth that covered some mummies that they were removing. I remember them giving him a strip of that ancient cloth, although I might be mistaken about that. This was my first contact with the magic of antiquity. The dryness of the Peruvian coastal desert can preserve cloth for hundreds and even thousands of years, and it was possible to touch that cloth, to interrogate it!

My grandparents did not accompany us to Cuzco nor on the rest of that trip, because of Misha's heart condition. There was once a photograph of my grandfather at that spot, but now I can't find it. I substitute it with another, of the selfsame Misha, but young and in a different locale in Peru. He has in his lap a skull, as if he were Hamlet posing with a pre-Incan Yorick.

Misha Adler at an unidentified archaeological site
on the coast of Peru, c. 1929.

To be or not to be indigenous? Or better put, as the great Brazilian modernist Oswald de Andrade would write at around that same time, "Tupí or not Tupí?" Was this perhaps the question my grandfather was asking? I doubt it. More likely, as the committed Jew and Marxist that he was at that time, he was inclined to see the present reflected in the mirror of Incan glory. Today's Indians, though subjugated, would once again become great. Though imperiled, the Jews were also once again becoming great. This was the source of his energy and enthusiasm for Hebrew, as well as for his passion for the emancipatory spark that he intuited in indigenous communalism.

My grandfather was not then a wavering prince like Hamlet; rather, he was a man compelled to create a future out of a present that was always precarious, and from a past that was crumbling around him. For him, the idea of a new world was a necessity. His idea of America had less to do with nostalgia for the past than with a reality that needed to be achieved. Our America, the America of my family, was a necessary place that one must inhabit and defend.

Even today we still live in a dangerous world that is constantly asking us to make decisions, yet we can only face our collective dilemmas by way of encrypted personal stories. Because, as Walter Benjamin put it, to tell the past is to take ownership of a memory "just as it glimmers in the instant of a danger." Thus peril is at once collective and deeply personal. We are no longer governed by tradition, so we can't simply rely on a collective past. For this reason family history is again relevant. It is no longer an aristocratic incantation of the glories of a lineage, but very simply our precondition: a matrix of past decisions that made us possible. And we stretch back to those decisions in moments of danger, as if we were migratory birds, flying in formation toward the south.

PART ONE

Citizens of the World

CHAPTER ONE

Unstable Affiliations

Provincial cosmopolitanism?

In his notable contribution to the first issue of the journal *Repertorio Hebreo*, edited in Lima in 1929, José Carlos Mariátegui writes: "Israel is not a race, a nation, a state, a language, a culture; it is the simultaneous transcendence of all of these things through something so modern, so unknown, that it still has no name."[2] What were the qualities or characteristics of this entity that was so modern and so unknown? Where did they come from? How had they been forged?

Mariátegui was well aware of the explosive effect of Jewish thought in modern culture. His own journal, *Amauta*, was an avant-garde project that was committed to the translation and circulation of texts from all over the world. Several key thinkers of this new globalism were Jewish — Marx, Freud, and Einstein, just to name a few — and there were a few noteworthy trends of the great current of modern Jewish thought that attracted Mariátegui especially: eccentric views, like that of Freud, who managed to adopt a certain irony with respect to the dominant morality and so pave the way for the blossoming of a universal critique.

José Carlos Mariátegui was arguably Latin America's most prominent radical thinker. His intellectual contributions have been compared — not unreasonably — to those of other Marxist contemporaries such as Antonio Gramsci or Rosa Luxemburg, although, in what is a very good example of the marginalization of Latin American thought from wide global recognition, the first English-language anthology of his work was only published in 2011, eighty-one years after his death.[3]

Maybe Mariátegui also identified with Jewish attitudes toward displacement. As a young man, he had spent two years in Italy as a political exile (1920–22), yet nothing interested Mariátegui less than devoting his time in Europe to the exhibition of his Peruvianness, either as stigma or as enigma. Frankly, he had bigger fish to fry. Rather than wallowing obsessively in Peru's singularities, Mariátegui threw himself headlong into European political and intellectual life. He gave testimony to key events during his Italian sojourn, such as the formation of the Communist Party and Mussolini's March on Rome. He fell in love and married the Italian Anna Chiappe, who would return with him to Lima, and he wrote feverishly for the Lima journal *El Tiempo*.

Mariátegui's reports to that paper reflected his conviction that, just as Peru belonged to the world, the world belonged to Peru. So, whereas conservative nationalists joined in the rallying cry of Charles Maurras, the anti-Semitic founder of Action

Française, clamoring "All that is national is ours!" Mariáte-gui's motto for his program of "Peruvianizing Peru" was "All that is human is ours!" Forging a genuine Peruvian nationality required tilting the lens of Peruvian history away from its colonial traditions and toward the Indians, who constituted four-fifths of the country's population. This involved uncovering the native past, certainly, but above all it required embracing the future over the past. "Our indigenism," Mariátegui wrote, "does not dream with utopian restoration. It views the past as root, not as program. Its conception of history is realistic and modern."[4] Turning outward, toward the world, was fully as necessary for socialist emancipation as turning inward, toward the nation.

Mariátegui's missives to *El Tiempo* from Italy were detailed accounts of the European order, which he knew was deeply relevant for Peru: discussions of the Soviets' situation, for instance, and of the tensions around the Adriatic; examinations of Italian politics, Germany's situation, the Russian famine, the rise of fascism, literature and the cultural scene. All of those things and many more.

A couple of years after his return to Peru in 1923, Mariátegui founded the socialist journal *Amauta*, a periodical dedicated to understanding Peruvian reality from a universal perspective, which is where he proclaimed, in the opening editorial, that "Everything human belongs to us." This became the rallying cry of a generation. And yet Mariátegui knew that committing to a universalist program exposed him to charges of perverting national traditions with alien thoughts. He knew about the challenge that comes with thinking globally from the margins, and for this reason especially he found much to admire in the Jews.

Besides, he understood the extreme rarity of the situation faced by Jews. "Upon losing its land," he wrote, "Judaism earned the right to make Europe and America its home." At another point in that same essay, he spoke in concrete terms of what he loved about Jewish culture: "[It] speaks neither Hebrew nor Yiddish exclusively; it is polyglot, itinerant, supranational. In an effort to identify itself with all races, it possesses the sentiments, the languages, and the arts of them all."[5]

Mariátegui also had a personal engagement with individual Jews, people with whom he interacted on a daily basis. The historian Osmar Gonzales has documented the friendships that Mariátegui had with a number of Jews who attended the "Red Corner," the discussion group that met during the afternoons in his house on Jirón Washington, in Lima.[6] Among these were two young "Romanian" Jews with whom he was especially close, Misha Adler and Noemí Milstein, who were then dating and would later launch the journal *Repertorio Hebreo*. These were my grandparents. But did these two youngsters really have anything ultramodern about them? Did they not come from the most backward regions of Europe? How, when, and from where was such a cosmopolitan aura generated among people of such provincial origins? What did these two young people have that made them so radically universal?

Borderlanders

Where were my grandparents actually from? At times they referred to the regions from which they came as Bessarabia, at others as Bukovina or Moldavia. Sometimes they came from

Russia or the USSR, at others from Ukraine or Romania. Until very recently, I had no understanding of this confusion, and I had to study a great deal just to answer one apparently simple question: Where were they from?

Misha (Miguel) Adler Altman was born in 1904, in Nova Sulitza, in the district of Hotin, Bessarabia. His house was on the Russian side of the main street that divided Bessarabia (Russian Empire) from Bukovina (Austro-Hungarian Empire). That is, my grandfather was born in a town that crossed, or was crossed by, an international border.

When my great-grandfather acquired his land, the area was sparsely populated, and he was able to purchase a large parcel. Misha grew up on a small farm, more than a house, on the Russian side of the town. There were trenches separating the main street from the property, and it was necessary to cross a small bridge to enter. At the back, the lot was close to a highway that led to the neighboring town of Hotin, the capital of the district known for its old fortified castle on the shores of the Dniester River.

According to information in the *Encyclopedia of Jewish Communities in Romania*, the population of Nova Sulitza was 4,156 in 1898, at the start of a period of economic growth that was triggered by the construction of a rail hub, and that continued unabated until the end of the First World War, when there began an era of prolonged economic decline. In 1930, the town still had a population of roughly seven thousand, 86 percent of which was Jewish.[7] Today there are likely no Jews in it at all. At the start of the Second World War, even after decades of emigration that was initially triggered by a series of pogroms, the Jewish population of Bessarabia still hovered around 270,000 people. Today the republic of Moldova, which corresponds to the territory that once made up Bessarabia, is home to only four thousand Jews.

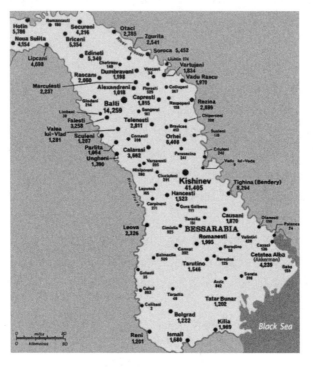

The Jewish population of Bessarabia in 1940,
community by community.
Nova Sulitza is at the northwest edge of the map.

The general culture of the Jews of Nova Sulitza was Yiddish and Russian. Indeed, the original name of the town, Novo-selitse, means "New Settlement" in Russian, and the term "Nova Sulitza," which is what I always heard, is a Romanization of that same name, which reflects the fact that the peasants of the region of Bessarabia spoke Romanian.

Diglossia

To get a better sense of what "provincial cosmopolitanism" might have meant for Eastern European Jews at the turn of the twentieth century, I need to discuss the question of language. It is worth reflecting, in particular, on the linguistic hierarchies in place in my grandparents' home region, and for this, the notion of diglossia is useful. The Russian critic Mikhail Bakhtin proposed this concept over a century ago, to refer to social formations in which there exists a "high" language—lettered and prestigious—and a vernacular "low" language, used primarily in informal contexts. The concept of diglossia thus refers to the relative prestige and the appropriate uses of languages when social hierarchies find themselves expressed in speech.

My grandparents moved between three adjacent regions: Bessarabia, Bukovina, and Ukraine. In 1904, when my grandfather was born, Bessarabia and Ukraine belonged to the Russian Empire, and Bukovina belonged to the Austro-Hungarian Empire. For the Jews of Nova Sulitza, which was, as I have mentioned, a town bisected by the Russo-Austrian border, there were at the time two "high" or prestigious languages: Russian and German. Each of these was supported by a powerful state (the Russian Empire and the Austro-Hungarian Empire, respectively), a school system, and a national literature that enjoyed great prestige. That is, my grandfather was born into a place in which there were not one but two "high" languages, even if knowledge of Russian was much more common than knowledge of German.

With respect to vernacular or "low" languages, the situation was even more complex. The peasants of the region spoke Moldovan or Romanian (two names for essentially the same thing). In Bessarabia, Moldovan had no support from the state: the Russian Empire did not allow schools to teach in that language, nor were there books printed in it except in neighboring Romania, which looked to annex Bessarabia precisely on the grounds of a shared language. Nevertheless, before Bessarabia became part of Romania (1919), Moldovan was a language of low prestige, and it was essentially only a spoken language.

In the neighboring regions of Ukraine and Bukovina, the peasants usually spoke Ukrainian, a language whose level of prestige was on a par with Moldovan. They were in both cases popular vernaculars that some urban nationalists wished to use to create new states, but that in principle lacked the prestige of Russian and German. There were, besides, other minority languages in these regions, such as Roma (spoken by Gypsies in the region) or Bulgarian.

Finally, there was the peculiar situation of the Jews, whose common vernacular language was Yiddish, which was spoken at home and on the street. A majority of the poorer Jews in the towns and small cities of Bessarabia were practically monolingual in Yiddish. There was also a movement that sought to transform Yiddish into a "national" language, and around the time my grandfather was born, Yiddish existed in print, due to the comparatively elevated level of literacy among the Jewish population. Indeed, there were newspapers in Yiddish, and a literature in that language was taking form. Nevertheless, Yiddish did not have the support of any state, and for this reason it was considered a "dialect."

Besides Yiddish, Jews had an additional language: Hebrew. This was a "high" language that was supported by religious tradition rather than by the state. It was studied in religious schools, attended almost universally by Jewish males in Russia and Poland, so that they might learn at least the basic prayers. Hebrew literacy also helped buttress modern Yiddish, because Yiddish is written with Hebrew characters, so literacy in one language supported reading in the other, and vice versa.

Thus, Misha came from a region in which a well-educated Jewish person undoubtedly aspired to speak and read Russian, and ideally also German. This person would also know Hebrew sufficiently well to read the Torah and Talmud. Besides this, they would speak at least one "low" language: Yiddish, and frequently also Romanian, which was useful for interacting with the local Christian population. In bourgeois families, a smattering of French was also desirable. In my grandmother's region, there was a similar logic in place, except the vernacular that was employed besides Yiddish was Ukrainian rather than Romanian. In other words, Eastern European Jewish "provincialism" implied having varying degrees of familiarity with multiple languages. My grandparents each spoke eight languages.

The Pale of Jewish Settlement

After acquiring the region that up to then had been known as "Southern Bukovina" from the Ottoman Empire in 1804, the

Russians changed its name and called it Bessarabia, to honor a certain Prince Bessaraab. They then conjoined the entire province to the so-called Pale of Jewish Settlement, where the czars had facilitated the settlement of Jews. The logic that underlay this supposed concession to the Jews was geopolitical.

The Russian Empire expanded enormously during the reign of Catherine the Great (1772–96). Among its new acquisitions were territories pulled from Poland and the Ottoman Empire, from Lithuania in the north to Ukraine in the south. Between them, these annexed regions had the greatest concentration of Jewish communities in Europe, so that the Russian Empire now came to contain the largest Jewish population in the world. The trouble was that Russia had always been averse to Jewish settlement, and the monarchy wished to preserve the kingdom's religious purity. The solution to this conundrum was to leave the newly annexed Jewish population in the acquired territories on the western fringe of the empire, in the so-called Pale of Settlement, and bar Jews from migrating into old Russia. The empire could thereby hold the largest Jewish population in Europe, while Russia itself remained religiously unblemished. Within the Pale of Jewish Settlement, the czars imposed rigorous conditions on the Jews. The Jews of Bessarabia lived under these conditions from 1804 until the region was annexed by Romania in 1919.

Social conditions in Bessarabia

Bessarabia was a rich agricultural region, but it was also one of the most underdeveloped provinces in all of Europe. A British study carried out immediately after the First World War offers a concise diagnosis: "Public health is in the same backward condition as in Ukraine, and it is especially poor in the cities. Medical services are very inadequate..."[8] The roads were dirt "and they become almost impassable when there is bad weather."[9] Indeed, the autumn and springtime mud is one of the recurrent motifs in writing on Bessarabia. Curzio Malaparte describes Bessarabia's muddy and rich black soil as dark dough saturated with yeast, swelling and filling the air with the heavy smell of rotten hay.[10]

The principal crops of the region were corn, wheat, barley, rye, oats, potatoes, and flax, as well as fruits such as plums, apples, pears, cherries, apricots, melons, and squash, which were exported to Russia as well as to Austria and Germany. The Bessarabian countryside was populated by Moldovans, but business in the towns and small cities of the region was in the hands of the Jews and, to a lesser extent, Germans and Greeks.

Yosef Govrin gives an account of Edinitz, a town in Bessarabia near Nova Sulitza and close to the same size, at the beginning of the 1930s. Through his text, one gets a general sense of the towns inhabited by the Jewish population:

> small stores, a bit of commerce, agriculture based on antiquated methods, a minor industry of soap and oil production. None of the roads are paved — the entire town is covered in thick mud... Frozen winters, with heat generated by burning sunflower stocks or, in the best of cases, with wood burned in primitive fireplaces embedded in the walls. Latrines. There was no telephone in any house, nor was there running water or drainage. There was

electricity only in the late afternoon. There was no public transportation, cinema, or theater (except for one or two annual performances put on by a traveling Jewish group). A very modest hospital and a pharmacy (both run by Jews). Two or three doctors (Jews), two or three attorneys (also Jews).[11]

As late as 1940, there was not even radio in Edinitz. The Jewish population, which made up 80 percent of the town, spoke Yiddish, and only a small educated minority also spoke Russian.

With respect to class structure, the British report adds that more than 43 percent of the land was still in the hands of the nobility, and that 48 percent belonged to Moldovan peasants. In Bessarabia, serfs were emancipated in 1861, but their actual release was delayed for decades. Malaparte speaks of their rustic mentality as late as 1941, when those peasants had become recruits for the Romanian army and formed part of the Nazi-led force that invaded the USSR. "They are peasants that don't even know what it means to be a peasant... They only know that they are Romanian and Greek Orthodox. They shout, 'Long Live the King' and also, 'Long Live Field-Marshall Antonescu!' They shout, 'Down with the USSR!' But they have no idea what a king is, who Antonescu is, nor what the USSR is."[12]

On the other hand, the towns of Bessarabia — it sometimes seems a stretch to call them "cities" — had no manufacturing industry, although these were quite developed in nearby cities such as Odessa, Kiev, and Czernowitz. Those who lived in town ran small businesses or were artisans, exporters of the rich agricultural production of the countryside, moneylenders for the peasants, or cobblers. Even the capital of Bessarabia, Kishinev ("Chisinau" in Romanian), was a bit of an outpost. Indeed, starting in the 1830s, the czarina used that city as a place to banish discontents. For a noble or burgher from St. Petersburg, being exiled to Kishinev was recognized as a form of punishment.

Despite the modesty of Bessarabia's cities, though, there were nonetheless tensions between the countryside and the towns, because commerce and credit were still concentrated there. These class tensions, characteristic of rural societies, were racialized in Bessarabia, where the countryside was Moldovan while the towns were, to a large extent, Jewish. So while the Jews constituted only 11 percent of the population of the so-called Pale of Settlement in the Russian Empire, which included Bessarabia, they made up between 25 percent and 90 percent of the urban population.[13] Almost half the population of Kishinev was Jewish (46 percent), and many of the towns of the region came to have an astonishing majority of Jews, as was the case in Nova Sulitza. There were rich people among this Jewish population, true, but the majority were poor and lived in squalor due in no small part to the many laws that limited their activity. In fact, an important percentage of the Jewish population of the urban centers of Bessarabia was indigent and relied on the charity of Jewish organizations.

Nova Sulitza

My great-great-grandfather on the Adler side arrived in Nova Sulitza as a purchase agent from a commercial house in Berlin.

Sent to do import-export business with Russia, he initially settled on the Austrian side of that border town. According to family lore, he was trained as a buyer and was a trusted figure for the businesses that sent him. He was also familiar with customs offices and international tariffs. His son, my great-grandfather Hershel, belonged to the first generation born in Nova Sulitza, and he joined his father's business. They were commission, storage, and duty agents.

Storage agents were needed in Nova Sulitza because Russian trains ran on rails of a different gauge than their Austrian counterparts, so it was necessary to transfer the payload, especially grain, from one side to the other. Transfer, purchase, store — that was the family business. Hershel's father decided at a certain point to move from the Austrian to the Russian side of the town, because it was cheaper and there was more activity there. He bought a large plot which was occupied by five families after the Second World War.

All of this information comes to me from my mother's and my uncles' memories, which in turn came to them from my grandfather, Misha. Although they retained a surprising amount of information, there were still too many unknowns, and I was not well placed to shed any light on them, not only because I lacked the language skills for archival work (Yiddish, Romanian, Russian, and German), but also because Jewish Nova Sulitza disappeared after 1941, so I could scarcely go there to interview people who had known that life.

Happily, a Jewish doctor from Nova Sulitza, Naphtoli Rabinovici, took it upon himself to publish a book on his home town, titled *Ich und Meine Shtetele* (Me and My Shtetl). It was printed in Yiddish and published in Tel Aviv in 1965. Through an Israeli colleague, I contacted a translator, Ms. Elisha Shaul, who provided me with detailed chapter summaries and literal translations of the portions that interested me especially. That material, added to family memories and photos and to a few supplementary sources, gave me a clearer picture of the town that my grandfather had left, and that his parents refused to abandon.

Nova Sulitza's "golden age" was brought on by the construction of a train line that linked Bukovina with Bessarabia through Nova Sulitza. It made its debut in 1894 and it ended with the First World War, after which the village went into decline. The Ribnitza-Bieltsy-Oknitsa-Novoselitsa railway line connected Nova Sulitza on one side of the city to Czernowitz, in Austrian Bukovina, and on the other to Odessa and Kiev, in Russian Ukraine.[14] Agricultural exports passed from Bessarabia to Austria, and from there also to Germany.

Eggs were Nova Sulitza's most important export product. They were collected on the Russian side and then packed and transported to Austria. Also important was the grain trade, and to a lesser extent that of fruits and vegetables, both fresh and preserved. Since manufactured products were cheaper on the Austrian side than on the Russian side, there was also a fair amount of business in contraband: agricultural exports from Russia to Austria, manufactured goods from Austria to Russia. These were the town's main sources of revenue during the "glory days" until the end of the First World War, when the map of Eastern Europe was redrawn and Nova Sulitza lost its place in international commerce.

Commerce, both legal and illicit, was a very important activity for the town's Jews, but it was not the only one. On the Russian side of town, there was a densely populated neighborhood of poor Jews who worked as servants or employees in the export warehouses of eggs and grain. There were also tailors, cobblers, and the like, as well as a constantly swelling number of unemployed. Poverty was severe, and yet the town's general population continued to grow.

The principal merchants were Jews, and they mostly bought agricultural products from Moldovan traders based in the neighboring towns. Those traders did not live on the international border, so they had no papers that would allow them to cross over. To cross from the Russian to the Austrian side, it was necessary to show papers that were stamped and valid for a period of twenty-eight days. Only the people who lived on the border itself had a right to these transit papers, although they were nonetheless routinely searched in order to "guarantee" that they had no contraband or, more accurately, to guarantee that the Russian soldiers received a portion of the income earned through the contraband trade, in the form of bribes taken to turn a blind eye.

The town's two most important economic institutions were both on the Austrian side of the border — the agricultural product exchange and the union of buyers of agricultural products. Rabinovici explains that the exchange had a numbered membership, and it was a sanctum sanctorum that only admitted the most important traders. It operated from eight a.m. to noon, and then again for an hour at four p.m. in order to wrap up its business. It also maintained a private library, where members read newspapers from Austria and Russia, as well as the Yiddish press and books in Russian and German. I'm not sure if Hershel Adler belonged to the Nova Sulitza Agricultural Exchange. There is really no way to be sure. Certainly my grandfather Misha belonged to the well-to-do sector of town, but, that said, Rabinovici—who was a prominent doctor himself—does not once mention the Adlers or the Altmans, even though he knew my grandfather personally, which suggests that the Adlers were not among the town's most prominent families. Rabinovici likewise wrote that there was a status hierarchy at work: the richest families lived in stone houses on the main street; after them came those with wooden houses; and then the families who rented. My great-grandparents owned a wooden house located on the main street; however, it was near the edge of town, so everything suggests that Misha belonged to a family that was economically comfortable but did not figure among the wealthiest of the town.

Romanian annexation

In March 1918, Russia quit the Great War. There was a revolution that took precedence. The following year, the Russian Empire, the Ottoman Empire, and the Austro-Hungarian Empire all ceased to exist. The Treaty of Versailles, which followed the surrender of Germany, redefined the political map of Europe and especially Eastern Europe, where the three defunct empires had intersected. It was at this time that Bessarabia ceased to belong to the Russian Empire and came to form part of Romania, a transfer prompted by the fact that

Romania had earned a reward for having sided with the Allies. And the peasants of Bessarabia spoke Romanian and the territory had long been the object of Romanian nationalist claims.

Romania was conceived in 1878 in the Treaty of Berlin, which was signed by the Ottoman Empire, the Russian Empire, France, Italy, the Austro-Hungarian Empire, and the United Kingdom, all under the orchestration of Otto von Bismarck. The monarchy thus created would conjoin two principalities of the Ottoman Empire, Wallachia and Moldovia, that were also known as the Romanian Old Kingdom.

Resting on ethnolinguistic claims, Romanian nationalists also wanted to annex Bessarabia, Bukovina, Transylvania, and the Dobruja, because these provinces had peasant populations that spoke Romanian. This claim, however, was not granted at the Berlin Conference, and it was thus not until 1919, by means of the Treaty of Versailles, that Romania finally gained the territory that its nationalists long felt belonged to them. With the acquisition of these new provinces, the Romanian Republic doubled both its population and its territory.

And yet, it would take no mean effort for these newly annexed provinces to glory in the national spirit. Bessarabia had belonged to the Russian Empire, Bukovina and Transylvania had formed part of the Austro-Hungarian Empire, and Dobruja had belonged to the Ottomans. Unlike the new national states, each one of these older empires was by tradition and necessity both multilingual and multiethnic. It is true that each empire also privileged a particular nation, but imperial identification with a historic heartland — like Castile for the Spanish Empire, England for the British Empire, Anatolia for the Ottomans, Austria for the Austro-Hungarian Empire, or Russia for the Russian Empire — still did not mean that the empire itself was as committed to linguistic and ethnic unity as nation-states were. Thus, the transition from empire to nation-state involved taking proactive measures to gain linguistic unity and national identification.

For this reason, the institutionalization of nationality in the new states tended to involve varying degrees of violence. The Turks carried out the first great genocide of the twentieth century, against the Armenian population, in anticipation of the imminent collapse of the empire and its passage to a national state (Turkey). They would later expel the Greeks and marginalize the Kurds. The formation of the Turkish Republic thus went hand in hand with a state-sponsored policy of ethnic cleansing.

Nationalist paranoia about real or alleged internal enemies also affected the Romanian Republic, especially with the expansion of the country after the First World War. This was so because each of the newly acquired provinces had important non-Romanian minorities: Magyars, Romani, Jews, Ukrainians, Germans, and Bulgarians, among others.

Romania had doubled its size with the annexed territories, and this meant that it would have to absorb populations that did not identify themselves as Romanian and in many cases did not speak the Romanian language. Some, like the Jews, Bulgarians, and Magyars, did not even share the Eastern Orthodox religion, the state religion of Romania. On the other hand, the Romanian-speaking populations of the acquired provinces were mostly illiterate, so even *their* conversion to the national ideal was not automatic.

According to British sources, the centennial celebration of the annexation of Bessarabia by Russia in 1912 "provoked indignation among nationalist circles in Romania, but there is no proof that this indignation found any echo among the population of Bessarabia,"[15] which suggests that not even Moldovan peasants fully identified with Romanian nationalism. It was necessary to create a national identity where there had been none, and to elevate the Romanian language and Romanian ethnicity above the languages and identities of the remaining minorities.

The tension between such nationalist impulses and the need to integrate minorities was already a well-known problem in Europe, and in recognition of this complication, the Treaty of Versailles required that the new "Greater Romania" respect the rights of its minorities. These rights were incorporated into the 1923 Romanian constitution and included (finally) a recognition of Jewish citizenship. Romania was thereby the last European country to emancipate Jews and give them full citizenship rights. Curiously, my grandfather Misha celebrated this supposed act of inclusion by emigrating to Peru.

CHAPTER TWO

Why Misha Left

So why exactly did Misha leave Romania? There's another simple question! But like so many of my questions, this one, too, was hard to answer.

Historians are fond of saying that the past is another country. And that is true enough: traveling in time does imply traveling in space. But in the case of my grandparents, I soon discovered that the past was always not one but two or more "other countries." This is because Misha and Noemí grew up in a world of crisscrossing languages and traditions, and each of these language communities had its own horizon of references. Each had its expectations and its own peculiar hang-ups. And yet these language communities sometimes overlapped and came together in the lives of the people who spoke or heard them. There is, for this reason, a kind of multifocal quality to my grandparents' stories—they are both Jewish and Romanian, for instance, or Jewish and Russian, or European and South American—and answering even simple questions to do with motives and motivations always involves looking at things from multiple points of view.

Romanian anti-Semitism

The sudden growth of Romania after the First World War exacerbated the anxieties of its nationalists. They feared that the inhabitants of the newly annexed provinces — Bessarabia, Transylvania, Bukovina — might wish to reattach themselves to their previous overlords. More than anything, though, they lived in dread of the possibility that the Russian revolutionary tide might sweep across Romania. For this reason, Bessarabia became a site of acute concern, since it had been a Russian province for more than one hundred years and so was a likely objective for Soviet expansionism.

These worries increased opportunistic Romanians' political reliance on anti-Semitism, since Jews could easily become scapegoated for communist agitation. Indeed, communism itself was often cast as an alien notion that was being driven forth by Jewish ambition. Such claims gained some veneer of local credibility because the Russian Revolution had in fact improved the Jews' situation, and many Jews were revolutionaries, especially in neighboring Ukraine. Some, such as Leon Trotsky, Lev Kamenev, and Grigory Zinoviev, played prominent roles. Furthermore, when read through the prism of the best-selling book *The Protocols of the Elders of Zion* (1903), a forged document that allegedly furnished incontrovertible proof of Jewish international conspiracy, communism could easily be interpreted as yet another Jewish stratagem in their determined effort to take over the world.

Moreover, the Soviet Union had not been conceived as a national state but rather as a confederation of socialist republics that together safeguarded the rights of each of its "nationalities" (while advancing the collective interests of the proletariat). In theory at least, this also involved protecting the collective rights of the Jews, who were also thought of as a "nationality." For this reason, the Soviet Union went so far as to recognize Yiddish as a national language, a step that no other country had previously taken. Even the Austro-Hungarian Empire, which had conceded full citizenship rights to its Jews as early as 1867, nonetheless had denied them collective rights as a national minority, which might have put them on a par with the empire's Hungarians, Ukrainians, or Poles.[16] Now the multinational Soviet Union had proven more innovative than even the modern Austro-Hungarian Empire in recognizing Jews as a properly *national* constituency.

As early as 1914, Lenin had argued that Russian Marxists should not shy away from the national question. Russian nationalists, Lenin contended, worked up a froth after the empire's humiliation in the Russo-Japanese War, and as a result they had adopted an oppressive and bellicose stance toward the minorities that so proliferated in the Russian Empire. Communists, Lenin wrote, should take their stand against Russian colonialism and support all of the empire's oppressed nations, even while insisting on the primacy of proletarian identification over and above any nationalist sentiment.[17]

That position was welcomed by many Jews, and especially those who identified both with socialism and with the struggle for the emancipation of their downtrodden community. After all, Russia's Jews were an obvious example of an oppressed nationality. And, indeed, in the Soviet Union of the 1920s, the government openly combated anti-Semitism, a policy that was quietly modified under Stalin, when the Soviet Union reverted to Russification, and to the occasional reliance on Jews as political scapegoats. Even so, it is undeniable that there was an official policy of critique of anti-Semitism in the USSR, a fact that led to a feeling of sympathy toward the Soviet Union among some sectors of Bessarabia's Jewish population.

On the other hand, even the anticommunist Jews of Bessarabia found it difficult to identify enthusiastically with Romania. As in czarist Russia, pogroms had long been used as a tactic of political distraction there. Indeed, even before attaining its independence, the Romanian principalities were notorious for mistreatment of Jews, and pogroms there had risen to the level of international scandal. For example, in 1867, Napoleon III sent a telegram to Prince Charles of Moldavia, in which he made reference to the French opinion with respect to this matter: "I should not fail to make Your Highness aware of the public outcry raised here by the persecution directed against the Jews of Moldavia. I cannot believe that an enlightened government such as that of Your Highness might authorize measures so opposed to humanity and civilization."[18] A couple of years later, President Ulysses S. Grant named a Sephardic Jewish attorney, Benjamin Franklin Peixotto, as the first American representative to the newly founded Romanian Republic.

Grant reminded Peixotto that "the suffering of the Hebrews of Romania profoundly touches every sensibility of our nature. It is one long series of outrage and wrong, and even if there be exaggeration in the accounts which have reached us, enough is evident to prove the imperative duty of all civilized nations to extend their moral aid on behalf of a people so unhappy."[19]

Peixotto thus arrived in Romania with the express mission of defending its Jews, and he indeed found them in a downtrodden state. The political class refused to grant them citizenship, and lack of access to education weighed heavily on their shoulders. Within a year of his arrival, there was also a small pogrom. Peixotto soon made inquiries to see whether the Romanian government might be open to authorizing the emigration of Jews to the United States, and to his astonishment, Romanian prime minister Lascăr Catargiu took advantage of the query to declare that the emigration of *all* Romanian Jews to the United States was a "perfect solution," adding that he would gladly provide a passport to every Jewish person who was willing to leave.[20]

This offer of exit visas for all was especially poignant, because since its foundation Romania had refused to offer nationality to Jews who wished to *stay*. Under the Treaty of Berlin, Romania had committed to granting Jews citizenship, but it had then passed laws that required them to undergo a cumbersome naturalization process. Romanians persistently represented Jews as foreigners — vagabonds who had encroached on Romanian lands.

Long-standing legal injunctions that barred Jews from owning agricultural land also made them vulnerable to these charges. Thus, the absence of Jewish farmers was also put to work as alleged proof of their foreignness, an argument that then served to limit Jewish access to the university, white-collar professions, and the government. Not surprisingly, few Jews passed the Romanian naturalization exam—exclusion was, after all, its sole purpose. So, between 1878 and 1912, only four thousand applicants—or roughly 1 to 2 percent of all Jews in Romania—obtained Romanian nationality. And yet now, when given the opportunity to usher them out of the country, the prime minister didn't flinch at offering them all passports!

The dream of ethnic cleansing, of eliminating all Jews, thus existed in Romania in an open and official way from the time of its independence, a political impulse that cannot be imputed to Germany at its foundation, for instance, for all of its crimes in the twentieth century: Bismarck never made any move to incentivize the mass emigration of German Jews to America.

Body matters

My grandparents dressed modestly. My grandmother scarcely wore necklaces, and she had no fancy jewelry that I can remember. My grandfather wore standard-issue gray pants and a jacket of the sort that in South America might mark him as a teacher, perhaps, or an office employee. They dressed like citizens, I suppose, which sounds completely bland, but in South America the figure of the citizen had long been an unobtainable collective obsession, so that such clothes could be worn with pride.

In the decades following independence, South America's much touted national citizens were about as rare as unicorns.

So, like unicorns, they were painted and embroidered just about everywhere. How could it be otherwise? Colonial society had been divided into castes. It was a society of masters and slaves, serfs and guilds, clerics and soldiers, Indians, Africans and Spaniards...Political subjects were anything but equal to one another, nor were they part of the same cultural communities. Even the region's lingua franca — Spanish — was comfortably spoken only by a minority. So that building a citizenry became a national obsession.

But creating citizens required nothing less than the rise of a new social class: the much pined-for "middle class." This is because the prototypical citizen could scarcely be culled from the old landed gentry any more than from its native serfs. When would those two ever be "equal"? When would either caste be in a position to represent the national interest as a whole? Never. Nor could the coveted new citizenry emerge from the cities' swollen "rabble" of half-naked porters and ragged prostitutes, street vendors, pickpockets, and drunks. A citizen had to be capable of holding his own, he had at the very least to *look* like a man who was independent, though not either like a man who was always surrounded by a throng of lackeys and dependents.

For these reasons, South American nationalists were confident that they could identify the citizen-unicorn when they saw him: a citizen's appearance was all-important. The citizen wore clothes, and didn't walk about half-naked. And he didn't dress like an Indian, either. In order to speed this process along, President Porfirio Díaz of Mexico even passed laws forcing rural folk to wear trousers whenever they entered a city, under penalty of a hefty fine. Though, then again, neither was the citizen an aristocrat. He had to wear clothes that were commonly available, and that signaled equality as a collective aspiration. So when I say that my grandparents dressed like citizens, it means that they embodied a political aspiration: in their generation, the unicorns had finally materialized!

Truth be told, though, something funny had already been happening with my grandparents' bearing even before they came to South America.

left: Lisa Noemí Milstein at eighteen years old. Lima, 1929.
right: Misha Adler at seventeen years old. Nova Sulitza, c. 1921.

The earliest image that I have of Misha is a photograph taken in Odessa: a studio portrait, wearing his school uniform. It has a certain martial air that I suppose was common in those times of high militarism: during the First World War, even students dressed like soldiers! The date on the photograph is December 6, 1917, so it was taken during the Russian Revolution. Misha was thirteen years old, and the dedication written on the back of the photo says, in Ukrainian, "A memento of Misha." The picture was taken to commemorate his bar mitzvah, which in those schools were group events, celebrated on the same day for an entire cohort, and not the sort of lavish extravaganzas that some of us have grown accustomed to.

Misha Adler in his school uniform, December 6, 1917.
Odessa is suggested in the marina on the studio backdrop.

The photograph provides a clue to the rebellion in which my grandfather's generation participated, for the military uniform counters the image of the Jews that then circulated in

Russia. One recurring anti-Semitic theme was that Jews were incapable of serving in the military, and therefore they did not deserve to be citizens. An entire physiognomy was invented to justify this prejudice, featuring flat, pigeon-toed feet, a stooping posture, and an overall sickliness.[21]

To be a citizen meant to be able to defend oneself, and it is without a doubt as an answer to the charge of being unfit for citizenship that at the First Zionist Congress (1898), Max Nordau called for the development of a "muscular Judaism." My grandfather entered adulthood at a moment of intense struggle for full Jewish citizenship, and his first photograph already announces active rejection of the stereotypical physiognomy of "his race." Although maybe by December 1917 that particular stereotype had already been debunked in revolutionary Russia, whose Red Army was being organized by a Jew (Leon Trotsky).

The rebellion against prototypical images of the Jewish body also implied a dismissal of the traditional forms of life, dress, and presentation of Eastern European Jews, who had long embraced the intensely segregated life of the shtetl, grounded for the most part around Hasidic religious communities. This was also the case of Nova Sulitza, whose principal religious community belonged to a Hasidic sect, the Sagidura. The town's basic education, especially that of the poor, was in their hands.

There was nothing more contrary to the Hasidic sensibility than the socialist ideology of the Hashomer Hatzair, a movement to which my grandparents belonged. Founded in Galicia (Poland) in 1913, the Hashomer Hatzair, which in English means "Youth Guard," had two components: one rooted in scouting, the other in Zionism. The focus on scouting was part of the spirit of the time. It combined the relatively recently consolidated idea of youth—which is a social category that supposes a break between the past and the future—with the discovery of nature and the consolidation of collective identity, especially national identity.

One of its first expressions was the Wandervogel movement, founded in Berlin in 1901. Shortly afterward, in 1908, Robert Baden Powell founded the Boy Scouts in Great Britain. In each case, the idea was to bring young people close to nature and thereby to know their own hearts. Scouting was of a piece with the Romantic sensibility, and it went hand in hand with the widespread mood of nationalism that was general at the time, and most especially in Eastern Europe. It cultivated the figure of youth as the foundation of a collective future.

All of the nationalisms of the period participated in this sensibility. In the United States, for example, the determination to strengthen the virility and health of the nation through nature manifested itself in a thousand ways, from the design of Central Park in New York and ordinances requiring houses to be properly ventilated, to the environmentalist ideas of John Muir, to Teddy Roosevelt's enthusiasm for founding national parks. Fresh air, exercise, and wide-open spaces were seen as keys to achieving national strength. In such a movement, the overcrowded environment of the Jewish ghetto and even of the shtetl seemed to be the very antithesis of public health, and so cultivating a relationship with "nature" was a poignant issue for Eastern European Jews. It was also for this very reason that to found a Jewish scouting movement implied a radicalism that was very specific, since it subverted the most deeply rooted and pernicious stereotypes regarding "the Jew."

Each of my grandparents, separately, joined the Hashomer Hatzair: my grandfather in Nova Sulitza, in the 1910s, and my grandmother in Czernowitz, in the 1920s. Maybe their early choice helps explain the paradox of their physical appearance, which was at once exuberant and austere.

Movements like the Hashomer Hatzair promoted athleticism, personal assuredness, and resilience, alongside a certain asceticism. For Jews, self-assuredness was itself exuberant, since it involved rejecting racial stigmata: athleticism flew in the face of reigning stereotypes of the Jew as crooked weakling and hysteric. For women, self-assuredness involved the added refusal of their subjection, which in traditional settings was often brutal. On the other hand, like the communist youth movements, the *shomrim* (members of the Hashomer Hatzair) rejected everything that reeked of "bourgeois vice," such as smoking or drinking. So it was both spartanism and rebelliousness, rolled into one.

Here is an early picture of Misha's scouting group, known in the movement as a *kvutzah*. Misha is the one in the shirt that was colored with crayons by my uncle. The ten boys, aged roughly fifteen years, wear uniforms inspired by those of the Boy Scouts.

And here is another photograph of the same *kvutzah*, with my grandfather a little bit older (about seventeen), at the center of the photo. He was a group leader.

Misha Adler (*second row, third from right*)
with other members of his *kvutzah*. Nova Sulitza, c. 1918.

The *madrij* Misha Adler (*center*) with the *janjim* of his *kvutzah*, c. 1921 or 1922.

Boys and girls are together even in their serious gazes, deliberately ignoring the religious norm of segregation between the sexes that was still dominant in Nova Sulitza. They are comrades, and camaraderie went hand in hand with socialism, which was the ideology of the movement, together with the aspiration of national liberation. Jewishness here was being vindicated as a collective identity rather than as a commitment to adhere to religious rules.

Misha Adler (*center*) with close friends from his *kvutzah*, all wearing some sort of political pin. Nova Sulitza, c. 1922.

And here, finally, is a third image, where the group has developed a touch of dandyism that contrasts with the image of the Jew in the anti-Semitic propaganda that circulated through Romania during this period.

As in many other cases, dandyism developed in an open rebellion against a society that sought to degrade a racialized minority. Misha was born at a time of intensification of scapegoat politics against Russia's Jewry, and that was the backdrop against which both dandyism and "muscular Judaism" developed. Indeed, the first Jewish militia in Nova Sulitza formed around the time of Misha's birth, after the pogroms in Kishinev and Japan's defeat of the Russian army. Later, around the time of the Russian Revolution, a second local militia formed to protect the community from the pillaging of soldiers who had deserted.[22] It is quite possible that young Misha was among them.

CHAPTER THREE

Emancipation and Emigration

Education

Misha was the first of his family to undertake advanced study. His father, Hershel, identified with the values of the Haskallah. This movement was launched in the eighteenth century by Moses Mendelssohn, who argued that enlightenment was not some peculiarly French thing, but rather that it was just a name for scientific and rational knowledge. Ideally, Mendelssohn argued, enlightenment should always go hand in hand with cultivation, that is with moral and practical refinement, but these two did not always advance in tandem. So, for instance, the French had more refinement than enlightenment, while the English and the Prussians had more enlightenment than refinement.[23] All nations of the world should strive for both.

Mendelssohn worked accordingly to bring Judaism into enlightened recognition by way of his translations of portions of the Hebrew Bible into German. More deeply, his work on the philosophy of Maimonides showed the way forward for the enlightened Jews: already in the twelfth century Maimonides had proved that every part of Jewish law serves a rational purpose. Judaism and rationality were thereby wedded in the holy scriptures themselves! Enlightened Jews took this as a cue, and turned their backs to the Hasidic enclosure; they preferred to see themselves as modern heirs to the tradition of Maimonides. Why should they play second fiddle to the Parisian *philosophes?* Enlightenment, rationality, and science belonged to the world and, as Maimonides had proved long ago, the Jews had long been there, and they'd long done that.

Jewish rationalism spread quickly during the nineteenth century. Periodicals associated with the Jewish Enlightenment had been arriving in Nova Sulitza even since Hershel's youth, journals such as *Ha-Melitz* from Odessa and *Ha-Tsefirah* from Warsaw. Although the village had no telephone or telegraph office, it was the terminus of one of the three railroad lines that existed in Bessarabia. Thanks to this, newspapers were available.

Even so, the high level of cultural accomplishment that developed in places like Nova Sulitza still baffles me. There were, after all, no public schools there, nor was there an integrated secular school where Jews and Christians might mingle and learn from one another. There was only a Jewish school (cheder) for boys and a Talmud Torah, which offered religious instruction. If girls wished to gain education, they had to train with private tutors. The policy of the Russian Empire had been to maintain only a small number of educational establishments in Bessarabia, so as to avoid any surge in Moldovan (or

Romanian) nationalism. The result was a high rate of illiteracy in the Bessarabian countryside. The urban minorities, for their part — Jews, Germans — relied on privately financed institutions, and they were better educated than the Moldovan population. According to British sources, in 1920 only 17 percent of Moldovan men and roughly 4 percent of women knew how to read, while 65 percent of Jewish men and 41 percent of Jewish women were literate.[24]

But educational aspirations often went well beyond mere literacy. Misha's father, for instance, had a soft spot for scientific education, so that Misha's schooling was not delivered by Hasids, as was the case for the poorer families of the village, who ended up learning little more than rudimentary Hebrew and error-filled Yiddish.[25] People of education and means, like the Adler family, fled from such educational establishments and sent their children away to study.

Although my grandfather first attended the Tarbut school in Nova Sulitza, he later boarded in a Gymnasium in Odessa, rather than the more usual option in German-speaking Czernowitz. Misha's first cousin on his mother's side, the well-known German and Yiddish writer Vera Haquen, was from Odessa, and the appeal of having family there might have been a factor in this decision. In any case, my grandfather came to speak and write Russian better than German, while my grandmother, who went to school in Czernowitz, spoke German better than Russian.

After the end of the First World War, Misha's father dispatched him to study engineering at the University of Vienna, but once there, Misha decided to abandon engineering and enrolled instead in the academy of Rabbi Zvi Peretz Chayes, who directed an institute dedicated to Hebrew linguistics and philology. Misha was not attracted to this topic for religious reasons. He was interested in the Bible, the Talmud, and the Mishna as literature, as language, and as an expression of national genius, but his deeper concern was with Hebrew as a feat of collective will.

After all, the rebirth of Hebrew had begun only very recently, and like Esperanto, it too emerged in the old Russian Empire. Its utopian horizon was the rebirth of a Jewish world that might bring together Yiddish, Ladino, and Arabic speakers into a single, vibrant, cultural community. So, for instance, the Lithuanian-born Eliezer Ben Yehuda (né Eliezer Perlman, 1854–1922), who authored the first Hebrew dictionary, got the idea of reviving Hebrew not in Lithuania or in Palestine (where he emigrated in 1881), but rather as a student in Paris, where he communicated with a Sephardic friend using the Hebrew that they both shared. Hebrew could thus be a language of unification that brought the potential of the past into the living present, and so opened up a horizon of national emancipation far beyond the old Pale of Settlement.

Zionism, immigration

The most famous rabbis from Nova Sulitza were Rabbi Faso and his son-in-law, Haim Hier. It was the latter's son-in-law, a rabbi from Radosimel, Ukraine, who began Zionist education in the village. On Friday nights, he gave sermons in Hebrew. He was also the director of the Tarbut school, which had a Zionist orientation. Rabbi Faso had attended the First Zionist

Congress in Basel (1897), and he wrote articles in *Ha-Tzfira* (The Siren), the first Hebrew-language newspaper to be published in Poland. I imagine that the rabbi may well have had an influence on my grandfather, although there would have been other sources from which to absorb Zionist ideology too, given Misha's involvement in the Hashomer Hatzair.

Around 1910, seven years before the founding of the first Romanian public library in Kishinev (the capital of Bessarabia), a clandestine — or at least somewhat discreet — Jewish public library was founded in Nova Sulitza. Czarist policy ran against such establishments. It had volumes in Yiddish, Russian, and Hebrew, hundreds of users, and several reading groups, some of which were oriented toward Jewish nationalism. One of these was called "Lovers of Zion," and another was "Languages of the Past."[26] I imagine that my grandfather must have belonged to one or both of these groups, perhaps Languages of the Past, since Misha and his friends took to speaking to one another in Hebrew in the village streets, which was an oddity and an affectation at the time.

Why was Misha so attracted to Zionism? Jewish emancipation had a central place in my grandfather's process of self-fashioning. I've already said that. And the ideals of universal emancipation — socialism — were identified with Jewish emancipation. That too. I think that a comparison between Misha and Zionism's founder, Theodor Herzl, may help round out the picture.

Like my grandfather, Herzl was from a relatively well-to-do family. Also like Misha, he aspired to be an engineer, but soon found his vocation in the humanities instead — in his case, in poetry and theater. Herzl was oriented toward the world rather than religion. He was an atheist, and his interest in Judaism was cultural, historical, and political rather than religious: religion for him mattered more than anything as a cultural accomplishment. In all of this, he resembled my grandfather, although there is admittedly an ocean of distance between Budapest, a metropolis, and Nova Sulitza, a shtetl in a remote and backward region. And also, of course, between Herzl's great fame and my grandfather's modest reputation.

Even so, there were parallels between the two men. In both cases, for example, Jewish nationalism took form as a response to the impossibility of genuine citizenship. Thus, the young Herzl had emigrated to Vienna to study law and tried to join a German nationalist group, which he later renounced over the group's anti-Semitism. Herzl found that he could not be admitted as a full contributor to the Germanic *Geist*, despite the Austro-Hungarian Empire's emancipation of Jews. There had been formal political emancipation, yes, but with it came a proliferation of informal expressions of anti-Semitism. The fullness of national identification thus remained frustrated.[27]

Like Herzl, my grandfather was also sent to study engineering at the University of Vienna, only to discover that his talent was in the humanities — in languages, philosophy, and journalism. Like Herzl, too, his turn toward Hebrew and Judaica was founded in a worldly orientation that had little to do with religion. Religion was for Misha an aspect of Jewish cultural history, but his aspirational aims were primarily oriented toward socialism. His community of reference for political action, though, could hardly be Romania, where anti-Semitism was so powerful.

Indeed, when the new Romanian constitution finally proclaimed Jewish emancipation, in 1923, a militantly anti-Semitic political party emerged, the League of National Christian Defense. It had been launched by Alexandru Cuza, a law professor at the University of Iasi. Four years later, a second organization was formed, the Legion of the Archangel Michael, known also as the Iron Guard, which was a militant group that also had many followers in the universities.

A stamp from the Romanian Republic, 1940, with an image
of the founder of the Iron Guard, Corneliu Codreanu.

It is no accident that anti-Semitism flourished in Romanian schools and universities. Jews there made up the most thriving portion of the middle classes, and they tended to do well in school. Romania was mainly an agrarian country, and the middle classes relied heavily on white-collar jobs and government posts. For this reason, nationalists looked to marginalize the participation of Jews in schools and universities, beating them, intimidating them, changing their grades, or blocking them from passing exams.

Little wonder that in Nova Sulitza there was a lot of support for the founding of a Jewish state in the period following the First World War, even though only a few people actually emigrated to Palestine at that time. Those who did were mostly idealists from the middle-class and upper-middle-class sectors of the village—the Herzls, one might say—many of whom ended up returning, due to the difficult material conditions that they often faced there.

The Balfour Declaration (1918) had unlatched Jewish immigration from Eastern Europe to Palestine. Known as the Third Aliyah, this population movement was provoked by factors that touched Misha's own life: the Russian Revolution, pogroms, the military draft, economic depression, and increased anti-Semitism after the First World War. Delegates from Hotin—the district in which Nova Sulitza was located—attended a Zionist conference in Brisheni (Bessarabia) in 1918, which generated a buzz in the village, most especially among children from "good families," like Misha's. A village history recounts how in those years young men and women from good families rushed to become pioneers:

> They left their homes and moved to a barracks called Pioneer House, where they ate and slept. They walked through the village daily, dressed in work clothing, carrying their work tools on their shoulders and performing heavy labor . . . [F]inally, on August 23, 1921, they made Aliyah [that is, they left for Palestine]. Large

numbers of villagers came to the train station to say their good-byes. They arrived in Haifa on September 24, 1921.[28]

Some of the pictures of my grandfather with his friends from Hashomer Hatzair were probably taken in the "Pioneer House" to which this history alludes, so they would have been camping in conditions designed to prepare them for kibbutz life, but it is likely that Misha missed the chance that he had been preparing for, because in 1923, the British Empire closed off Jewish immigration to Palestine and so brought the Third Aliyah to an end, though only after some forty thousand Jews had moved to the region. Misha and his cohort at the Hashomer Hatzair could not wait around Nova Sulitza for a second chance to go to Palestine, either, because they were collectively threatened with a military draft that especially targeted the regions recently annexed by the new Greater Romania.

With the Palestine option taken off the table, Misha and his whole *kvutzah* boarded a ship headed for Peru, a country that was looking for European workers as a eugenics-inspired counterbalance to the large number of Chinese immigrants that it had previously received. In doing so, Misha followed the preferred migration pattern of the overwhelming majority of the village, because as a rule Nova Sulitza's migrants did better in South America than they did in Palestine. Indeed, by the late 1920s there was not a single Nova Sulitzer family that didn't have at least one relative in South America, with the greatest concentration of them in Lima. Remittances from these migrants effectively saved the village from starvation during the economic depression that struck after the close of the First World War.[29]

CHAPTER FOUR

Their First America

How they arrived

Misha arrived in Lima when he was nineteen years old. What was it like? What were his impressions? I only know a little about all of this. Misha's ship left Europe from the port of La Pallice (La Rochelle), France. In those days, passenger liners also transported cargo, so they probably stopped either in Havana or Santo Domingo and Cartagena (Colombia) before crossing the Panama Canal, which had only just been inaugurated nine years before that. The canal was universally admired as an awesome feat of modern engineering as well as a resounding triumph for the new field of tropical medicine, without which it could never have been built. After Panama, Misha's ship probably stopped in Guayaquil and then went finally on to the port of Callao, just outside Lima, where the vessel either concluded its journey or went on to Valparaíso for a final stop. Peru and Chile were the farthermost destinations for shipping along the South American Pacific, and they were about as far from Nova Sulitza as anywhere on the planet.

The ships docked for a couple of days at each port to load and unload cargo, so my grandfather had received early impressions of the tropics before reaching Peru's dry coastal plane: the luminous colors of Havana and Cartagena, the cool shade of the jungle canopy in Panama and Colombia, the bustle of vendors peddling tropical fruits, dolphins racing at the bow of the ship... Misha saw black people, possibly for the first time in his life. And Indians, certainly for the first time. He heard the gentle cadence of South American Spanish, so tantalizingly close to Romanian, and yet never quite intelligible either.

My grandfather loved the tropics. In fact, he was still fascinated by Amazonia when I knew him, four decades later. I found some of his reading notes from the early 1960s on John Collier's *The Indians of the Americas* (1947), where Misha writes: "Cast into the wilderness and hidden there for generations, hungry, the groups of Indians managed to keep their languages alive, their religion, their cultural systems, symbols, and mental and emotional faculties with regard to their sense of self and the world." The jungles of South America were a place in which cultures had persisted in ways that had an uncanny resonance — almost like a counterfactual — to the crumbling lifeworld of the shtetl: the Indians "did not remain fossilized, unadapted or enclosed in the past but rather remodeled, assimilated but remaining true to their ancient values, these societies kept their idiosyncrasies." I still have in my library a few of his old books: vocabularies of the Warao language, *La musique des*

Incas et ces survivances, ethnographic reports on the Indians of the Colombian Amazon, that sort of thing.

I think that Misha had fallen in love with America even before reaching Peru, or navigating the frigid Antarctic current that brings Lima its rich fishing stock and its coastal dryness. I imagine that Lima was a gray city then. In my mind that city has always been gray, though also beautiful in its fashion. It had been built by the conquerors, so all of its people were migrants — descendants of African slaves, of Spaniards, of Indians from the Sierra. A Chinese population was brought in as indentured plantation labor, and also many Japanese migrants, who were sometimes confused with them. Some Italians too. With the First World War a new wave of Europeans came from that continent's collapsed empires: migrants from Aleppo, Damascus, and Beirut, and now, too, from Romania, Hungary, and Poland.

Misha arrived in Lima on November 19, 1924.[30] He had been supported in his travel by his father, and with the notion that he would work there for a couple of years, until the danger of the military draft had passed. The idea of going to Peru, specifically, supposedly came from a friend from the Hashomer Hatzair whose last name was Peker, who was already in Lima selling clothing door-to-door. He sent postcards to his friends, bragging about his charm with Lima's widows, who not only opened up their doors to his wares but were also happy to welcome him into their beds. No doubt the young man added these embellishments to encourage his friends to come.

Jewish emigration from Nova Sulitza to South America began around 1918, owing to the economic depression that was brought on by the Great War. In the case of Nova Sulitza, the crisis was acute, because after the collapse of the Austro-Hungarian and Russian Empires, the town no longer sat on an international border, since it had passed into Romanian hands instead. A goodly portion of Nova Sulitza's import-export business died as a result. Moreover, the Romanian government raised taxes on Bessarabian Jews. And to complete the picture, there was a drought.[31]

But they say that when God closes the door, he opens a window, and Nova Sulitza's economic downturn coincided with the implementation of a new wave of settlement policies in South America. In Peru, the newly instated president Augusto Leguía passed a decree on October 10, 1919, guaranteeing Europeans, with the exception of Gypsies, a free boat ride to Lima for themselves and up to three family members, and thence to cover all transportation costs to the Peruvian interior that they were meant to "colonize." This offer proved to be attractive to Romanian and Hungarian Jews.[32]

The Eastern European Jews who arrived in Peru had to operate in a complicated racial hierarchy that was new to them. When I asked Misha what it had been like to land in Peru he said that it was wonderful to arrive to a place where "no one knew what a Jew was." The nation's chief polarity had always been between Spaniards and Indians, a division that was expressed in regional terms as animosity between the Coast and the Andes, and most especially between Lima — a walled town built by and for conquistadors — and the Sierra. Indeed, until very recently, the term *serrano* (native of the Sierra) was used in Lima as a slur that meant "Indian." This was Peru's core drama. But there were also other, less salient, racial distinctions that were also relevant for the new Jewish immigrants.

After independence, the Spanish American republics had stagnated. Indeed, that was the period when the distance between the wealth of the United States and that of Latin America became a chasm, and the United States emerged as an empire, while Latin America became its imperial "sphere of influence." There was a demographic dimension to this story, too, for while the population of the United States almost tripled between 1820 and 1850 — from a little over nine million to over twenty-three million — the population of Mexico, which was Spanish America's most populous republic, stagnated at around fourteen million. The other Spanish American republics pretty much followed suit.

In response to this prolonged demographic slump, the Argentine statesman Juan Bautista Alberdi famously pronounced the formula *gobernar es poblar* (to govern is to populate), which became a byword for progressive politics throughout the continent. The guiding idea was to foster "civilized," that is, European, immigration that might settle (i.e., "colonize") the countryside, and so substitute a quasi-feudal landscape of semiruined estates, miserable peons, and enormous fallows with productive farms, white-picket fences, and an upright and properly informed citizenry. In the final quarter of the nineteenth century, the rise of Social Darwinism provided a second, supplementary rationale for fostering European migration, which was to "improve the (national) race." Some countries, such as Argentina, Uruguay, and Brazil, attracted massive numbers of European migrants, especially from Southern Europe. However, places like Mexico or Peru, which had an abundant and very poorly paid (indigenous or black) labor force, were less successful.

Peru's situation was somewhat peculiar, though. Geographically, the country is composed of a coastal desert that, when watered, is propitious for highly productive commercial agriculture; a massive, difficult-to-access Andean region which was once the center of the Inca empire and is the heartland of Peru's indigenous population; and vast Amazonian territories east of the Andes. During the colonial period, Peru's coastal agriculture relied on African slave labor, but after the slave trade came to a close at the start of the nineteenth century, coastal plantation owners turned to southern China for indentured labor. Between 1847 and 1876 Peruvian entrepreneurs imported around 100,000 Chinese "coolies" (indentured servants) to work on the sugar and cotton plantations, build the country's railroads, and mine guano (bird excrement that was profitably exported to Europe as fertilizer). Nearly half of these workers died of exhaustion, malnutrition, or suicide, in addition to the many thousands who died on the overcrowded ships that traveled to Callao from Hong Kong, an ordeal that is said to have been as deadly as the Middle Passage of the African slave trade.

After the end of the coolie trade, in 1876, the "Chinese race" was still considered inferior, so Peruvian migratory policy tended to discourage Asian immigration and levied all sorts of duties and limitations to the traffic. Moreover, as the Chinese established themselves in Lima, they became occasional political targets. Thus, in May 1909, a rabble of supporters of ousted president Nicolás de Piérola destroyed twenty-four Chinese businesses. Public opinion enthusiastically sided with the rabble, so Lima's entrepreneurial mayor Guillermo Billinghurst chimed in on the xenophobic spirit with an ordinance to destroy the Callejón Otaiza, an overcrowded tenement, and ousted the five hundred Chinese immigrants who lived there. Sensing a political opportunity, President Augusto Leguía, who was in his first term in office, also endorsed the anti-Chinese mood by suspending admission of all Chinese into the country.[33]

Peru's desire to foster European — over Chinese — immigration was thus such that it was willing to embrace migrants from backward Eastern Europe, and did not even care whether those who came were Jews. Its limit, tellingly, was Gypsies, who were excepted from the invitation to colonize the Peruvian interior on account of their transhumance and reputation for thievery. In other words, despite the fact that Misha arrived in a country where Catholicism was the official religion, and that Jews were understood by eugenicists of the period as being a far cry from any optimal race, their situation in the local racial hierarchy was actually pretty good, since they could blend in with the European minority to a considerable degree, and not be confused with Lima's underclass of Indian, African, and Chinese migrants.

This did not mean that they had it easy, though. Migrants to Lima were at first almost completely men, and they tended to work as door-to-door salesmen (known in Yiddish as *klappers*) selling clothes on installments, which was a new sales method back then. The Jewish peddler was thus simultaneously a seller, a credit appraiser, and a payments collector, and his work life was exhausting. The Colombian-Yiddish writer (and former peddler) Salomón Brainski invokes the solitude of these salesmen in a story of a peddler who speaks of missing his only friend "in this far-off land, where one feels at times as alone as a lost dog, barking with a howl in its innards, behind a wall, on a dark night."[34]

Jewish peddlers in the Bogotá press.
left: El Tiempo, September 13, 1941.
right: El Espectador, February 27, 1936.

Peker's story about the merry widows of Lima was likely a youthful exaggeration, penned more or less transparently to coax his far-flung friends to come join him. But with no future in Bessarabia and the imminent threat of forced military recruitment, even the improbable promise of *Arabian Nights*–style erotic encounters may have interested the young men of Misha's *kvutzah*: it offered them adventure in the face of the unknown. Besides, they had no better alternative than to migrate; any glimmer of hope or adventure was welcome.

Indeed, with or without such erotic enticements, my uncle Zuñe ("Alfonso"), Misha's younger brother, emigrated to South America at roughly the same time as Misha, but to Cumaná (Venezuela) to work as a peddler. His friend Susye (Israel Mailijson) went with him, and ended up marrying one of Misha's sisters, my aunt Ana. The other sister, Rebeca, later married Sima Vurgait, who arrived in Peru on the same ship as my grandfather. By the mid-1920s long-distance migration was widespread among the male youth of Nova Sulitza, and in many cases these young men ended up marrying each other's sisters and cousins, and taking them to South America as well.

Beginnings

Upon arriving in Peru, Misha didn't work as a peddler like most of his shipmates. He had a talent for languages. When I met him, he spoke Hebrew, Yiddish, Russian, German, Romanian, French, English, and Spanish. He had begun to study Spanish on the ship, so that when he arrived in Lima he spoke it well enough that a Sephardic businessman, whose name was Sarfaty, hired him to mediate with the other "Romanians."

Lima was growing at the time of Misha's arrival, but it still only had about 200,000 inhabitants. Around 80 percent of the Peruvian population still lived in the countryside. Indians made up around four-fifths of the national population, and only half of all Peruvians even understood Spanish. Still, the 1920s were a moment of cultural effervescence in Peru. Thus, in his study of the Mariátegui Circle, Oscar Terán notes that between 1918 and 1930 the number of publications tripled, and there was a surge in centers of cultural production in each of the principal cities of the Peruvian provinces.[35]

In the middle of this (slow) cultural awakening, there was then arriving in Peru a very modest, but nonetheless consequential, number of Jews. In 1898, there were scarcely forty-three Jews in Peru. Around the time of the First World War, roughly 120 Sephardic immigrants arrived there from the collapsing Ottoman Empire, among whom was Sarfaty. The Sephardim had the advantage of speaking Ladino, which is an old Spanish dialect. Shortly afterward, Ashkenazi Jews began to arrive, mainly from Romania (55 percent) and to a lesser degree from Poland, Russia, and Hungary.[36] The majority of these settled in Lima's Chirimoyo neighborhood, and they founded the Unión Israelita del Perú in 1923, just before Misha's arrival. The first Peruvian synagogue was established in 1934, but this came after Misha and Noemí had left.

The Jews of these generations alternated residence between Lima and the provinces. As the majority were traveling salesmen, they tended to establish themselves in commercial centers such as Trujillo, Huancayo, Arequipa, Lambeyeque, and Piura. This was in keeping with President Leguía's intent, which had been for European migrants to colonize the interior. If they happened to be doctors or dentists, it was also easier to find clients in these provincial towns. In all, and despite continued Jewish migration to Peru during the 1930s, as late as 1948 there were scarcely 2,800 Jews in all of Peru, of which about half (1,200) lived outside of Lima.

My uncle Sima, for example, traveled extensively through the country. He gave music lessons and established a small studio in Huancayo. It turns out that he also had a flair for entertainment. Misha even worked as his part-time manager at one point, and arranged a few public performances by the "King of the Mandolin and Unicycle." When I met him, my uncle Sima was old and sedate — a bit depressed, as I remember him. I never suspected that he could play the mandolin while riding on his unicycle! Age can change you, I suppose.

Isaac Perlman, with the look of an officer in some European army, and his indigenous helpers, carrying merchandise. Cerro de Pasco, Peru, 1920s.

Isaac Perlman, who would marry the younger sister of my grandmother Noemí, is another example of Jewish migration to the Peruvian provinces. He arrived with all of his family from Hotin, Bessarabia. Perlman had been an officer in the Romanian army, which was an exceptional situation that suggests a high degree of assimilation and wealth. The Perlman family emigrated with some resources, and Isaac was able to set up a business shortly after his arrival, in the mining town of Cerro del Pasco (Peru) and later in Cúcuta, on the border between Colombia and Venezuela. For his part, Misha helped Sarfaty manage his Yiddish-speaking vendors, so he didn't go to live outside the capital. He negotiated an arrangement with his boss that allowed him time to study at the Universidad Mayor de San Marcos.

San Marcos

Founded in 1551, Lima's Universidad de San Marcos was the oldest in the Western Hemisphere, and yet this noble aura was manifest mainly in the form of a kind of smug conformity. At the start of the twentieth century, Peru's greatest university was just a provincial backwater. Run by lawyers and petty clerks, it was acutely portrayed by Mariátegui as "a static university; a mediocre center of indolent and priggish bourgeois culture that offers a sampling of dead ideas."[37] Sodom and Gomorra had been lost for want of ten just men; the Universidad de San Marcos, according to Mariátegui, was lost because it did not have a single great teacher.[38]

Even so, the university remained a neuralgic point for Peruvian politics. The country had never had a civilian president who had not studied there.[39] Given its political centrality, then, one might consider the decline of San Marcos as a symptom of the general decline of Peru. At the time of San Marcos's founding, in the mid-sixteenth century, Lima was

Spain's viceregal capital for the whole of South America, and it was a commercial hub for the richest silver and gold mining region in the world. But Lima later underwent a process of slow decline, due in part to that city's cumbersome location. By the eighteenth century silver exports from Upper Peru (today Bolivia) bypassed Lima, and began to be shipped to Europe by way of Buenos Aires, on the Atlantic. By the end of that century, Spain carved out two new South American viceroyalties at Peru's expense, New Granada and Río de la Plata, with capitals in Bogotá and Buenos Aires.

Lima's decline was later exacerbated during the War of the Pacific (1879–84), when Peru lost its southernmost province of Tarapacá, and Bolivia lost Antofagasta to the Chileans. The Peruvian war against Chilean imperialism is in some ways reminiscent of the Mexican-American War (1846–48), and it hit Peru very hard indeed. The country was ruined economically and socially upended, and it lost its rich saltpeter mines as well as major copper repositories. Saltpeter was a necessary ingredient for gunpowder and there was a major market for that product, driven by militarism in Europe, the United States, and Asia. Copper, for its part, was about to begin its meteoric rise as an export commodity, owing to Thomas Edison's development of electric lighting in 1879, and Peru was unable to reap those benefits. In addition, Lima itself was occupied and ravaged by Chilean forces.

The form of governance that emerged in Peru after this debacle is often referred to as the Aristocratic Republic, an arrangement that lasted from 1895 until the election of Augusto Leguía, in 1919. The period is roughly contemporary with the Belle Epoque in Europe, though it begins later and then runs on through to the end of the First World War. Essentially, the national government was now run by a coterie of businessmen, mostly members of the Partido Civil, and therefore antagonistic to military rule. The principal actors in the reigning coalition were owners of the rich sugar and cotton plantations of the Peruvian coast, bankers, newspaper owners, landowners, and rentiers. This was also a time when the tension between Lima and the Andean region had grown even stronger, because the collapse of the Peruvian army during the Chilean invasion prompted peasant rebellions in the southern Andes that were then quelled from Lima. Indeed, the República Aristocrática developed as an adamantly Lima-centered variant of the positivist-inspired progressivism that was general in Latin America in this period, with its power tied to financial capital, the rentier economy, and commercial agriculture.

The *civilistas* (members of the Partido Civil) promoted the virtues of a civilian-led democracy, as against military dictatorship, but theirs was a democracy that excluded Peru's Indian majority. So, for instance, in 1896 the *civilistas* passed an electoral law restricting voting rights to citizens who could read and write. It is likely that illiteracy rates hovered around 80 percent in those years. Even in Lima there was considerable illiteracy, especially in the nonwhite population.[40]

Civilismo was thus run by a minuscule coterie known, revealingly, as Los Veinticuatro Amigos (The Twenty-Four Friends), a group that met on Fridays at Lima's Club Nacional, a gentlemen's club that had been founded in 1855, at the height of Peru's guano boom, and that was modeled on London's famous men's clubs. Top-hat-and-cane-bearing civilians were now running the show, and indeed the sleepy self-congratulatory comfort at the Universidad de San Marcos that Mariátegui decried was very much of a piece with *civilismo*'s overall social and cultural enclosure. Indeed, all twenty of the university's permanent professorships were occupied by members of just three *civilista* families: the Pardos, the Prados, and the Miró Quesadas.[41]

Civilista president Manuel Pardo y Lavalle.

Still, all good things must come to an end, and Peru's rather anemic counterpart to the Belle Epoque entered a final stage of decline immediately after the First World War. On the social front, the *pax civilista* had provided some conditions for modest growth and economic improvement, and so new middle sectors emerged in Lima as well as in provincial cities. A new working class also sprung up around textiles, mining, and the sugar industry. Taken together, this change proved sufficient for the emergence of a new kind of government, which was no longer an oligarchy, but a more or less benign populist dictatorship, built on fragile interclass coalitions and a fair modicum of repression.

At its head was Augusto Leguía, a man who had once been a regular at the Club Nacional. Leguía had made his fortune in the sugar industry, and was later a pioneer in Peruvian insurance sales. He served as secretary of the Treasury under three different *civilista* presidents, and finally became president in 1908. During his first term, however, Leguía faced down an attempted coup, and left the *civilista* party. He later self-exiled to the United States, where he worked for the New York Insurance Company and learned American business methods. Leguía returned to Peru and to political life in 1919, won the presidential election against the *civilista* candidate José Pardo, and then led his own military coup to guarantee that his triumph at the ballot would be respected.

Leguía built himself up as a Wilsonian figure, and countered the Anglophilia of the *civilista* party and the Club Nacional by way of an American alliance. Great Britain had been Peru's imperial tutor for the whole of the nineteenth century; it had financed the railroads and it controlled the guano industry. But now, the Great War was over, and Peru's key patron was the United States, with its investments in sugar, rubber, mining, and tropical products.

left: Augusto Leguía. *right:* Woodrow Wilson.

It was in this context that the Universidad de San Marcos began to boil over. By the time of Leguía's ascent to power, the university's student body finally included members of the new middle classes, and not just Lima aristocrats. People like firebrand Víctor Haya de la Torre, from Trujillo, who was among the leaders for student reform, and who soon founded the Alianza Popular Revolucionaria Americana (APRA), often considered Latin America's first populist political party. Initially supportive of Leguía's bid for the presidency, that generation exploded the cultural cocoon of *civilismo*, and looked outward, to Mexico's Revolution, with its example of agrarian reform and its cultural rennaissance, for instance, or to Russia, and to the cultural ferment in Europe and Latin America. But it also looked inward, and asked one core question: Why was the Indian absent from Peruvian nationality and culture?

In 1919, San Marcos had its first student movement, which sought to oust a group of especially incompetent professors, and demanded student participation in the selection of new faculty. The students made some gains, but the university remained in *civilista* control, so that in 1923 there was a second movement, with similar claims. By then, the university had become a site for oppositional politics, which could give voice to a wide range of issues. So, for instance, a few months before Misha's arrival in Peru, Victor Haya de la Torre led a socialist and secularist protest movement against President Leguía, the students' erstwhile ally, in protest against his intention to "enshrine the Sacred Heart of Jesus as the patron saint of Peru." The protests ended with at least one casualty, and with Haya going into exile in Mexico.

Leguía's presidency was built on unstable coalitions, and it developed in dynamic tension with key actors. He had sent both Mariátegui and César Falcón into a gentle but compulsory exile (on government scholarship), and shut down their paper, *La Razón*, Lima's first left-wing daily. In 1923 Mariátegui returned from exile and was invited to be a teacher at a new institution, the Universidad Obrera Gonzales Prada, a night school for workers that had been founded by Haya de la Torre in 1921 in recognition of the structural limitations of the Universidad de San Marcos. At the Universidad Obrera, Mariátegui gave lectures on topics including the European war, the Russian Revolution, the German revolution, the Peace of Versailles, proletarian agitation in Europe, the crisis of democracy, and the crisis in philosophy. These were all topics unrepresented by the faculty at San Marcos, but that had plenty of interest among its students.

In this environment of cultural ebullience, Misha began to study philosophy, a subject in which he would receive his doctorate in 1930, with a dissertation on Karl Marx. I haven't been able to find my grandfather's thesis, because my grandfather had to leave Peru under complicated circumstances, and my friends in Lima have not yet found it in the university archives. I've no idea who in that faculty might have directed it. Maybe it will reappear one day. According to my uncle, it was the first thesis written on Karl Marx in any Peruvian university, which seems very likely to me. Marx would never have been a viable topic for a San Marcos thesis before the student movements of the early 1920s.

Misha Adler's doctorate certificate
from the Universidad de San Marcos, 1930.

Undoubtedly, Misha brought his interest in Marx from Europe. He was also at the time a sympathizer of the Russian Revolution, which he had witnessed firsthand while a young student in Odessa, and was himself a committed socialist. It is thus very likely that he would have read at least something by Marx in his youth, even if only the *Communist Manifesto*. He had very likely read a fair deal more than that.

Even so, it is likely that Misha decided to specialize in Marxist thought owing to his involvement in José Carlos Mariátegui's political movement. Jorge del Campo, a communist painter who was part of Mariátegui's inner circle, laid out the movement's organizational strategy:

> José Carlos organized the work in such a way that the comrades from *petit bourgeois* backgrounds, whether university students or young intellectuals, were required to adopt Marxism-Leninism — scientific socialism — in a systematic, theoretical, and practical way. This was not only an individual necessity but a function of the constructive labor that we were developing. It revolved around, as I've said, transmitting our theoretical knowledge to the worker groups then in the process of organization, collaborating with them where we might be useful.[42]

My grandfather's commitment to Mariátegui's course of action implied that, for him, the study of Marx was as much a practical matter of political militancy as a theoretically motivated choice. In any case, it is certain that Misha's interest in Marx took root in Peru, and in his participation in the group that met in the so-called Red Corner of Mariátegui's house.

The klapper *and national consciousness*

Misha had a number of qualities to bring to the discussions and activities that developed in Mariátegui's salon: translation, certainly, and formal training in Marx's thought, which was shared and transmitted in workers' circles. But there was also a third and more subtle contribution, I think, which was the fresh intensity with which Misha appreciated local reality.

Misha's generation embedded itself into Peruvian national society in a peculiar way. Jewish peddlers moved through the poorer neighborhoods and slums of capital cities such as Lima, and also in a far-flung network of provincial towns. Communication was effective in these networks, because the salesmen working in the provinces were connected to those in the capital, since they worked with the same suppliers. Moreover, they were in touch with a broader South American network through connections of family, place of origin, and language: Jews from villages such as Nova Sulitza had acquaintances and relatives in various South American countries.

This helps us grasp the almost incredible migratory trajectories of many of these migrants. For example, Boris Milstein, my great-grandfather, left Lima for Tuluá (Colombia), without first residing in Bogotá. Such a leap would have been unthinkable without a preexisting ethnic network that stretched from Lima to Bogotá, and from each of these capital cities to the provinces. Similarly, Isaac Perlman, who married my aunt Pupe, moved from Bessarabia to Cerro de Pasco (Peru), and from there to Cúcuta, on the border between Colombia and Venezuela. These places are thousands of miles apart, and they were entirely disconnected from one another. My uncles Zuñe and Susye, for their part, moved first to Cumaná (Venezuela), then returned to Bessarabia, and later moved to Bogotá and Caracas respectively.

Long-distance communication within the community had its commercial uses, but it was also vital for the social reproduction of the ethnic group, including for the arrangement of marriages, which was challenging for such a minuscule minority. In the case of Peru, door-to-door sales also provided opportunities for political observation and development, and so for leadership. So, for instance, one of the Bessarabian Jews who was close to Mariátegui, Bernardo Regman, was a *klapper* and then became a cofounder of the Socialist Party of Peru. He later would be the treasurer of the Peruvian Communist Party. Regman probably knew the poorer neighborhoods of Lima better even than Mariátegui, as he had spent years there knocking on every door.

The depth of knowledge that the small and hardworking community of Ashkenazi peddlers gained of the Peruvian "national reality" was extraordinary, although this knowledge was mostly unreciprocated: people tended to refer to them indiscriminately as "Turks," "Poles," "Russians," or "Germans," and they were commonly addressed as "Míster" (pronounced *meester*). Nonetheless, Jewish peddlers acquired close-up knowledge that, exceptionally, even spilled into the literary field. Thus, in his forward to the Spanish translation of a book of stories written by Brainski in Yiddish, the avant-garde Colombian poet Luis Vidales wrote: "I believe that Brainski has not received the attention in Colombia that he deserves...In a good portion of American literature (short stories and novels), the landscape is everything. Humans are only incidental playthings." For Vidales, this situation contrasted with the stories of Brainski, which emerged "from the daily customs of humble people, in their natural, logical, and realistic practice."[43] The point of view is symptomatic rather than exceptional. Young immigrant merchants and peddlers tended to reflect on the realities that they encountered. They had prejudices of their own, certainly, but at least their impressions were not governed by the preconceptions of the local middle classes.

So, while one of the reasons for Mariátegui's attraction to my grandparents had to do with his enthusiasm for Jewish high culture, the depth of their own "discovery of America" was also important, because it enriched everyday experience with a gaze from a remote and deeply cosmopolitan elsewhere. A gaze that came to know the lives of the local poor, but that was not blighted by illiteracy or devoid of cultural aspiration.

CHAPTER FIVE

Lisa Noemí Milstein

My grandparents met in Lima near the end of 1927, when my grandmother was fifteen years old.

Lisa Noemí Milstein was born on January 22, 1911, in Mogilev (district of Podolia, Ukraine), a small city on the Dniester River that then marked the border between Ukraine and Bessarabia. Her father, my great-grandfather Boris, was a small-scale industrialist and merchant. He came from a place near Mogilev called Jaruga, which is also on the Dniester, just a bit farther south. Boris had even served for a time as representative of the village. According to my uncle Manuel, "he sometimes had a drink with the goyim (the Christians)," which is a way of saying that he had ties in local spheres of power.

Boris had two trades that came to him from his father, and maybe also from his grandfather. He made soap, and he ran a sawmill that cut railroad ties according to the very precise specifications required for such work. After his marriage to Tania Greisser, Boris moved from Jaruga to Mogilev, which was the main city of that small region, and he bought a large house that my uncle characterizes as "a mansion." In Mogilev, Boris built his soap mill.[44]

Noemí thus came from a provincial bourgeois family. In her house, they spoke Russian rather than Ukrainian (the latter being the language of the peasants), as well as Yiddish. There are also other signs of the comfort in which she was raised: Boris hired her a private tutor, who gave her lessons in French and piano. What could be more Russian than that?

When Noemí was six, the Russian Revolution broke out. Her family remained in Mogilev until 1920 or 1921, the period that corresponded to the ongoing civil war between the White Russians and the Bolsheviks. It was also during this time that Ukrainian nationalists organized large-scale pogroms. According to what I've been told, the revolution hardened at this time, and the Bolsheviks sent a commissar from Kiev with orders to hang a member of the bourgeoisie in the public square of each town in the region. Boris had been selected for hanging in Mogilev. I'm not sure if this was mainly because of his mansion or also because he was Jewish, but the official making the arrest knew Boris and liked him, since a relative had worked at the soap mill. He advised Boris to take his family and all the money he could gather up and leave Mogilev that same night, without any delay.

And so it was that Boris, Tania, their three daughters, and Tania's mother, Revka, left secretly and in a hurry. Their immediate goal was to cross the Dniester, the border between the Soviet Union and Romania, in order to get to the city of Czernowitz, which had become a gathering point for Soviet refugees.

Shura

The crossing of the Dniester, in 1921, marked the first devastating loss that my family suffered because of European conflict. It was the loss of Shura, in an episode that has remained engraved in my family's memory, and one that has had repercussions that reach into my own generation.

The Dniester River near Mogilev, Ukraine,
looking into Bessarabia.

My grandmother's family had to flee secretly in a small boat loaded with refugees. The plan was to cross the Dniester clothed in darkness. The Milstein girls — Noemí (ten years old), Shura (born on February 27, 1919, and then only two), and Pupe (born on March 21, 1921, and then a baby in her mother's arms) — traveled with a group that included their parents, Boris and Tania, and their maternal grandmother, Revka. As they started to cross the river, little Shura, who was scared, began to cry. The boat captain threatened to drown her, so that her cries wouldn't cause the whole group to be discovered. Revka got out of the boat and saved Shura, while the rest of the family crossed the river.

According to the version of the story that Shura's daughter Rita tells, and which undoubtedly comes from Shura herself, Tania had wanted to stay on the Ukrainian side when Shura began to cry, but Boris stopped her. It was too risky. So, in an instant, they left their daughter behind. As the plan was to get both Revka and Shura across later, the family settled in Czernowitz, not all that far from Mogilev. But the border quickly became uncrossable, and the Milsteins remained in Czernowitz for six years without being able to reunite with their daughter.

Czernowitz was filled with Ukrainian émigrés at the time. In 1921, the Romanian authorities reported that 100,000 refugees from Ukraine had arrived in their country, many of them Jews.[45] A significant percentage had established themselves in Czernowitz, which was natural given that city's importance and location. The economic situation there was not tenable over the long term, however, and the Romanian authorities exerted pressure so that the migrants might move on as soon as possible. Officially, the presence of Ukrainian refugees was only provisional and merely a stop on the way to another destination, such as the United States, Canada, Palestine, or South America.[46] In the end, with resources shrinking, no realistic hope of getting their daughter out of Russia, and no possibility of remaining in Czernowitz either, Boris, Tania, my grandmother Noemí, and her youngest sister, Pupe, embarked for Peru.

Tania (center), Noemí (right), and Pupe (left),
with Shura absent. Lima, 1929.

Czernowitz

When Noemí and her parents arrived in Czernowitz, the city
no longer belonged to the Austro-Hungarian Empire but to
Romania. The Romanian language was made mandatory in the
schools, even though most schoolteachers didn't know how to
speak it.[47] Even the town's name had changed: now it was called
Cernauti. From a Jewish perspective, the transfer of Czernowitz to Romania was a step in the wrong direction. Austrian
Czernowitz had had a Jewish mayor, and it had sent Jewish
representatives to the Reichsrat in Vienna, whereas Romania's
grudging emancipation of its Jews prompted the creation of
anti-Semitic political parties. This translated into discrimination in the schools of Cernauti.

In 1926, for example, there was an incident that became
famous: a group of Jewish boys verbally assaulted a Romanian

schoolteacher, whose last name was Diaconescu, because he had denied entry to ninety-two of the ninety-four Jewish students who had applied for admission into the Aaron Pumnul school. There was a rowdy political movement that demanded strict quotas on the number of Jews who could study in the schools and universities at that time, and these political groups had significant influence on public opinion but also in the government. So it was that twenty-four of the teacher's Jewish "attackers" were convicted by Romanian courts. A few weeks later, a fascist student murdered the Jewish students' ringleader, and the (confessed) murderer was declared innocent in court and treated as a hero in the national press.[48] Such events reflect the pronounced reversal of fortune for the Jews of Czernowitz.

Noemí began her schooling in that place and time. The Gymnasium where she studied must have been private, because she learned very good German there, so she added that language to her advanced proficiency in Russian, French, and Yiddish. Noemí was also an avid reader, and Czernowitz offered much greater intellectual stimulation than Mogilev. On the other hand, the feeling of uncertainty must also have been acute: Noemí was, after all, one of tens of thousands of "temporary" Ukrainian refugees in Czernowitz; moreover, although they had fled the Russian Revolution, Ukrainian Jews were nonetheless suspected of being Soviet agents.

According to the history of the city authored by Marianne Hirsch and Leo Spitzer, there was also a Zionist school in Czernowitz that served as a platform for various youth organizations (Hazmonah, Zephira, and Hebronia). It is possible that Noemí studied there, because it was in Czernowitz that she joined Hashomer Hatzair, the organization that brought my grandparents together.

Noemí Milstein (left) at sixteen, with her friend
from Hashomer Hatzair, Bruria Steinmetz.*

Also Lima

Before his departure for Peru, Misha Adler had been part of the *Hagannah* (executive committee) of Hashomer Hatzair. The head of the organization in Romania was Yitzhak

---

* The back of the photo reads, "For the eternal memory of your beloved *kvutzah* sister, Bruria Steinmetz, with heartfelt greetings. *Chazak Veemac* [the Hashomer Hatzair salute, meaning 'Be Strong and Brave']. Signed in Czernowitz on August 12, 1927."

Nussenbaum, better known as Yitzhak Ben-Aharon. He would leave Romania for Palestine in 1928 and later become a founding member of the leftist party Mapam and long-standing member of the Israeli Knesset. Ben-Aharon had also gone to school in Czernowitz, and when the Milstein family decided to leave for Peru, he sent a letter by hand to Misha, using Noemí as the messenger and asking him to look after her. That was how the couple first met: in Lima, but introduced from a distance by Ben-Aharon, of Nova Sulitza and Chernowitz. Misha would be the only boyfriend that my grandmother would ever have.

In Lima, Noemí enrolled in the Rodó girls' school, where she either completed the high school diploma she had begun in Czernowitz or started from scratch in order to learn Spanish and earned the certification she needed to enter the university, I'm not really sure.

Noemí Milstein's exam certificate.

Inscription document for the Faculty of Economics
at the Universidad de San Marcos in Lima, 1930. Noemí
would not be able to continue her studies at the university,
as she was expelled from Peru that same year.

Noemí was committed both to her studies and to political struggle. Like Misha, she too would form part of Mariátegui's Red Corner, and she became a charismatic member of the Socialist Party, which they were putting together. Jorge del Campo speaks frequently of Noemí, starting with an admission that he was secretly in love with her:

> Soon after joining the group, I felt an intense spiritual love for Noemí, who, due to my scruples, surely only came to intuit with gratitude and sympathy what I felt for her without ever admitting it. I loved her as a woman and as a comrade, respecting her conjugal situation and her loyalty to her spouse, who was also one of our esteemed comrades. I think issues of this type

occurred with other comrades. We have never spoken about it, and one could certainly find similar facts and others that reflect very clearly the great humanity and morality of the communists trained by Mariátegui.[49]

Mariátegui also recognized Noemí's talents. This was reflected above all in the fact that she formed part of his innermost circle, but in his correspondence, too, he spoke warmly of her as "very intelligent."[50] And she really was. In 1929, my grandmother would work as the managing editor of the journal *Repertorio Hebreo*, which she founded together with Misha, and as a translator for the journal *Amauta*, of which I'll speak in the next chapter.

CHAPTER SIX

The *Amauta*

Blinding lights

My grandparents knew many famous people in their day, but José Carlos Mariátegui was the person who touched them most deeply. One might think that explaining this influence is made easy by Mariátegui's reputation. His short life was dazzlingly brilliant, like a bolt of lightning. When my grandfather published his first journal, *Repertorio Hebreo*, he referred to Mariátegui as "the largest brain and the clearest spirit on the continent," an opinion that was by no means rare. "The greatest mind in Latin America has ceased forever to work."[51] This is how the journal *Amauta* announced Mariátegui's death. In 1994, when Mariátegui's sons published an invaluable edition of his complete works, they wrote that his book *Seven Interpretive Essays on Peruvian Reality* had sold over two million copies, which is unparalleled in Latin America for any serious and conceptually rigorous work of economic, social, and cultural analysis.

Born in the southern town of Moquegua, José Carlos was a descendant of Francisco Javier Mariátegui, a leader in the Peruvian independence movement and member of that nation's first constituent assembly. His father abandoned him when José Carlos was very young and his family soon emigrated to Lima. José Carlos was in this regard a typical Latin American déclassé intellectual: born in a distantly grand provincial family, but raised without a father and with meager resources. To top it off, Mariátegui was afflicted with ankylosis at age seven, a condition that was not treatable in Peru at the time, and his leg was more or less useless thereafter. José Carlos was forced to abandon school at fourteen for financial reasons, and began working as an errand boy at the well-known Lima newspaper *La Prensa*. He was soon promoted to reading copy and working with the typesetters. José Carlos took advantage of that position to sneak his first article into publication. It was an urban chronicle, published under the pseudonym of Juan Croniqueur, that turned out to be so promising that in a few months, Alberto Ulloa, *La Prensa*'s much revered editor, offered "Juan Croniqueur" a regular slot.[52]

During his years as Juan Croniqueur, Mariátegui covered Lima's social and cultural life — horse races, films, urban scenes, personalities. He developed an innovative style and distinctive voice, which he perfected after dropping the Chroniqueur moniker, when he turned his attention squarely to political, social, and cultural analysis. It is fair to say that Mariátegui is one of Latin America's most remarkable journalists of all time, comparable to — in my opinion, even superior to — figures such as the Cuban José Martí. He is also one of Spanish America's greatest editors, and his journal *Amauta*, which I will discuss below, is certainly one of twentieth-century Latin America's two or three most innovative and influential cultural and political journals. Finally, Mariátegui was a deeply original thinker, comparable in scope and depth to contemporaries such as Leon Trotsky, Antonio Gramsci, and Rosa Luxemburg.

José Carlos Mariátegui at twenty (June 1914),
in his Juan Croniqueur days.

It has not been easy for me to develop my own interpretation and understanding of Mariátegui. His name is too personal to me, because my grandparents were among his closest friends. Such illustrious connections can be blinding, because their grandeur is easily grafted onto fantasies of one's own potential. Thanks to my grandparents, Mariátegui's aura touches mine, but it is not as if Mariátegui's genius somehow rubbed off on me. Genealogical proximity to greatness is an inheritance, an unalienable possession that gains a mysterious power over us, as if it were a fetish image in which origin and destiny become one and the same thing. Such a fetish makes the past luminous, true, but also darkly impenetrable. It can be experienced both as a boon and as a burden. And as a result, I've had to read José Carlos Mariátegui's work rather slowly.

Architecture of experience

The light that emanated from Mariátegui can be more easily captured if one thinks of his collective projects: his discussion group, the editorial work on the journal *Amauta*, his political work toward the creation of Peru's Socialist Party, and the spaces of intimacy and friendship that he cultivated. Mariátegui led a life in which home and work, the public and the private, the aesthetic and the political all breathed together. Indeed, his dazzling intelligence must be qualified if we are to understand him for what he really was; for it is even more useful to imagine him as an experience, as a praxis, than as an innate and individual ability (a "brain") or even as the author of original interpretations. Mariátegui was a collectivist at heart. He did not wish to be an isolated genius. His work sought to bring Peru with him, and this involved inventing a variegated and intricate set of habits.

Mariátegui's house is a useful place to start to understand the way in which he organized this mode of existence. Until he turned thirty, José Carlos had been highly mobile, despite the ankylosis that afflicted his left leg. In 1920 he was exiled to Italy, and he traveled through portions of central and Western Europe until his return to Lima in 1923. Only a year later, though, his condition deteriorated to such a degree that his leg was amputated, and he was thereafter confined to a wheelchair. For this reason, Mariátegui's house became even more central; his mobility had been seriously reduced precisely in the years in which his influence was peaking, so that he became reliant on correspondence and print, but also on social contacts in his home space.

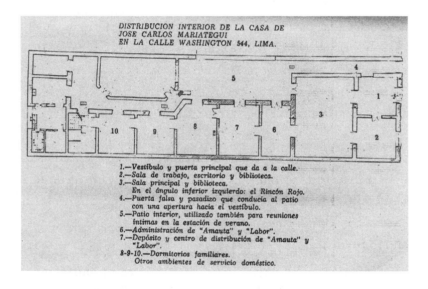

DISTRIBUCION INTERIOR DE LA CASA DE JOSE CARLOS MARIATEGUI EN LA CALLE WASHINGTON 544, LIMA.

1.—Vestíbulo y puerta principal que da a la calle.
2.—Sala de trabajo, escritorio y biblioteca.
3.—Sala principal y biblioteca.
    En el ángulo inferior izquierdo: el Rincón Rojo.
4.—Puerta falsa y pasadizo que conducía al patio
    con una apertura hacia el vestíbulo.
5.—Patio interior, utilizado también para reuniones
    íntimas en la estación de verano.
6.—Administración de "Amauta" y "Labor".
7.—Depósito y centro de distribución de "Amauta" y "Labor".
8-9-10.—Dormitorios familiares.
    Otros ambientes de servicio doméstico.

This is a drawing of the house that specifies the use to which each room was dedicated while it was still inhabited by José Carlos and his family. Today the house is a museum, archive, and cultural center. In the late 1920s one went into the house from the street through an entryway that led on one side to Mariátegui's study and on the other to the living room, where at six p.m. the discussion group would meet in the so-called Red Corner. Beyond this, there was a room that served as an editorial office, first for *Amauta* and later also for the political journal *Labor*, followed in turn by another room that served as a storage space for back issues of these journals. Beyond this, there were three bedrooms for the family, the kitchen, and the spaces reserved for the domestic help.

The communist painter Jorge del Prado shares a telling memory of the Red Corner discussion group: "Mariátegui had gotten out of his wheelchair to sit on the sofa, where he spoke with other members of the group. In another part of the room, a group of workers leafed through books taken from the shelves. On a small table there was a stack of journals and newspapers received through exchange that—I later discovered—José Carlos would consult during his work hours, but which he would also make available to his visitors."[53] In other words, Mariátegui would be seated in a corner while people circulated through the room, leafing through journals and talking among themselves until the time came for them to sit down near to him. Those evenings often stretched out well into the night, especially for those who had some private matter to discuss with Mariátegui. Intellectuals, political militants, and workers filed through the house on a daily basis.

Mariátegui's house was an interclass space, where people met friends and acquaintances or at least came into contact with interesting strangers. It offered a site for the interchange of knowledge, with workers leafing through books and journals and artists exchanging ideas with political activists. The scene brought together the combustible possibilities of the moment, no longer as logical propositions but as actual lived experience.

These meetings had the imprint of the house's owner, who didn't require that participants forget their origins, but quite to the contrary, asked that they consider the differences between them so as to find ways to move forward together. Workers felt no embarrassment regarding their class status, and neither did Romanian Jews need to pretend to have been born and raised in Peru. It is as if Marx's maxim "From each according to their ability, to each according to their needs," had been embraced by Mariátegui's circle without waiting for the communist utopia to arrive.

A bohemian undertow

To capture the flavor of this alloy between a modern political party and an eighteenth-century salon, it serves to know that, in his youth, Mariátegui was a player in the "decadentist" culture that fascinated Lima's flaneurs during its Belle Epoque. In the 1910s, Lima's intelligentsia made its rendezvous at establishments such as the Palais Concert confectionery, described by Oscar Terán as an art nouveau structure "with an orchestra of young women who played Viennese waltzes and German *lied*."[54] Lima's young communists of the 1920s had come of age in or near public spaces that had been shaped by and for a highly aestheticized sensibility that was the cornerstone of Latin American *modernismo*, a literary movement and aesthetic that converged with French currents such as Parnassianism and Symbolism.

The figure of Juan Croniqueur is an example of this spirit. The chronicles that Mariátegui signed under that name frequently came in the form of short poems that invoked feelings generated by well-appreciated urbane scenes and relationships, and that sought to indulge youthful pleasure, while providing cameo portraits of an idealized bourgeois world. This stanza of "Emotions at the Race Track" provides a taste of the style in question:

> *Disquiet. Negligence. Aristocracy. Laughter.*
> *Smile. Comment. Rumor. Languor.*
> *The afternoon faints and is made spiritual*
> *By a woman's inexplicable swoon.*

Mariátegui later referred somewhat dismissively to his youthful preoccupation with this sort of entertainment, and called it his "Stone Age." Still, his intense involvement in Lima's city life and its literary culture became an ingredient of his mature style when he realized, probably in Italy, that Peru was an idea that had yet to be invented, and that it needed to be created out of the world that had been entirely excluded from Lima's Parnassus.[55] On the other hand, engagement with the aesthetic requirements of *modernismo* had raised the bar for journalistic writing, and its refined affectations breathed life into a salon culture that had existed in South America's capitals since the late eighteenth century. City life came hand in glove with spaces of anonymity and with the invention of meeting grounds for those who might be driven there by their elective affinities. This combination of anonymity and selection was ordered in socially exclusive spaces such as the Club Nacional, the race tracks, the cinema, fashionable coffee houses, and confectioneries, theaters, newspaper offices, bars, churches, and squares. The very nineteenth-century habit of taking on authorial pen names is of a piece with this sort of topography, for it created a kind of imaginary Parnassus where strangers and friends came together as characters, shedding their familial baggage in order to engage in public life more freely.

This was still mainly a space for male sociality—newspapers then were even more male-dominated than salons—in which writers were free to engage in a rarified exercise of self-fashioning to such a degree that they sometimes created pseudonyms even for their pseudonym. Juan Croniqueur, for instance, at times took on second-order pen names, including "Jack," "Monsieur de Camomille," "Val D'Or," "Kendal," "Kendalif," "Kendeliz Cadet," "Cyranno III" (after a horse named Cyrano II), and "Revoltoso."[56]

Of course, Mariátegui's Red Corner was a very different sort of place from Lima's aristocratic Club Nacional. Peru's Socialist Party—which later morphed into its Communist Party—was pretty much created there, and a magazine for the working class, *Labor*, was laid out in the room next door. Above all, the people that came together at the Red Corner were not selected for class affinity or according to shared origin and tradition. In Mariátegui's house, Lima's textile workers met an intellectual elite, and young students mingled with agrarian militants from Cuzco. And yet there was also a lot of refinement there. The Red Corner was the antithesis of Lima's bourgeois culture, and as a result it retained some elements of its opposite: it retained the amiable and refined respect that marked Lima's older salon culture.

Friendship and tradition

Those who were touched by Mariátegui spoke of his humanity and his engaging way, his warmth and empathy. My grandmother, who was generally disinclined to idealize anyone
or anything, compared Mariátegui to Jesus of Nazareth. For
Noemí, José Carlos had the kind of touch of divinity that she
imagined Jesus may have had.

Painter Jorge del Prado described José Carlos on the day
that they first met, in 1928. Prado mentions José Carlos's angu-
lar profile and his wheelchair. He notes the amputated leg and
then lingers on his eyes: "Everything made him resemble a
large child, except, of course, the slow and halting motion of
his body, the mature persuasion in his voice, the tremendous
vital persuasion in how he'd look at you, which gave him an
undeniable authority, which was in no way lessened but rather
heightened by his natural simplicity and his permanent and
spontaneous extension of friendship."[57]

Friendship was a core value in Mariátegui's circle, but what
exactly did Mariátegui's predisposition to friendship consist
of? Where did it come from? Jorge del Prado's memoir provides us with a valuable clue. That painter was nineteen when
he arrived in Lima from his native Arequipa. He had only
recently turned into a communist, and as a result he decided
to abandon painting, which seemed to him to be a superfluous
pastime. He wished instead to dedicate his life to the pressing
needs of the working people, and proudly expressed this determination to Mariátegui at their first meeting. José Carlos had

already founded the Socialist Party by then, and was indisputably Peru's leading Marxist, and yet his reaction took Prado by surprise: "Politics," Mariátegui said, "is fed and ennobled by science and art. There can thus be no contradiction nor antinomy between being a revolutionary and being a painter or sculptor, writer or scientist. Neither is it right to imagine that marching in the ranks of the Revolution requires a total break with the past."

There was a lot at stake in his view. Devoting oneself to "The Cause" frequently involves turning one's back on one's parents and old friends, and bracketing off one's own sensibilities as if they were a deformity, a selfish petit-bourgeois petulance that must be purged in order to transform oneself into a pure and chaste servant of The Cause. Mariátegui had no use for this position. There was no justification for approaching the revolutionary ideal as if it were a jealous lover, nor did it require a categorical break with tradition. Indeed, José Carlos viewed "a total break with the past" with great suspicion, because he believed in the integration of the past and the future. It was from tradition and myth that the revolution would necessarily spring.

So, for instance, in an essay on the role of tradition in revolution, Mariátegui began with a reflection on the Castillian medieval poet Jorge Manrique: "Manrique's poetry is tied to tradition, but not to traditionalism. Against what the traditionalists want, tradition is alive and changing. It is created by those who deny it, so that they can renew and enrich it. And it is murdered by those who want to fix it, by those who seek the extension of the past in a feeble present..."[58] Mariátegui then goes on to say that, contrary to the usual view of revolutionaries as iconoclasts, "true revolutionaries never proceed as if history started with them," and he offered as examples Karl Marx's assimilation of the ideas of the bourgeois economists Adam Smith and David Ricardo, and Proudhon's reliance on ancient community institutions in order to formulate his critique of private property. Tradition, in other words, is alive and is always the ground from which the present and the future are shaped. Therefore, tradition's penetrating force should never be confused with the dead weight of traditionalism.

Indeed, Peru's malady rested on a Lima-based traditionalism that sought to suffuse the present with the culture of the conquistadors, while breaking Indian participation off from national culture, relegating always the Incas to prehistory, to a time before time. It was this traditionalism that had reduced the nation to its European or mestizo component, and that excluded its Indian majority. As a result, Peru itself was a concept that had yet to be created, yet to be forged.[59] In such a moment, tradition needed to be heard, seen, and recognized, and an openness toward friendship was necessary for any of this to happen. Otherwise, diverging traditions would continue to fold in on themselves, rather than to open up to the transformative possibilities of the present.

I think that Mariátegui understood that, more than a relationship, friendship is an event. It happens when people do something together, and it involves recognizing what each friend has experienced. In the Lima in the 1920s, obliterating tradition involved ignoring others. Friendship was a way of bringing various traditions back into play, and so of fostering an entirely new discussion. It is certainly for this reason that the people touched by Mariátegui tended to feel that he changed them, since he facilitated the incorporation of their past into a future-oriented project. I think that it was this transformative spirit that moved my grandmother to compare José Carlos to Jesus. Knowing José Carlos changed her.

The Amauta

In his life in exile, Mariátegui came to understand that Peru lacked one thing: a true teacher. José Carlos had been edged out of Peru in the aftermath of Lima's 1919 student movement, an episode that formed part of a pan–Latin American uprising for university reform that had started at the University of Córdoba, in Argentina, but that spread to many South American capitals. José Carlos had dropped out of school early, so he was not involved in the student movement. Rather, he and his friend César Falcón had recently founded the paper *La Razón*, Lima's first leftist daily. That paper was the first venue to criticize Augusto Leguía, who was instated as president in July of that year, and it supported both labor and the student movement. Leguía shut down *La Razón* as a result, and exiled Falcón and Mariátegui to Italy.

When Mariátegui returned to Peru in 1923, there was a sequel to the 1919 student movement, and he took the occasion to express his ideas on the subject of university reform. To Mariátegui, the Universidad de San Marcos was a decrepit institution. Stuck in the past, and stifled by the elite's stranglehold on its faculty, it could not rise to the challenges that emerged after the close of the Great War. The most painful symptom of San Marcos's deficiencies was the lack of a teacher or guide who might rise to the task of opening the world up to Peru's student youth: "The university has a few valuable professors, who teach their courses faithfully and intelligently, but there is not a single exemplar of a true leader and teacher (*maestro*) for the youth. There isn't a single faculty member who could be a conductor. Not one prophetic voice, no leader, director or apostol."[60] Germany had figures like Einstein and Spengler, Spain had Miguel de Unamuno, Mexico José Vasconcelos and Antonio Caso, Argentina had José Ingenieros. Peru's university had no one. At some intimate level, Mariátegui decided to occupy that position.

Obviously, he could not do that from the university, but Mariátegui knew perfectly well that in Peru that institution could not be the mainspring of intellectual creativity and ferment. The nation's university — San Marcos — had closed itself off to the country's people, to the Indians, and elitist enclosure led inevitably to foundering in a sea of hypotheses. Thus, José Carlos wrote that "illiterate people find their own path more easily than their lettered counterparts or than the philosopher. Given that they must act, they act. Given that they must believe, they believe... Their instinct steers them away from sterile doubt."[61] So instead of turning to the university for teaching, Mariátegui relied on his writing, and he used the newspaper as his podium.

He began the arduous work of opening up the world for Peru in his weekly dispatches from Italy. Upon Mariátegui's return to Lima, in 1923, his lessons were so appreciated that he was invited to teach at a new alternative space for higher learning, opened for workers and a general public as a night school, the Universidad Popular González Prada. That school had been launched in 1921 by the student leader and anti-imperialist militant Víctor Manuel Haya de la Torre, and it was Haya himself who invited Mariátegui to teach. Mariátegui's twenty-or-so lectures on the crisis of the West would be his one and only experience as a lecturer. His approach to his classes is summed up in a sentence from his opening session: "Comrades, I am not here to teach you the history of the world's current crisis, I am here to study it with you." Mariátegui was critical of educational philosophies that relied on disciplining students. The true teacher, he wrote, is recognized by his students wherever he might be: "surrounded familiarly by his students, he is always their teacher." Rather than relying on the classroom, the podium, and disciplinary measures, the true teacher's authority "is a moral fact."[62] And indeed Mariátegui's authority was a moral fact that was offered openly and generously, in friendship.

The results of his lectures at the Universidad Popular were compiled in Mariátegui's first book, *La escena contemporánea*. Published in 1925, it is a densely packed and carefully curated tour of the contemporary world, with concise and sharply analytical essays on its key figures, political processes, and national contexts. Gandhi, Ataturk, Einstein, Tagore, Mussolini, Lloyd George, fascism, the Mexican Revolution, the Third International, Trotsky, Lunacharsky, Zinoviev, Rosa Luxemburg, Gabriele D'Annunzio, the situation in Poland, Hungary, Romania, China, Turkey, India...*La escena contemporánea* is a remarkable feat both of concretion and synthesis that combines useful information, insight, and political critique in a way that instantiated and performed precisely what the Universidad Mayor de San Marcos lacked: teaching.

Mariátegui's diagnostic exploration of the economic, political, and cultural condition of the world in the aftermath of the Great War was his only foray into university education. It was followed by the launching of a new op-ed column, titled "Peruanizar el Perú" (Peruvianizing Peru), that was dedicated to thinking about Peru as a province of the world. The work developed in that series laid the foundations for Mariátegui's second and final book, the famous *Seven Interpretive Essays on Peruvian Reality*, which was published in 1929, a year before his death, but the op-ed column also generated parameters for what was to be perhaps Mariátegui's greatest creation: the cultural, literary, and political journal *Amauta*.

Launched in 1926, the journal was originally going to take the name *Vanguardia*, but it finally adopted a different one, *Amauta*, which means "teacher" in Quechua.[63] Teaching was thus proposed as a collective endeavor, best realized in a journal rather than through any one individual's efforts. The impulse to rescue and mobilize the past for the present informed this decision, as did Mariátegui's insistence on the role of reading for an enlightened, universalist understanding of the world and of one's position in it. More than this, Mariátegui's view of his own action and creation perhaps retained a dash of the early influence that Gabriele D'Annunzio had on his generation: work was either transformative or it was dead.

Mariátegui was a Peruvian, and Peru's people needed to understand how to build a future for themselves in the world.

This involved collective exercises of reflection and discussion. People came to recognize and acknowledge all of this, I think, and so they began to refer to Mariátegui himself as "*El Amauta*": the teacher.

Revista Amauta

Amauta understood itself to be a space of convergence within the cultural field. Despite its political commitment, there was no sectarianism in it, and many of its collaborators weren't Marxists, even though everyone "contributed to a significant degree to the purpose of the journal, which was to modify substantially the cultural environment in a progressive and transformative sense."[64] What this meant was that the journal respected the trajectory of its collaborators and created a space in which a *modernista* poet such as José María Eguren, a communist activist such as Ricardo Martínez de la Torre, a translated article on the painting of George Grosz, an essay by Georges Sorel on Lenin, and a reflection on the meaning of dancing the Charleston could all be read together. Mariátegui's editorial zeal thus echoed his embrace of friendship as a political stance. In such a space, the knowledge that Misha and Noemí brought with them was very welcome, and they both contributed to *Amauta* as translators.

Beyond all of this, there was a vivid conviction regarding the importance of the world's margins for the development of alternative ideas at that moment of universal revolution. Mariátegui also understood this marginality firsthand. The knowledge that Mariátegui had of privation allowed him to envision the culture of the people as a creative force from which Peru might emerge as a vibrant national society, and then contribute something original to the international revolution that was raging since the triumph of the Bolsheviks in Russia. He saw Peru's redemption figured in the religious life of Peru's indigenous communities, and he understood that the best thinking emanated from need. "Europe," he once wrote, "revealed to me the extent to which I belonged to a primitive and chaotic world; and at the same time it made clear to me my responsibility to an American project."[65]

Russia had opened the window to world revolution, but its manifestation in Peru required a deliberate effort of self-recognition and self-expression. Peru had spent centuries turning its back on its native communities. Even Lima's love affair with its colonial traditions ignored the true, raunchy, and mixed-race city in favor of a fanciful obsession with the cultural lineage of the conquistador.[66] For Mariátegui, as for Lenin, universalism required the emancipation of oppressed nations, and this meant that his socialism was expressed in a double movement: it looked "inward" to consider the indigenous world and the political movement in Lima as spaces of innovative cultural creation, and "outward," to the world, in an effort that required commitment to translation and calling attention to the texts, authors, and discussions that were most relevant for Peru's radical transformation. As the historian Martin Bergel has pointed out, Mariátegui's project attached to Goethe's old idea of living in the era of "world literature" — that is, it derived from the recognition of a radical contemporaneity between what was happening in Peru and in the rest of the world.[67] Peru, Mariátegui insisted, was just one of the world's provinces, and not a unique and incommensurable world unto itself. Thus, Mariátegui writes in the introduction to the first volume of *Amauta*: "The object of this journal is to address, clarify, and come to know the problems of Peru from a learned and scientific point of view. But we will always consider Peru within the broader panorama of the world…All that is human is ours."[68]

And for Mariátegui, there were no more cosmopolitan social subjects than the Jews. In the first volume of *Amauta*, there appears a translated essay by Sigmund Freud on resistance to psychoanalysis (translated by my grandfather), in which Freud asks whether it is a coincidence that the inventor of psychoanalysis is Jewish. He concludes: "to make psychoanalysis viable, it was necessary to be fully prepared to accept the isolation to which the opposition condemns one, a fate that is familiar to Jews more than anyone else."[69] This point of view coincides with that of Mariátegui. In an article published in my grandparents' journal, *Repertorio Hebreo*, he writes: "the Jewish world I love does not speak Hebrew or Yiddish exclusively; it is polyglot, mobile, transnational. Given its need to identify with all races, it possesses the feelings, the languages, and the arts of all of them." And later he adds: "internationalism is not, as many obtuse figures on the right and left imagine it to be, the negation of nationalism; rather, it is its transcendence."[70]

CHAPTER SEVEN

Jewish Americanism

Noemí and Misha identified with Mariátegui, in part because they had lived through obverse processes. Europe had revealed Peru's ideological disjointedness ("I belonged to a primitive and chaotic world" is how Mariátegui described this epiphany), but it had also sharpened his commitment to America. My grandparents, for their part, understood the aporia of the Jewish experience much more fully in Peru, a country where, as my grandfather told me, "they didn't even know what a Jew was." Noemí and Misha had moved from a world in which Jews were segregated and marked as a race, to one in which they were ambiguously identified as Europeans. And yet the Indian world that they could therefore sit atop was so deeply segregated and pauperized, but also so very much alive, that the disjuncture was conducive to thinking universally, rather than to exploiting their new superior position to improve their own lot. The American lens would help them visualize emancipation from a genuinely universal perspective.

Tradition and transformation

And, indeed, there were areas of confluence between the Jewish conscience and that of Amerindian national emancipation (conceived by socialists of the period as being identical to Peruvian national emancipation). Both the Indians and the Jews were coming out of an era in which they had tried to develop self-contained communities—the Hasidic movement of Eastern Europe was the main symptom of this enclosure—but both groups were also compelled to negotiate with, fight against, or break into the dominant society. For European Jews, there were two main paths to facing discrimination. The first was to try to pass as non-Jewish, a strategy that was not necessarily a first step toward assimilation, given that blending could be a sporadic tactic, mobilized to deal with social impediments of different kinds, without it constituting an attempt to abjure one's identity.

The strategy of dissembling was occasionally viable in Peru's Indo-mestizo world, too. Migration to Lima, in particular, could in some contexts mitigate the hardships that came with being identified as Indian, and in Lima an indigenous person might manage in some instances to blend in with other members of its new but growing working class.[71] On the other hand, the possibilities of dissimulation for the indigenous in Peru were limited in ways that recalled those faced by Misha and Noemí in Romania, where violence and even legally sanctioned discrimination was never far from the surface.

The second Jewish coping strategy was political militancy, in either communist or nationalist movements or both. Militancy involved either the affirmation or the transcendence of one's identity in the face of discrimination. It could take the form of Jewish labor militancy in organizations such as the Bund, which supported the consolidation and widespread use of Yiddish in its communications while rejecting Zionism, or Poale Zion, a Marxist-Zionist labor movement. And it could take the form of either a liberal or a communist militancy, committed to achieving equality, defined either in terms of equal political rights or as economic equality. There was thus a lot of Jewish energy invested in politics in this period—supporting the Russian Revolution or Zionism or equal rights in various liberal parties. Whether assimilationist or committed to achieving Jewish national sovereignty, though, Jewish militancy involved breaking out of the ghetto or the shtetl and into the broader world of national or universal claims.

Misha and Noemí found an active space for thinking about such matters in the pages of *Amauta*, which was devoted to creating a new idea of Peru, and therefore alive with debates on literature and painting, and a persistent search for aesthetic languages that distanced themselves from dominant canons of beauty. Also, the enormity and depth of the indigenous Andean universe was very exciting: Noemí and Misha came from a world in which the traditional culture of the shtetl was in decline or even dissolving, within the Soviet Union, for instance, where collective farms and new modes of work and life were quickly developing. It must have been moving for a proud Jew like my grandfather, who had worked to revive Hebrew as a modern language, to find himself facing an alternative world—very deeply oppressed, without a doubt, but also vital in its native communal forms. How to break the chains of oppressed nations? How to channel the force of tradition into a genuinely modern and revolutionary project? Those were the great questions of the time.

Woodcut by painter José Sabogal,
one of many published in *Amauta* in its
search for Peruvian artistic idioms.

In Peru, the majority of the population still did not speak Spanish, but rather the language of the Incas. It was a traditional world. Mariátegui distinguished a revolutionary seed in those traditions: "it is not civilization, nor is it the alphabet of whites that raises the soul of the Indian. It is myth, the idea of the socialist revolution."[72] Myth, an element of living, breathing, tradition, could fuse into an entirely modern idea: socialist revolution. Such a dialectic resonated with Eastern European

Jews, for whom it had been natural to pass from the messianism of "backward" religious traditions such as Hasidism, to a zeal for redemption in social revolution.

Another important point of confluence between the Indo-American world and Jewish cultural formations is that both of them predated Christianity, and they had managed to survive its forceful imposition without completely assimilating. This eccentricity could readily morph into irony, that is, into a distance that facilitated a notable cultural flourish in the case of the Jews, but that had yet to erupt into cultural modernism for the Indians. Eccentricity was perhaps more radical for the Indians than for the Jews, since the marginalization of Jews in the Middle Ages had denied them land and turned them into city folk, and therefore into the yeast of the bourgeois revolutions. The Jews were, after all, part of the vanguard of modernity, either as tradesmen, financiers, artisans, or workers, whereas Peru's Indians were for the most part peasants. Still, there was a point of empathy that Misha felt with the rising Indo-Peruvian nationalism, stemming from disidentification with the dominant Christian and Eurocentric nationalist chauvinisms.

Beyond the question of a shared penchant for irony, the fact of their anteriority and independence prior to having been brutally (but always only partially) subjugated made it so that Amerindians and their Jewish counterparts could each draw on a cultural repertoire that reached back before Christianity, from which they could imagine a different world. For them, revolution meant recovering a voice that had been lost to the "civilized" world. It was for this reason that the rescue of Hebrew, the rescue of the sacred places of Jewish antiquity, the aesthetic discovery of the indigenous world, the exultation of its languages, and the recovery of its ruins were taken in like fresh air from a new world. It was the breath of a revolution.

Friendship

My grandparents collaborated on *Amauta* as translators but never as authors. There isn't a single original contribution signed by Misha or Noemí in the thirty-two volumes of the journal that were published between September 1926 and its closure shortly after Mariátegui's death in 1930. Why not? Honestly, I don't know. Maybe Mariátegui considered Misha and Noemí to be too young and inexperienced. The pages of the journal were usually opened to people who had already made their mark in the cultural world. Misha and Noemí had arrived in Peru too recently to have acquired such accomplishments, and it is possible that Mariátegui hoped for them to take an active authorial role in the future.

It is also conceivable that Misha lacked the boldness that is needed to be writer; that is, maybe he had more of an editorial eye than a writer's spirit. This could indeed have been the case, because even though Misha did eventually publish articles, he did not end up being a prolific author, though he did constantly invent and try to launch new journals. Noemí, for her part, was unquestionably too young. She was only fifteen years old when *Amauta* began its five-year run, and seventeen when she was first introduced to its editor. Besides the question of age, though, it doesn't seem impossible to me that my grandfather might have wished to monopolize the talents of his young and beautiful girlfriend, having Noemí collaborate as managing editor for *Repertorio Hebreo* and giving her little time for other creative work, apart from her political activities in Mariátegui's political party. Once again, I can't be sure. It is certain, in any case, that Noemí was considered to be a kind of muse and a rising star in Mariátegui's circle, and that this potential of hers would never be as fully recognized later in her life, after she was exiled from Peru.

Announcement of the imminent appearance of
Repertorio Hebreo, directed by Misha Ben Tzvi Adler.

Even without their having made formal contributions to the journal (apart from translations), one can ascertain the close friendship that Misha and Noemí had with the members of the editorial group easily enough, and with Mariátegui and his family in particular. For example, when the journal *Repertorio Hebreo* was first released, Mariátegui announced it on the first page of issue 21 of *Amauta*, rather than relegating the notice to the back of the volume, as was customary for such announcements. *Repertorio Hebreo* had a special place for Mariátegui, which he also signaled by contributing an original piece to each published issue of that journal.

My grandmother, for her part, appears only once in *Amauta*, in an issue honoring José María Eguren that included some of the poet's drawings, along with a gallery of photos that he had taken of his friends. Noemí is included there, in a company that bespeaks the esteem that she had garnered in the intellectual circles of the time, for they include four famous poets (Juana de Ibarbourou, Blanca Luz Brum, Martín Adán, and the Surrealist poet and painter César Moro), Argentine diva Berta Singerman, and the distinguished Peruvian historian Jorge Basadre.

Noemí was one of the muses of Mariátegui's circle, and she was also one of the first women who were active in Peru's socialist cause. Prado recalls this generation's particular modus operandi:

> With respect to the role of women in revolutionary and progressive intellectualism, our influence — which was also that of Mariátegui — was channeled through the activity and growing prestige of figures as notable as Carmen Saco and Angela Ramos. However, in reality, these comrades, along with those who participated during the early years — such as Noemí Milstein and my sisters Alicia and Blanca — as well as those who later joined, did

not initiate their revolutionary path by means of feminism, such as normally occurs, but rather through their own experience in the fight against social injustice, which became transformed later into proletariat class consciousness in light of a Marxist-Leninist analysis of our reality, carried out by Mariátegui.[73]

What remains of a photo taken during one of the trips to the country, with Mariátegui in the car. The woman next to my grandmother is poet Carmen Ramos. The man in the hat behind Ramos is Jorge del Prado.

Lima offered Noemí possibilities for herself as a personality in her own right. True, she had already been in the Hashomer Hatzair while in Czernowitz, which was certainly a very different sort of organization on the gender front than, say, the Colegio de Señoritas Rodó in which her parents enrolled her in Lima. In the Hashomer, women and men mixed freely and debated, and they'd long broken with the sort of traditionalism that was still preponderant in the often Catholic girls' schools in South America. Indeed, there were several Eastern European Jewish women with backgrounds like Noemí's—including participation in Hashomer Hatzair and then socialist or communist organizations—who went on to have robust careers in politics and literature.

Nonetheless, Noemí was only fifteen years old when she arrived in Lima, so it was not exclusively in her early involvement in the Hashomer in Czernowitz, but above all in Peruvian cultural and political life that she was first taken seriously as a woman. And this was in fact a great space for that to happen, since Mariátegui's circle boasted an impressive group of female artists and activists—Carmen Saco, Blanca Luz Brum, Anna Chiappe de Mariátegui, the sisters Alicia and Blanca del Prado, and others. Mariátegui was a loyal friend to these women, and he held them in high esteem, published their work, took an interest in their careers, and supported them informally as well. Del Prado relates as an example how Mariátegui helped his sister Blanca and two young friends when they made the daring decision to move to Santiago de Chile on their own; José Carlos introduced them to his contacts so that they might find work and be introduced in local cultural and political circles. In a letter of introduction for Blanca, which Mariátegui sent to Sara Hubner in Chile, he characterized his young friend as a spiritual representative of Peruvian youth and of its women, and as an ambassador from *Amauta* to Santiago.[74] José Carlos helped his friends so that they might act on their dreams.

In his classic book *Seven Interpretive Essays on Peruvian Reality*, Mariátegui devotes a chapter to literature, where he focuses particularly on the creative force of women, and there is no condescending or paternalistic attitude in that, either. He says, for instance, that "in Spanish American poetry, two women, Gabriela Mistral and Juana de Ibarbourou, have garnered for some time more attention than any other poet of the period. Delmira Agustini has, in her country and in all America, a long and noble line of descent. Blanca Luz Brum has brought her message to Peru." And he quickly adds, "and these are not solitary or exceptional cases."[75]

A day in the countryside with Mariátegui.
Seated to the left are Noemí, Misha, and Anna.

The Repertorio Hebreo

The journal *Repertorio Hebreo* began and ended in 1929. My grandfather, who at that point signed his name as "Miguel Ben Tzvi Adler," was its director, and my grandmother, Noemí Milstein, served as managing editor. *Repertorio Hebreo* was published at Minerva, the press that printed *Amauta*, and which belonged to Mariátegui, although Misha was also a partner with some shares. They were able to publish three issues of the journal before Misha's sudden arrest and jailing put an end to things.

Cover of the first issue of *Repertorio Hebreo*.

Repertorio Hebreo had many points in common with *Amauta*: both journals were devoted to the understanding and transformation of a people. In its inaugural issue, my grandfather wrote that *Repertorio Hebreo* "proposes, above all, to be an exponent of high Jewish culture. It will teach. It will investigate. It will make a fair revision to the supreme values that constitute the basis of our culture, it will be a free tribune, a true laboratory of ideological experimentation: debate, critique, legends, episodes, anecdotes."[76] Misha also pointed out that there did not exist at that time a journal devoted to contemporary Jewish ideas and art in Spanish, and he made it clear that the journal would "group together the most representative elements of the new Jewish spirit: writers and artists, Jews and non-Jews, who support and duly appreciate the Jewish contribution to universal culture."[77]

Just as *Amauta* sought both to consider Peru from a global vantage point and to examine the world from Peru, *Repertorio Hebreo* too sought to discuss and critique contemporary Jewish culture seen from any angle, provided that it avoided chauvinism, which was, according to Misha, "the most destructive element of civilization and of human well-being."[78] In the first issue, a small table presents the journal's collaborators. There are Peruvians, who were mostly contributors to *Amauta* and almost entirely not Jewish; foreign contributors from the broader Jewish world; and Jewish cultural institutions in Berlin, Warsaw, Buenos Aires, and Moscow, with which the journal had a relation of exchange. *Repertorio Hebreo* sought to unite and not separate: "to sow love and comprehension in place of customary racial hatred and stupid vengeance."[79] And it would do it by teaching and evaluating new Jewish thought through critique.

The first issue of the journal opened with Misha's manifesto, followed by a penetrating article by Mariátegui titled "Israel y Occidente, Israel y el mundo" (Israel and the West, Israel and the World). Always going straight to the heart of things, Mariátegui begins by restating his position from 1925, namely that the modern mission of the Jewish people is "to assist, through its ecumenical and cosmopolitan activity, in the advent of a universal civilization." He explains that the national claims of the Jewish people do not interest him; rather, his focus is the Jewish contribution to the formation of an international society in which the oppression of national minorities and racial prejudice would be proscribed, given that the Jewish people had suffered more than any other. He finishes: "If Jews can believe that they are destined for something, it must be to act as the yeast in the rise of a new international society."[80]

For Mariátegui, the British policy of reducing the Jewish people to a national state was possibly a form of unconscious persecution, given that it "offers the Jews a new ghetto," although "since Marx, the last of its prophets, Israel has transcended capitalism, both spiritually and ideologically. Capitalist society declines due to its inability to organize production on an international scale."[81]

At the same time, these conclusions did not lead Mariátegui to turn his back on the nationalist claims of Jews. After all, his internationalism was rooted in oppressed peoples' struggle for emancipation, and that included national emancipation as well. Nevertheless, "Jewish patriotism cannot resolve itself in nationalism... Israel cannot now deny Christianity nor renounce the West, in order to close itself off sullenly in its native soil and pre-Christian history."[82] Mariátegui recognized in Zionism the secret desire of European anti-Semites to rid themselves of the Jews and their internationalism, to reduce their number, and to rip them from the heart of the West, where they occupied and made up the vanguard. "Upon losing its land, Judaism earned the right to make Europe and

America its home," he wrote, and then concluded his notable essay sounding a Hegelian note: "Jewish ostracism has lasted for so long and has so expanded the Jewish people that they no longer can fit in their land of origin, and since Marx, their last great prophet, their homeland is the world."[83] The work of my grandparents' journal was launched with these high expectations ringing out, and from distant Lima of all places.

Networks

Producing only three issues, *Repertorio Hebreo* never fully established itself as *Amauta* had done. Indeed, to understand the journal one must focus on what it had hoped to accomplish. This project would be both a memory and an unfulfilled aspiration that took root in my grandfather and accompanied him throughout his life.

I have already mentioned the first success of the journal, namely, that *Repertorio Hebreo* developed out of a collaboration between Peruvian intellectuals and Jewish intellectuals dispersed throughout the world. This already makes the journal interesting. In its second and third issues, *Repertorio Hebreo* shared some of the letters of congratulations that it had received after the publication of its first issue; among these there are some from Peruvian personalities such as Ricardo Martínez de la Torre, Carlos Alberto Izaguirre, Dora Mayer de Zulen, and Humberto Traverso, but there are also letters from European and North American figures such as Sigmund Freud, Waldo Frank, Maurice Parijanine, and the Italian editor Agénore Magno, as well as from

South American intellectuals such as Samuel Glusberg and Manuel Ugarte. In their private correspondence, my family also preserved a short note from the Chilean Nobel laureate Gabriela Mistral, which surely would have appeared in the journal's fourth issue if it had ever come to see the light of day.

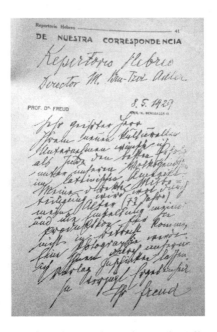

Letter from Sigmund Freud to Misha Adler.*

The creation of a network was thus an almost immediate result of this journal's publication. After offering his congratulations, the Argentine socialist leader Manuel Ugarte brought

* The letter reads: "My dear Sir: As a Jew, I wish your cultural enterprise the greatest success among our coreligionists in Latin America. Due to my age (73 years) and the interruption of my production, you should not count on my direct participation. I shall send a photograph through my editor. Yours truly, Freud."

to my grandfather's attention that "the new spirit that begins to animate the life of each one of our republics rejects selfish prejudices and traditional hatreds; it promises to bring about the broadest reconciliation of all the inhabitants of our America under the sign of justice and solidarity." Humberto Traverso, for his part, contributes a poem, in which he proposes a parallel and dialogue between the Jews and the indigenous communities of the Americas. The poem is called, "Indian Soul," and it begins as follows: "Portrait of a martyr / image of genius / the Jew who wanders. / The Jew who suffers, / look at the Indian, / your traveling companion."

In a different vein, the Argentine writer and editor Samuel Glusberg shared with Misha his experience as a Jewish editor in Buenos Aires. Glusberg began by confiding that he had received positive reports about Misha and Noemí from their common friend, José Carlos Mariátegui. Given this connection, Glusberg offered the younger Misha some advice, though not before having praised the new publication effusively: "I have no plans *ever* to restart the publication of *Cuadernos de Oriente y Occidente*. Your *Repertorio* makes it pointless." He went on, however, to share some less auspicious information: "I frankly believe the Jews of Buenos Aires are not yet prepared to sustain an undertaking of this sort and much less an Argentinian Institute of Jewish Culture, in the style of the French, Italian, English, German, and North American cultural institutes that now exist in the city."[84] He later explained how his own Jewish journal, *Cuadernos de Oriente y Occidente*, had been very well received in Argentine and South American literary circles, but had been "berated in the Jewish newspapers and journals."

Unfortunately, I've not been able to find the reviews that Glusberg was referring to, but his editorial idea for *Cuadernos de Oriente y Occidente* had much in common with those of my grandfather. Both published literary works from Spanish American writers, next to works by European and US Jews, for instance. I'm not sure whether Buenos Aires's Jewish journals objected to the high level of integration between Jewish and non-Jewish writers (i.e., that they sought a journal that was less open to South America's literary currents), or that they disliked its communist leanings. I think that there was something unsettling about the mode of integration between Judaism and South America that might have irritated a few Jewish critics.

This is all speculation, of course, but Glusberg later made an intriguing personal decision that I believe provides a clue in this regard. He changed his name to Enrique Espinoza. Superficially, the change appears as a denial of his Jewish roots, and a conversion to America. The identifiably Jewish Samuel Glusberg becomes the inconspicuous (presumably Catholic) South American Enrique Espinoza. Maybe there is an element of conversion in the case; however, Glusberg renamed himself after his two favorite authors, Heinrich ("Enrique") Heine and Baruch Spinoza (Espinoza), both of them Jews. I believe that both my grandfather and Glusberg were involved in a transformative dialogue between Jewish and Spanish American culture. The most explicit statement that I found of this is from a 1965 notebook of Misha's, where he jotted down the following phrase: "Americanism and Judaica, Zionism and Americanism have ended up harmonizing and fusing into one another in my intimate thoughts and feelings, to such a degree that they have been reduced to one and the same thing."[85] My intuition is that Glusberg, who by the way was also from Bessarabia, was undergoing a parallel process, and that there were segments of the Jewish community that saw it as an (undesirable) symptom of assimilation.

However that may be, Glusberg decided to shut down his journal with an unpublished issue of the journal all prepared, which contained poems by prominent Argentine writers including Horacio Quiroga, Lugones, and Fernández Moreno, as well as an essay by Martínez Estrada. He sent Misha the materials for them to appear in *Repertorio Hebreo* instead. Sadly, these valuable materials were lost in the shuffle of the years, and have never been recovered.

It is interesting to speculate on whether the fact that Buenos Aires's Jewish community was so much larger than Lima's might have ended up being a disadvantage for Glusberg's magazine and an advantage for *Repertorio Hebreo*. We will never know whether Lima might not have been more hospitable grounds for this kind of publication. What is clear is that both *Repertorio Hebreo* and *Cuadernos de Oriente y Occidente* managed to forge a network that connected the continent's intelligentsia to Jewish intellectuals and journals in Europe and the United States.

In that context, the brief exchange between Misha and Freud is also meaningful, I think. Unlike the correspondence that Misha maintained with Spanish American authors, which was more or less natural, or even with Waldo Frank, a New York intellectual who was deeply connected to the Latin American left, writing to Freud was a brazen act of *chutzpah*. True, Misha had translated a text by Freud for *Amauta*, but in

1929 the Viennese doctor was already at the height of his fame, and he had translators all over the world. Freud had revolutionized the field of psychology in a way that paralleled Einstein's revolution in physics or Darwin's in biology, and yet Misha presumed to ask him to contribute writings to a very modest Jewish journal that was being published out of Lima.

Beyond the *chutzpah* factor, though (and I do think that Misha had it), my grandfather's Viennese foray was in a deep way not at all impertinent. Even from eleven thousand miles away—and Peru was pretty much the end of the world then, like Australia or New Zealand—Misha recognized that he and Freud had the world in common. In fact, it was precisely this feature of recognition that Mariátegui most admired about the Jewish people: their radically global contemporaneity, which transcended national enclosures with their self-serving and pompous traditions. It is interesting that Freud too seems to have understood this connection, answering with a brief note of recognition and a signed photograph, which my family has unfortunately lost. In 1929, Austrian Jews were facing Nazism not just across their northern border, in Germany, but also within their own country. A cultural journal devoted to Jewish topics coming out of Lima, where at the time there were no more than a thousand Jews, was a fact that deserved some recognition, even if only through a brief note.

Misha

What were Misha and Noemí hoping to accomplish with *Repertorio Hebreo?* It has taken me some time to get an adequate understanding of this editorial adventure, which was as short-lived in reality as it was lasting as an ideal.

There was, in the first place, a need for collective self-recognition. There was undoubtedly a revolution then taking place in the Jewish world, but there was also in place a rich, centuries-old tradition. For my grandfather, it was necessary to explore both, come to know them, and discuss them. For this reason, *Repertorio Hebreo* was eclectic in spirit and scope. In all of this Misha was a faithful *mariateguista*.

The journal's first issue begins with pronouncements by Einstein, Freud, and Tagore celebrating the foundation of the Hebrew University of Jerusalem. There are also texts by poets such as Gabriela Mistral and José María Eguren, contemplating Jewish culture from an American vantage point, and an essay on modern Jewish musicians that begins by reminding readers that Jews are not only good interpreters of other people's music but also original composers (it then mentions as examples Arnold Schoenberg, Darius Milhaud, Gustav Mahler, and Ernest Bloch). There are presentations of painters who were still unknown in Lima, such as Georg Ehrlich, and critiques of racism by Jewish artists. There are discussions of the cultural transformation taking place in the United States thanks to Jewish immigrants, and of the new Jewish theater in the Soviet Union. Finally, there are reviews of new literature in Yiddish...All of that.

Together with this, there was marked interest in pursuing the dialogue with the group from *Amauta*, only now in a space focused on Jewish, rather than Peruvian, culture. There was at least one article or commentary by Mariátegui in each issue, of

course, but *Repertorio Hebreo* also published poems and drawings by Eguren, poems by Angela Ramos and Blanca Luz Brum,
and essays by Waldo Frank, Maria Wiesse, and Dora Mayer
de Zulen. *Repertorio Hebreo* thus presented an opportunity to
which South American intellectuals perhaps did not usually
have that much access, namely, to comment on subjects related
to the Jewish phenomenon in a space that proclaimed itself Jewish and looked to explore Jewish culture in a reflexive manner.

Jewish theater in the Soviet Union.

With the exception of some of the texts by Mariátegui, the
majority of these contributions on Jewish culture were often not
so very robust; still, the exercise must have had some meaning,
if only with respect to the collective effort to live, reflect upon,

and take charge of the world's radical contemporaneity. For in the end, many of the intellectuals who had first understood the phenomenon of global contemporaneity were Jews. To give an example, one essay published in *Repertorio Hebreo* discussed Ludwik Zamenhof, the Judeo-Polish philologist who invented Esperanto. It affirms that "our century marches toward internationalization: the material means of communication are extraordinarily developed; there is no reason to prolong Babel."[86]

The sculptor Jacob Epstein next to his bust of Paul Robeson.

Noemí, then eighteen years old, was in charge of the books and notices section that capped each issue. Her job was to select articles from the Yiddish, German, Russian, or French press (and sometimes the North American press), and translate interesting reviews. She did good work, and I think that had she continued, she eventually would have acquired her own voice and authority, either as a writer or as an editor. This unfortunately did not happen.

The third aspect of Misha's editorial work had to do with his support for Zionism. This is a complex subject for the period during which the journal was published — before the Holocaust but already at a time when powerful anti-Semitic currents were gaining ground in much of Europe, and also with all the promise of universal emancipation brought on by the Russian Revolution. Misha's ideological work concentrated on supporting the Soviet policy with respect to its constituent nationalities (such as the Jews) and arguing for the creation of a Jewish republic in Palestine, founded on the Soviet model.

The first issue of the journal is ambiguous with respect to the theme of Jewish nationalism. While it prints Einstein's, Freud's, and Tagore's praise for the creation of the Hebrew University of Jerusalem, there is also the aforementioned article by Mariátegui, in which he makes it clear that while he is not against the foundation of a Jewish state, the people of Israel should not be reduced to a national state, neither in Palestine nor anywhere else.

Mariátegui had already laid out the general parameters of his position on this subject in his 1925 book *La escena contemporánea*. To him, Zionism was only one of a number of currents of the exciting Jewish resurgence that followed the Great War, and, though justifiable, it was not its highest form, because it represented a nationalist reaction that was symmetrical to the rise of nationalism in Europe, while the Jewish experience in Europe had already transcended those nationalisms in practice. Moreover, Mariátegui believed that Zionism was to a large

degree a British project, and that it had an anti-Semitic under-
tow, in that its aim was to remove the Jews from Europe, where
they were a formidable force for transformation. On the other
hand, he conceded that, especially in the cases of Romania and
Poland, anti-Semitism had become so fierce that the Jews were
now unassimilable there, and so a Jewish homeland was needed
as an alternative. He also believed that the Jews were a mod-
ernizing force in Palestine, and that this was in itself very positive. But he also felt that Jews, who at the time constituted
only 10 percent of the population in Palestine, were destined to
remain a minority there, because outside of Poland and Romania, the vast majority of the Jewish population preferred to live
in Europe or in the Americas.

And there was another thing. For Mariátegui the Jewish
renaissance "is not the rebirth of a nationality. It is also not the
renaissance of a religion. It is, rather, the rebirth of the Jewish
genius, spirit, and sentiment."[87] The reconstruction of a Jewish homeland was but an episode of this flourishing. Humanity owed the Jewish renaissance a debt of gratitude, not for its
nationalism, which was perhaps not that different from other
nationalisms, but rather for the spiritual and intellectual work
of its humanists, scientists, and artists, and the work of its great
revolutionaries and social reformers.

The systematic discrimination of Jews had made it possible
for them to transcend the national formula and make themselves into the vanguard of internationalism. This didn't mean
that the subject of nationalism should not be explored — on the
contrary, Mariátegui felt that universal emancipation passed
through the liberation of all oppressed peoples, including Jews.

He simply believed that Zionism was not the greatest Jewish value, and that it should not be the cultural mission of a periodical such as *Repertorio Hebreo*.

The second issue of that journal opens with an article by Misha on the situation of the Jews in Russia. It criticizes those who had made much of anti-Semitism in the Soviet Union with no recognition of the enormous progress that had been achieved with respect to the Jewish question since the fall of the czars. Misha carefully enumerates the relevant changes: official support for publications in Yiddish; the creation of political autonomy for Jews; the translation into Yiddish of children's books and scientific publications; official financing for a Yiddish encyclopedia; the formation of professorships in Yiddish at some universities; and support for two Jewish theaters (Habima and Granovsky). All of this had taken place since 1917, alongside the distribution of agricultural land to Jews, a move that had been anathema for centuries.

None of this fully eradicated anti-Semitism in the Soviet Union, and Misha declares himself cognizant of this fact. Nevertheless, he reminds his readers that in the time of the czars, Russia had been the country with the greatest level of anti-Semitism and the worst conditions for Jewish people in the entire world, while now, in the Soviet Union, the situation for Jews was better than in most of Europe. As he puts it: "It is now time to recognize that the October Revolution has performed a true miracle with respect to the Jewish problem."[88]

The third issue of *Repertorio Hebreo* was published shortly after a massacre of Jewish colonists in Palestine, an episode referred to in Hebrew as *Meora'ot Tarpat* and in Arabic as the

Buraq uprising. During the violence, Palestinians killed more than 130 Jews, and British authorities killed roughly the same number of Palestinians in their attempt to put down the rebellion. The murder of Jewish colonists and the destruction of their property reminded Misha of the pogroms he had witnessed in Russia and Romania, so he published a written protest. In this, he was supported by the principal actors of the *Amauta* group, with Mariátegui front and center. The protest also prompted Misha to solidify his position with respect to the foundation of a Jewish state in Palestine:

> The creation of an independent Jewish state in Palestine — a single country in which all Jewish expatriates, dispersed throughout the world, have inalienable rights "in a territory historically their own" and under the auspices of a socialist regime — founded on the principles in force, and with great success, with respect to Jewish colonization in the union of the new Soviet republics, would indisputably be an event of great historical transcendence…Zionism and communism are not mutually exclusive. And as the learned Einstein has said: "A Jew who strives to impregnate his spirit with humanitarian ideals can call himself a Zionist without contradiction."[89]

I'd like to comment on two or three of the points made here. First, the claim for a Jewish land in Palestine takes place through two channels. The first is historical, as Palestine was originally Jewish land, and the second is pragmatic, in that it is the only territory in the world to which expatriated Jews have any sort of claim. That is, what is dominant here is not a religious argument but rather a legal one — that Jews had a historical claim to that territory—and a more pragmatic and urgent one—that Jews were being expelled from Europe, where they being denied even the most basic rights. The best solution, from Misha's point of view, would be to imitate the Soviet Union, but now for the persecuted Jewish population that was outside of the USSR: the creation of a Jewish soviet in Palestine.

Misha insists that Zionism and communism are not mutually exclusive, and he supports the establishment of a communist Jewish homeland. His solution bears some resemblance to Mariátegui's ideas on political reform in Peru, spelled out in his extraordinary *Seven Interpretive Essays on Peruvian Reality*. Mariátegui had only just published that book, and it was being enthusiastically promoted in the pages of *Repertorio Hebreo*. In short, the communist revolution would necessarily imply the emancipation of oppressed nations, and the Jewish people had been expelled and excluded, persecuted and discriminated against across all of Eastern Europe. They had nowhere to go, nor could they develop their national identity without some territory to call their own. That was his reasoning.

Misha's arguments nonetheless reveal a degree of tension with Mariátegui's ideas. For the latter, the Jewish people had more fully earned the right to be European and American than any other, and their transnational culture was much closer to that of New York, London, Berlin, or Lima than that of the rural Palestinians or the semi-nomadic Bedouins. For Mariátegui, it would likewise be an error to reduce Jewish culture to the internal traditions of Judaism (the use of Hebrew and Yiddish, the religion of Abraham, the Talmud, etc.). As he saw it, the Jews had achieved a genuinely universal value, and their mission was now humanity itself, with Marx as their prophet, and not nationalism.

Misha agreed with this, but he likely saw the formation of a Jewish state as a pressing practical matter. This sense of urgency undoubtedly came from his experience in Romania, a country that had by then become one of the worst for Jews in all of Europe — a competition that was not so easy to "win." Misha knew that the conditions for Jews were deplorable in the region that stretched from the Baltic Sea in the north to the Adriatic Sea in the south. He had seen these conditions first-hand. This prompted him to promote a Jewish state, but he did so without abandoning the internationalist messianism he and Mariátegui both associated with Marx.

CHAPTER EIGHT

Expulsion

Prison

I read a number of entertaining period pieces while conducting research on the Lima of my grandparents, but one that really stands out is the pamphlet "I: Tyrant and Thief" (*Yo tirano, yo ladrón*), written by the at-that-point recently ousted president Augusto Leguía from his jail cell. It is a minor classic in the very Latin American genre of political self-tribute. Inevitably, it opens with a flourish: "He who speaks to you through this poorly conceived book (filled, nonetheless, with sincere truths), is a prisoner on the brink of settling his accounts before God's Divine Tribunal, a figure insulted and vilified by public opinion, the same public that so recently expressed to him its unmeasured adulation."[90] The tone intimates both the pathetic and the picaresque sides of Peruvian politics, which have been a recurrent subject for imperialist lampooning of Latin America and its "banana republics."

Augusto Leguía's pompous apology and self-defense before his Maker seem almost to justify the taunting that *Time* magazine was fond of, in its oh-so-superior style of commentary on Peruvian political chicanery. Today, we're no longer used to reading mainstream journalists write quite so derisively (or so frankly) about their subjects, but even bearing that in mind, the degree to which the magazine reveled in the insignificance of Peruvian politics is striking.

The first note was published in 1925, and its lead sentence delighted in Leguía's light weight no fewer than three times: "Last week came tidings of that benevolent dictator, that bantam Mussolini, the diminutive yet lion-hearted President Augusto B. Leguía y Salcedo of Peru, who 'tips the scales at 98 pounds of dynamite and determination.'"[91] *Time*'s second note, published five years later, just a few months before Leguía's fall, again leads with the diminutive: "Once employed by New York Life Insurance Co., courageous little Señor Augusto B. Leguía ('The Bantam Roosevelt of Peru') is now in his fourth term as president."[92]

Unfamiliar as I was with the term "bantam" (*Time* characterized Leguía first as a bantam Mussolini and later as a bantam Teddy Roosevelt), I looked it up, and found that it means "a chicken of a small breed, the male of which is noted for its aggression." I don't entirely disagree with *Time*'s disdainful characterization, but still, it means something that *Time* was so confidently derisive with regard to South America that it felt that it did not require much more than a few maliciously crafted paragraphs to cover Peruvian politics over Leguía's entire eleven-year reign.

Peru, in American eyes, was quaint and exotic, fascinating and ridiculous. The country could not be taken seriously, at least not in its own terms. What it needed was a new generation of benign but firm captains of industry and politics (US, or at least US-trained), who might recognize Peru's true potential in a way that the descendants of conquistador Francisco Pizarro could not.

After the Inca empire fell to the Spaniards in 1532, Lima became the capital of a viceroyalty that encompassed the whole of Spanish South America, and Limeño society became the nervous center of a sprawling quasi-feudal system, with the Indians playing the part of the serfs. Its Counter-Reformation political order was militantly conservative, and its social life pivoted on religiously inflected rituals and on the daily performance of fine-grained status distinctions. In other words, Peru was a society of manners, where deference and the exercise of authority were practically an art form. For early twentieth-century US observers, Peruvian obsession with form, status, and family needed to be replaced with pragmatism, entrepreneurial acumen, and rational discovery.

Still, American coolheaded rationality was not so easily attained in the face of an "unknown continent" that still shimmered with legends of gold. Indeed, gold was firmly tied to the national imaginary in the lands of the Incas; even today, both Lima and Bogotá proudly house major archaeological collections in museums called Museo del Oro—Gold Museum. The image of precious discoveries overwhelms everything: pre-Columbian cultures have their golden aura, but they are also reduced to gold, because Peruvian gold and silver transformed everything. It created and destroyed everything.

When Spanish conquistador (and Jewish *converso*) Pedro Cieza de León published the first volume of his famous chronicles of the conquest of Peru in 1553, he introduced his work with a remark on the astounding size of Peruvian treasure: "[W]here have men seen what they see today, fleets entering loaded with gold and silver as if it were iron? Or where was it known or read that so much wealth could come from one kingdom?"[93] And the conquistador immediately goes on to say that Peruvian gold transformed the status hierarchy in Spain's cities, which were now all full of rich *peruleros* (Spaniards who had returned from Peru) whose conspicuous expenditures had so inflated local prices that it was no longer clear how normal people would get by. Peruvian treasure had impoverished Spain's poor, but it had also made princes out of swineherds. And neither was the impact of Inca gold and silver confined to Spain alone; rather it held sway in all of Europe and, Cieza continued, it had proved providential for the True Faith, since Emperor Charles V was able to wage war against the Lutherans in Germany thanks only to Peruvian treasure.

Although twentieth-century Americans fancied themselves as the enlightened discoverers of a kingdom that had been lost to reason by the closed-minded heirs of the Spanish conquest, they were still no less seduced by tales of Peruvian gold. American author and famed explorer Richard Halliburton offers a colorful example of this. In his 1929 book on his South American travels, he introduced Peru with precisely such an image of a golden discovery. After dwelling first on the well-known story of the Inca Atahualpa's ransom and of Inca sunworshippers holding their rituals in a court of shimmering gold—and then on the sterile futility of Pizarro's cruel looting—Halliburton turns to his first adventure in the Peruvian jungle.

He had wandered away from the trail, and suddenly found himself alone in a golden glade. "I rubbed my eyes. Perhaps I was bewitched...I was as rich as Atahualpa...Into the sea of gold I plunged...Magic! But the treasure, each countless coin, suddenly came to life, leaped from the earth in a blinding cloud, blotted out the scene, hid the sun, rose and fell and buried me in flame. And then I knew. I had not found the Inca gold at all. I had found the butterflies."[94]

Americans were eager to discover South America's true wonders, and these were, at times, every bit as awe-inspiring as legend. But they existed in a different plane, for inherited images had to give way to lived experience, as gold had given way to butterflies in Halliburton's story. For the new American conquistador, Peruvian vanity and self-infatuation stood in the way of the spirit of exploration, but this made Peruvians naturally submissive in the face of any power that was capable of transforming raw material into value, through investment, industry, and commerce. Thus they had kowtowed to the British after independence was gained from Spain, and the British had dominated Peruvian finance through the whole of the nineteenth century and until the First World War. This allowed them to profit from new mining discoveries. They had made millions from guano fertilizer mining in the 1840s, 1850s, and 1860s, and had again reaped the profits of the saltpeter nitrate boom, until the richest mines were annexed by Chile, in its 1879–84 war with Peru and Bolivia. The British also financed the first railway concerns.

Now, with the decline of Britain's influence in the Western Hemisphere, it was the Americans who held sway over Peru's finances and export economy. In US narratives on early twentieth-century Peru, the Americans' unimpeachable rationality is cast in sharp relief with Peruvian idiosyncrasies, which generally oscillate between the quaintly charming and the outdated, a treatment that extended to everything from courting to politics and scientific curiosity to common daily routines.

American observations tended to divorce the Peruvian mentalities that so fascinated them from their material context. If Lima's middle and upper sectors embraced their somewhat decrepit glories, this was due in large part to the long-standing embattled relationship that existed between the nation's coastal elites and the Andes. The coastal plane was a mixed-race society, composed principally of Afro-Peruvians, Chinese, and Peruvian-born Europeans ("Creoles"), while the Andes were the Indian heartland of the country, where indigenous communities were harshly dominated by Creole landowning overlords, known as *gamonales*.

Lima's elites had failed to integrate the Andean region into the nation, except by extending neocolonial forms of subjection through violence. During Peru's war with Chile, when Lima's power faltered, Andean militias rose up, and there were again intimations of native rebellion in the highlands. They then had to be put down yet again, by a government that was nearly broke. There was a long history of Peruvian elites putting down Andean social movements, and then turning in on themselves. Lima's closed society reflected the country's inability to integrate its native peasantry.

Perhaps the most consequential example of this dynamic is the so-called Túpac Amaru rebellion. In 1778, an Indian nobleman named José Gabriel Condorcanqui adopted the name of the last Inca emperor, Túpac Amaru, and rebelled against the colonial order, seeking British support for the reinstatement of the Inca empire. Native revolts were especially dangerous when they had powerful allies who might provide guns, and the idea that there might be an independence movement, orchestrated as a caste war and leading to the re-emergence of the long-repressed Inca empire, frightened Peruvian elites, while it became a kind of messianic referent for its revolutionaries.

Túpac Amaru led a broad-based rebellion of a scale that was unprecedented in colonial times, and it took the authorities almost two years and a large standing army to put it down. One effect of this rebellion was that it made Lima's elite especially fearful of class warfare and Indian uprisings. Indeed, when the wars of independence began throughout Spanish America, thirty years later, Lima's Euro-American elites cast their lot with the Spaniards and mostly remained passive. As a result, Peruvian national independence occurred by conquest, and it was claimed by an Argentine *criollo*, José de San Martín, who led what was essentially an invading army in order to "free" Peru.

It is true that the specter of caste war and slave rebellion made *criollos* anxious everywhere in Spanish America. Haiti's 1803 slave revolt and independence in particular was mobilized as an instrument of royalist propaganda, but many *criollos* supported independence regardless of these fears, and worked to build alliances with sectors of their popular classes. In Peru, however, recent memory of the Túpac Amaru rebellion made native elites especially fearful and conservative.

And neither was Lima's fear of the natives dispelled after independence, because Indian rebellion always remained a latent possibility that reared itself in moments of elite fragmentation, such as during the war against Chile, for instance. In other words, Lima's traditionalism was at least in part a defense mechanism of a ruling class that governed a deeply fragmented, neocolonial society, where native serfs were often suspected of pining for reinstating the Inca kingdom, the Tawantinsuyu.

But in times of peace, like the 1920s, Lima's traditionalism was more apt to be read by Americans as just a quaint and ineffectual relic. So, for instance, in Hans Otto Storm's rather tedious novel *Pity the Tyrant*, which is set in Lima during the final days of Augusto Leguía's regime, the author dwells on the romance between an American business traveler and a Chilean woman "from a good family" (*de buena familia*), who cedes to his sexual advances with disarming ease, only later to flare up in anger, in what for the American is an irrational show of jealousy, prompted by the fact that he has begun courting another woman.[95] First the woman is loose, then she is possessive. Above all, she is nonsensical, while the eminently reasonable American guiltlessly profits from her absurdity.

To my mind, there is an interesting side to this particular instance of imperialist superiority, which is its playful instrumentality. The traveler is never really lost in his passion, never ensnared by it. He is at once earnest and self-interested, good-hearted and abusive. More than the all-consuming passions that one finds, say, in Joseph Conrad's *Heart of Darkness*, where the main character's alter ego, Kurtz, is forever lost to the "darkness" of the Congo River, American writing and reportage on Peru rarely seems to break ties with American belonging. Peru provided mementos and trophies that would all be enjoyed back at home in good time.

The strains of *Jolly Farmer* entice Manuella out into the patio, where she shows me how a guitar really should be played.

Richard Halliburton showing his
"beautiful señorita" to the American public
after enticing her to dress up as an "authentic Limeña."

This logic of conquest was not confined to sex. Machu Picchu had been discovered by the world just recently, in 1911, by American explorer, Yale professor, and Indiana Jones prototype Hiram Bingham III. That stunningly beautiful place, the "lost city of the Incas," gained instant fame as a beacon of the grandeur that the jungle hid away, and of all that remained to be discovered in Peru: the heights of Machu Picchu.

For the Peruvian radicals of Mariátegui's circle the Andes were then rumbling with a new consciousness, the rumor of Indian revolt, which were also the birth pangs of a new nation. In 1915, Peruvian Sergeant Major Teodomiro Gutiérrez Cuevas returned from exile in Argentina having embraced anarchism: he took on the Quechua nom de guerre Rumi Maqui (Hand of Stone) and led a broad-based Indian rebellion against the landowning class, with the goal of distributing land among the peasants, reinstating the Tawantinsuyu, the Inca state, and seceding from Lima's control. The movement was brutally quashed, but not before touching the young Mariátegui and other Limeño intellectuals. In fact, Rumi Maqui's revolt was one of the events that marked the close of Mariátegui's bohemian moment as Juan Croniqueur, and initiated his definitive turn to revolutionary politics. Rumi Maqui also led Mariátegui to understand and defend the revolutionary power of Indian restoration, in other words, the revolutionary potential of myth, tradition, and native belief.

The first major writerly rendition of the immanence of Indian revolt was Luis Valcárcel's *Tempestad en los Andes* (Tempest in the Andes), which was published around the same time as Halliburton's entertaining but trivial book. It is a poetic account, narrated as an epic and myth, of the return of the repressed, wherein the Indians awake from the long night of colonial dominion: "It was a formless mass, ahistorical. It did not live, it seemed eternal like the mountains, like the sky. In its sphynx-like face, the empty sockets said it all: its absent eyes did not witness the procession of things. It was a people of stone."[96]

Valcárcel created a poetry of native revolt, which began with such descriptions of a petrified Indian society, turned in on itself and living in the pain of conquest and oppression, and then finally awaking to a storm of revolution and collective affirmation. Machu Picchu was the most perfect image of that petrified existence: it was a secret, long-abandoned Inca city that had finally come out into the open.

The political awakening of the Peruvian countryside rang true for at least some — perhaps even many — Peruvians. But for most Americans, Peru's greatness was thought to be lost in the past, and it could not be recovered by its own people, who were mired in endless, intractable, but also trivial and venial conflict. Thus *Time* magazine's 1925 story tells of an American Episcopalian physician who was Leguía's personal doctor, and who was rewarded for this service by the president in true banana republic fashion, with the bestowal of the mayoralty of Callao. *Time* then used the occasion to characterize the political situation in broad strokes: "Without becoming lurid, it may be baldly stated that no less than nine major revolutions and at least a score of minor revolts have been put down during the ten odd years in which Señor Leguía has worn the presidential sash of Peru."

Time's second article on Leguía, published with the fitting title "I... Eternal," ridicules the president by quoting from an impassioned speech that he pronounced in the Chamber of Deputies while a coup against him was being set into motion:

"No assassin's bullet can destroy my work. It is eternal. Should I die, the assassin's own hand will inscribe my name in history." The American magazine's naughty disdain for Peru's president went hand in glove with its almost nonexistent coverage of Peruvian politics. It is in this respect a classic expression of the imperialist hubris that has accumulated over the years in America's good-humored ignorance of the "Other America."

Of course, there is no denying that Leguía, who characterized Peruvians as "a naive people with the mentality of a child, easy prey for the tricks of any clever or heartless person, like my detractors," did his own bit in favor of the view that Spanish American politics was one continuous operetta. Socially, Peru was a bisected society, which meant that democratic politics could only develop with an authoritarian ingredient that relied heavily on inventing enemies and adversaries. Sadly, one of his farcical twists involved my grandparents directly. It took place on November 11, 1929.

The Jewish-communist plot

In keeping with all good farces, there were cosmic forces at work in the background of this one. The New York Stock Exchange had collapsed a few weeks prior, destabilized the Peruvian economy, and with it Leguía's eleven-year reign. To emerge from this trouble, Leguía invented a useful distraction: a "Jewish-communist plot" that was allegedly being hatched in Mariátegui's house.

The scandal was meant to draw public attention away from the governmental crisis long enough for Leguía to find allies who might prolong his tenure in office, such as the archbishop of Lima, Emilio Lissón. It also provided him with an excuse to arrest a couple of union leaders who were neither communists nor Jews but who were a thorn in his side, alongside a handful of Jews who might play the part of suspects in the public eye.[97] There were several Jews in Mariátegui's circle, but the closest to him were undoubtedly Misha Adler and Noemí Milstein. Both were arrested. Ironically, so was my great-grandfather Boris, who was a businessman who had fled the Russian Revolution, and could hardly be characterized as a communist.

On November 21, 1929, Mariátegui wrote a letter to his friend in Buenos Aires, the writer and editor Samuel Glusberg, telling him of the raid on his house and how the police had arrested members of his group and seized *Amauta*'s correspondence. He then mentioned that "among those arrested are Adler and his girlfriend, Noemí Milstein; and the persecution has a curious anti-Semitic character. It seems that all the Jewish peddlers are to be imprisoned, along with their suppliers and others. They are absurdly suspected of constituting an organization of agitators."[98]

On day fifteen of the raid, Mariátegui wrote again, this time to the Peruvian poet César Vallejo, who was living in Paris at the time, telling him that "many Jews remain in jail, among them Miguel Adler, director of *Repertorio Hebreo*, against whom there exists no other charge except for the leftist ideological tenor of his journal, his international correspondence, and his friendship with me. His girlfriend's father has also been detained, a merchant distant from any ideological concerns."[99] And in yet another letter, Mariátegui writes to Costa Rican writer Joaquín García Monge, explaining that "the majority of those imprisoned have now been freed. Some still remain in police custody, such as Miguel Adler, director of *Repertorio Hebreo* and the principal victim of this first anti-Semitic gesture by the Peruvian police, and E. Saldías, a textile worker who represented different worker organizations in the Union Conference of Montevideo."[100]

Leguía's idea of stirring up an anti-Semitic demonstration may well have been inspired by an earlier experience: Lima's 1909 anti-Chinese riots, which I brought up a couple of chapters ago. These had occurred during Leguía's first presidency (1908–12). On that occasion, a rabble of Carlos de Piérola's frustrated supporters against Leguía vented their frustration on Lima's Chinese merchants, looting many businesses. Lima's aristocratic mayor, Guillermo Billinghurst, condemned the violence, surely, but he also moved immediately to raze an alley of seedy tenements that were inhabited by as many as five hundred Chinese. The popularity of Billinghurst's anti-Chinese one-upmanship was not lost on President Leguía, who then jumped onto the jingoistic bandwagon himself, and banned Chinese immigration from Peru altogether. Billinghurst, for his part, consolidated his popular base and later went on to be elected president. This experience with the political usefulness of xenophobia may have tempted Leguía to concoct his phony Jewish-communist plot.

There were, of course, risks that the ploy against Jewish communists might not work as well as the one against the Chinese. The Jews of Lima had not yet garnered the kind of popular animosity that was aimed at the Chinese, possibly because their numbers were more modest and they had not been in Peru as long, and because, despite the growing international influence of fascism and anti-Semitism, there was not yet much popular racism directed against them. This is probably the reason why Mariátegui was puzzled by the anti-Semitic turn that the government raid had taken. The move, in short, was more desperate and less effective than the government's opportunistic co-optation of the 1909 anti-Chinese riots had been. Still, the specter of a Judeo-communist plot seemed like it might gain some traction in the press and in Lima's middle classes, and in this way earn the government the one thing that it needed the most: time.

Based on chronologies that I tallied from Mariátegui's correspondence, we know that the young Noemí perhaps spent around ten days in police custody. But Misha was cast as the principal suspect, and was sent to the island prison of El Frontón, where he spent perhaps two or three months.

El Frontón was Lima's answer to Alcatraz. Sitting opposite the port of Callao, the island might have been seen by both Misha and Noemí from the ship when they first arrived in Peru, and then again on the occasions that took them to the baths or eateries of Callao, La Punta, or Chorrillos. Still, it was a dreaded place for all Limeños. Peruvian historian Carlos Aguirre writes that El Frontón prison was run like a slave plantation, down to the detail of having its own illegal cemetery for those who perished while working there. Prisoners were employed making pavement stones for the city of Lima, which was growing under Leguía, and Aguirre shows that the quarries turned a profit.[101] But El Frontón needed at least 250 inmates at any given time to keep the business profitable, which meant that Lima's vagrants were sometimes rounded up to provide workers for the island's quarries.

Although the prison had only been inaugurated about a dozen years prior, by the time Misha was imprisoned the place was already a bit of a ruin. A 1932 official public health report found the jail's buildings to be overcrowded, dilapidated, and filled with rodents and other vermin.[102] One of my grandparents' friends, the communist poet and journalist Angela Ramos, published an exposé of the living conditions in the prison just three years before Misha was sent there: prisoners ambled about like walking corpses, often bleeding because of poor working conditions in the quarries. Many inmates did not even know why they had been detained. The prison needed captives to get by, so its purpose was not limited to containing criminality.[103]

It seems that my grandfather was occupied there filling sacks of guano. I'm not sure whether that guano was locally mined or shipped in from other islands. In any case, this work involved breathing guano dust, so it caused a lot of illness. Misha was released from prison probably in January or February 1930, thanks to the intervention of his old friends from Nova Sulitza, several of whom had done well in the six years that had elapsed since their arrival in Lima, and were now in a position either to coax or to bribe government officials into releasing him. The condition, though, was deportation.

It is painful that the Peruvian government's first-ever anti-Semitic intervention — an act that Peruvian historian Alberto Flores Galindo has characterized as "Peru's first pogrom" — affected Misha and Noemí so directly.[104] It led to their expulsion from Peru, a country that they had come to love. Personal

tragedy aside, the episode's sinister nature also had its predictably farcical side. Leguía had orchestrated his little power
grab by making use of the stereotypical figure of the Jewish-
communist conspirator, using the Jew as a stock character, lifted
in this case from the anti-Semitic literature that had begun cir-
culating through Latin America since the days of the Dreyfus
affair, in the 1880s and 1890s, and that culminated with the 1903
publication of the *Protocols of the Elders of Zion*, which cast Jews
as a secret cabal whose mission was to take over the world.

Such prefabricated images might have seemed a bit out
of place in Peru, where nineteenth-century anti-Semitism
was not an issue, since there were practically no Jews there,
but in fact their effectiveness sprung precisely from their
novelty. Starting in the mid-1890s, when the telegraph connected Europe to America via a transatlantic cable, in the daily
news South America's capitals became suffused with images
of events and characters that had few or no local precedents:
homosexual scandals, anarchist assassins, serial killers. Jewish
plots and plotters were among such news items. So although
Leguía's claim of a Jewish-communist conspiracy seemed quite
dubious, since it had no local precedent, it was credible to the
extent that it was making a claim for Peru as a modern country, with all of the complicated problems of modern countries,
including dealing with Jewish intrigue. The use of an image
that was at once prefabricated and imported could distract and
entertain the public, and thus buy the wily Augusto Leguía a
little time to get out of a tight spot (yet again!).

Jorge del Prado, who was detained for two days in Lima's
El Sexto jail along with my grandparents, speaks of yet another

aspect of Leguía's operetta, namely the extortion to which the police subjected the Jewish peddlers that they had detained so that they might provide the plot with at least some vague semblance of credibility. Prado relates how Fernandez Oliva, "the shady chief of the state police during the Leguía regime, together with the Minister of Government, converted the farce into a lucrative business, particularly at the expense of Jewish merchants."[105] The police charged somewhere between one thousand and ten thousand Peruvian *soles* (between roughly US $5,000 and $42,000, adjusted for inflation) for each Jew to be allowed to leave jail.

But then again, there wasn't much that was so very original in this part of the script either. The use of the stereotypical Jew as a player in one political opera buffa or another went hand in hand with the extortion of actual real-live Jews in Europe as well as in America. In this case, Jews like Noemí's father, Boris, who had nothing to do either with communism or with politics, were nonetheless rounded up in order to prove the physical existence of alleged conspirators. Without their actual material presence, the farce would be incomplete, but since rounding them up meant making them vulnerable, extortion came as a welcome secondary benefit. And while the story of a Jewish Red Scare was just a hoax authored by an unscrupulous president, its effects, in the end, were real enough.

Of nationalities and passports

Misha was released from prison with an agreement, brokered by the local Jewish community, that he and Noemí would leave the country. But the Leguía government was unstable by then, and teetering on the brink, so Misha and Noemí found ways to delay their departure. Except that before going on with that story, I need to discuss the question of my grandparents' nationality.

Misha's and Noemí's Peruvian expulsion papers (November 1930) identified them as Romanian. However, as Mariátegui had told Glusberg, neither could expect any protection from that government, because there was no Romanian legation in Peru.[106] But the truth was that even if there had been an embassy, Romanian policy toward its Jews was not oriented to providing them with protection but rather to stimulating their permanent emigration. My grandmother's Romanian identity was, if anything, even more problematic than my grandfather's, because she had been born in Ukraine, and the attitude of the Romanian government toward Jewish refugees who had arrived from Russia after the revolution was that they could only stay temporarily. For this reason, and in exchange (as always) for money, the government expedited passports only with the expressed goal of ushering them out of the country.

What all this means is that my grandparents may not have had renewable Romanian passports that might have permitted them to move about the world freely, and it is in this context that they figure as having applied for Peruvian citizenship.

Even so, there are a number of murky points in the case. My uncle Manuel remembers that Misha had a valid Peruvian passport when he and Noemí traveled to Peru on a visit, in the early 1960s. This was the visit that is engraved in my childhood memory of Misha with the archaeologist in ruins on the outskirts of Lima. So how do we explain the fact that he was denied Peruvian nationality, and then years later used a Peruvian passport?

I can think of only two possibilities. The first is that Misha and Noemí bribed somebody to get either a Peruvian passport or a Peruvian birth certificate that might years later have been used to gain a passport. The second is that Peru might have given both Misha and Noemí Peruvian nationality upon their arrival from Europe, because the spirit of Peru's policy of European colonization was precisely that these immigrants would eventually become Peruvians. It was also the case, though, that Peruvian officials had only agreed to release Misha from prison on the condition that he be expelled from the country. Except that you can't legally expel a citizen from his or her own country.

My hypothesis is, then, that government officials ignored a previous nationalization, if it existed, treated Noemí and Misha as Romanian foreigners who were applying for citizenship, proceeded to deny their application on account of their communism and their subversive political activities, and so immediately moved to deport them. By the time all of this happened, Leguía had already been toppled and General Luis Miguel Sánchez Cerro was president. Being, as he was, a fascist sympathizer, Sánchez Cerro was much more earnestly anticommunist than his predecessor, so his government definitely wanted them out. Misha and Noemí probably then held on to their Peruvian (at this point, illegal) passports in order to be admitted to Colombia, and may have renewed those passports decades later, when Sánchez Cerro was long gone. End of my lengthy, but necessary, parenthesis on my grandparents' nationality.

The death of Mariátegui

Starting around 1928, Mariátegui's standing with the government got progressively worse, and Lima was becoming unlivable for him. The Mariáteguis and my grandparents seem to have nurtured a fantasy that they would all go to live in Switzerland. More realistically, though, plans were being made to leave Peru for Buenos Aires. In July 1929, a few months before Leguía's *razzia*, Mariátegui had sent Misha to Bolivia, Chile, Argentina, and Uruguay as a representative of *Amauta* (probably with a Peruvian passport?).[107] It is possible that during that trip Misha toyed with the idea of moving with Noemí and the Mariáteguis to Buenos Aires. What we know for sure is that by February 1930, with Samuel Glusberg's help, Mariátegui had already made the necessary arrangements to leave Lima.

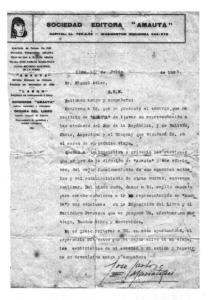

A letter from José Carlos Mariátegui
to Misha Adler, July 13, 1929.

In March of that same year, though, Mariátegui had a relapse of the mysterious illness that had afflicted him from childhood, and that had already forced the amputation of his leg. He was hospitalized in the Villarán Clinic. My grandparents were by his side during his final weeks and at the moment of his death on April 16, 1930. My uncle Manuel shared with me the following version of the events leading up to Mariátegui's death, which my grandmother had told him:

> When José Carlos was on his deathbed, a group of relatives and friends gathered around him. At one point, Anita, who was propping up José Carlos's head, asked Noemí to take her place while she took a saucepan off the stove. When my mother took her place, José Carlos said to her, "Noemí, let's go to Switzerland; let's go to Switzerland." Seeing that he was getting worse, Noemí sent someone to tell Anita to come quickly. As soon as she arrived and took Noemí's place, José Carlos entered his final moments of life... Told by my mother to me. End of story.[108]

I'd like to share photographs from my family's collection of the death of the great Peruvian intellectual.

José Carlos Mariátegui on his deathbed.
Villarán Clinic, April 1930.

top: Misha Adler next to the bed where Mariátegui lies dying.
bottom: Noemí Milstein is standing on the left; kneeling
beside Mariátegui is probably his wife, Anna Chiappe.

And to complement these pictures of the final days and
death of the *Amauta* with a photo of Mariátegui's funeral taken
from Prado's book. Misha is there, walking just behind the
coffin with his head turned and wearing a white shirt.

top: Pallbearers (including Misha, on the left) next to Mariátegui's coffin. *bottom:* Mariátegui's funeral procession.

The fall of Leguía

When I was sixteen years old, my grandmother and I were talking about something, I don't remember what, and in the course of our conversation she told me that she could well imagine the kind of charisma that Jesus had during his life because she had known a man with those qualities, José Carlos Mariátegui. This is the only time that my grandma spoke of José Carlos to me, even though I spent quite a lot of time with her. Noemí was rankled by any kind of name-dropping, and she was also not one to dwell much on the past. Noemí preferred to be in the present and in the future. In this case, though, she was offering evidence for a very specific point, which was that personalities like Jesus exist in the real world.

After Mariátegui's death, the Lima that my grandparents knew began to close in around them. Everything was hanging by a thread: that world in which "nobody knew what a Jew was" and in which "there was no anti-Semitism" seemed to be waning, too. But above all they faced the close of exciting collective discussions in the Red Corner of the house on Jirón Washington, the end of their political activism in Peru's unions, no more translations of German and Russian for *Amauta*, which also would fold very soon. *Repertorio Hebreo*, the journal that they had created, was also in an untenable situation, and their many remarkable friends, such as José María Eguren, Blanca Luz Brum, and Jorge del Prado, would soon become distant.

On August 22, 1930, four months after Mariátegui's death, there was a coup d'état. As it turns out, Augusto Leguía did not fall from power because of a Jewish-communist plot, but rather because of a much more (for South America) humdrum military coup, at the hands of a subordinate with fascist tendencies, Lieutenant Colonel Luis Miguel Sánchez Cerro. After a few days, this "Traitor from Arequipa" (in the ever-fatuous rhetoric of Leguía) took power with the help of a portion of Peru's "childlike" public opinion, hectored by "vegetarian bipeds, writers with no morals or scruples."[109]

Immediately after the coup, a mob sacked Leguía's house in Miraflores. After the crowd departed, my grandparents decided to take a walk to see the wreckage. And they had the good luck to find a small ivory statuette lying on the sidewalk, in front of Leguía's house. It was a small Chinese antiquity that, I speculate, may have been offered to the president as a sign of goodwill by members of the Chinese legation. A peace offering from one of Peru's at times persecuted minorities, and also a memento from the house of the man who had my grandparents arrested, following the anti-Chinese script. I grew up with that statuette, without knowing what it was or where it came from. It was when I began writing this book that my mother told me that story.

Expulsion

The military coup d'état did not improve things for my grandparents. Sánchez Cerro and his group were xenophobes and
committed anticommunists, and on November 14 the Peruvian
government denied Misha's and Noemí's applications for citizenship, expelled each of them from the country as communists, and declared them personae non gratae.

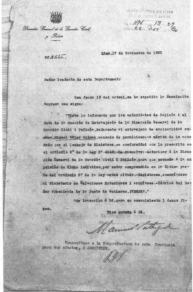

left: Noemí Milstein in Huancayo on November 23, 1930, shortly before her
deportation from Peru. *right:* Misha Adler's order of expulsion from Peru, 1930.

The police dossier that closes with the expulsion of my
grandfather mentions his assets, which, apart from his doctorate from the Universidad de San Marcos, consisted solely

of the shares that he owned as one of Mariátegui's partners in the Minerva publishing house, which printed both *Amauta* and *Repertorio Hebreo*. Upon his expulsion from Peru, Misha donated these shares to Anna, Mariátegui's widow, a gesture that sealed my grandparents' bittersweet goodbyes to a time that had been one of great happiness.

A trip to the country with José Carlos and Anna, c. 1928. Misha is to the left of Anna, and Noemí is on Mariátegui's right. The back of the photo, written in Noemí's handwriting, reads: "A memento of times past."

PART TWO

The Debacle

CHAPTER NINE

Adulthood

Marriage

Reconstructing the sequence of events after my grandfather's release from jail requires some conjecture. I think that what happened is that a few months after Misha and Noemí's arrest in Lima, Noemí's father, Boris, who had also been briefly detained, traveled to Tuluá, Colombia, to pave the way for yet a new migration, while his wife, Tania, and his daughters Noemí and Pupe waited in Lima. Financial records in Tuluá state that Boris set up a soap mill there in September 1929.[110] It is not entirely clear why he chose to leave Lima at that point. There is no living memory of this in my family, but it seems likely that Boris had plans to leave Peru even before his daughter's expulsion. And he might have had several reasons for that.

To begin with, Boris might not have thought that Misha was such a good match for his daughter. Misha was a communist sympathizer, and the Milstein family had lost a daughter,

Shura, while escaping communist persecution. Misha was also
an intellectual in a world that offered few options to intellectuals. Would he be able to support Noemí and their future
children? Finally, the government raid in November 1929 had
landed Boris and Noemí herself in jail, leading ultimately to
her expulsion from Peru. Did Misha's influence not have something to do with this misfortune?

I'm not really sure if these questions regarding Noemí's
relationship with Misha weighed heavily on Boris's and
Tania's minds in their decision to move to Colombia, though
I do know, from my mother, that things were tense between
Misha and Noemí's father. Boris's decision to move may also
have been guided by economic considerations. Possibly there
was too much competition in the soap business in Lima. He
may have been searching for a more isolated provincial town in
which to set up business, and found an ideal spot in Colombia's
agriculturally rich Valle del Cauca. Whatever the case, the fact
is that after Noemí's expulsion from Peru in November 1930,
Boris and family moved to Tuluá.

Misha, for his part, went to Buenos Aires. This was perhaps
the journey that they had previously planned out with Mariátegui. Even so, it is not clear what Misha planned to do in Buenos
Aires without him. Maybe he was waiting for Noemí to talk
to her parents and persuade them to bless their marriage plans;
or maybe he was looking to establish himself in Buenos Aires
after marrying Noemí. I don't really know. In any case, it certainly wouldn't have been easy to survive in a foreign city in
1931; the global Depression had set in, and Buenos Aires was
by no means excepted from it. Whatever the reason, though,

Misha left Argentina for Colombia after a couple of months, married Noemí (with Boris and Tania in attendance), and the two of them passed briefly through Cali, which was the nearest city to Tuluá, before moving on to Paris.

Misha and Noemí, married and expecting Larissa.
Cali, Colombia, late 1931 or early 1932.

Paris

Noemí and Misha arrived in Paris at the beginning of 1932. Misha enrolled for doctoral studies in the Institut d'Ethnologie, which was at that time located in the Trocadero Palace.

He was interested in three topics: Indo-American ethnology, Jewish ethnology, and the scientific and humanistic critique of racism. To tackle these issues, he studied under the direction of Paul Rivet, who led the institute at the time and was its leading figure together with Marcel Mauss. Rivet was what the French called an Americanist, that is, a specialist in South American ethnology, and he had done a great deal of fieldwork in Ecuador. He was also a member of the Socialist Party, an antiracist, and in 1934 he was named president of the Vigilance Committee for Intellectuals Against Fascism.

Misha Adler's certificates for registration at
the University of Paris (*above;* 1932) and membership in
the International Institute of Anthropology (*opposite;* 1934).

Paris must have been a powerful experience for my grandparents; such an extraordinary city, with so much cultural effervescence. In the only letter I've found from Misha to Rivet, written twenty years later from Israel, Misha speaks of "the center of the civilized world that beloved Paris always represents," and he looks still to create a "center for ethnological investigation, built around an Archive/Museum of Man, following the style and perfect model" that Rivet had created in Paris.[111] After his studies with Rivet, Misha would identify himself as an ethnologist, and he would write for Americanist publications that were more or less specialized and coincided with the goals and methods of the so-called sciences of man. Each of these was oriented, according to my grandfather's own expression, toward "the mutual comprehension of the races and peoples of the world."

In Paris, there was also then a striking synthesis of aesthetics and politics. Exoticism — the influence first of African art, followed by the art of the so-called primitive peoples of Oceania and America — had been a central aspect of modernism.

The critique of Europe's rational pretensions, and in particular of its self-image as the height of civilization, became acute with the disastrous events of the First World War, while critical movements as diverse as Bolshevism, Dadaism, and Surrealism moved to center stage. Primitive art was thus the herald of a movement that shook modern aesthetics to its roots, and the Institut d'Ethnologie's anthropologists — Marcel Mauss, Paul Rivet, Alfred Métreaux — were closely connected and engaged with figures of the Surrealist movement such as Georges Bataille, Michel Leiris, and André Breton, to name a few. Indeed, as anthropologist and historian James Clifford has pointed out, the Institut d'Ethnologie and the Surrealist Manifesto were launched just months apart from one another (1924–25), and their interconnection was intensive from the beginning.[112]

Noemí and Misha were in Paris between 1932 and 1934, which were also years during which Surrealist artists frequently attended classes at the Institut d'Ethnologie. Here those artists learned of the rationality of the people whom colonialism had tagged as irrational, while they exhibited the West's own deeply seated irrationality in their work.[113]

The aesthetic rendering of pre-Hispanic and Indo-American objects, exhibited not only in the museum of the institute but also in art galleries and disseminated in the world in fashion, must also have made a big impression on my grandparents. The modern indigenous aesthetic of *Amauta* had in Paris an enormous stage that was brighter than anything that could exist in Lima, where cultural institutions, museums, galleries, and fashion industry were still very modestly funded. I imagine that the Parisian experience must have strengthened Misha's conviction that the other America could be a space of redemption for Europe.

Paris would also introduce him to the sort of professional platform that is necessary to develop research and teaching, something that was then beyond the built capabilities of the Universidad de San Marcos in Lima. In his 1953 letter to Rivet, Misha tells him, "You continue, my dear professor, being for me the most convincing example of what we are capable of on this difficult path, always ascending toward the perfection of our many innate capacities." The excellence that Misha found in his teacher could not be disassociated from the material conditions that made it possible, and these could be summarized, perhaps in a slightly mystified way, in one word: Paris.

Alongside the excitement, though, the young couple also found a good deal of disquiet in Paris. These were the years of the Great Depression, and they were very difficult in economic terms. At the start of 1933, Adolf Hitler became chancellor of Germany, and the Nazi threat closed in on them from several points. Predictably, Hitler's victory emboldened the anti-Semitic parties of Romania, where Misha's parents, brothers, and other relatives still lived. The Hitlerian menace thus touched Misha and Noemí directly though Eastern Europe. But also, Paris itself was threatened. On February 6, 1934, activists of the French extreme right marched on the National Assembly, leaving fifteen people dead and two thousand wounded. The rightist march was sufficiently threatening to provoke a general strike in protest, organized by the General Confederation of Labor.[114]

My grandparents also experienced the insecurity of the times in a private way. On June 17, 1932, my mother was born. They named her Larissa, in honor of the journalist Larissa Reisner, about whom an article or two had been published in *Amauta*. From a very young age, Reisner had edited a journal opposed to the Great War; later she had joined the Bolshevik Party and married Fyodor Raskolnikov, a naval officer who had helped organize the Kronstadt Mutiny, although they later divorced. She also collaborated with Leon Trotsky, was a correspondent for *Izvestiya* and *Novaia Zhizn*, Maxim Gorky's newspaper, and covered the 1923 revolts in Germany, where she fell in love with the Marxist leader Karl Radek, a man who would later be arrested by Stalin. Reisner died from typhoid in 1926 when she was only thirty years old. Six years later, my grandparents gave her name to their firstborn.

My mother's name speaks of the spirit of the times, and of the closeness people felt to lives shaken by the storms of war and revolution. But there was another thing: because she was born in France to Judeo-Romanian students, Larissa Adler had no nationality. This was in part because the status of her parents as Romanians gave them no protection whatsoever from the Romanian government, which issued travel papers to Jews only so that they might leave and not so that their children might inherit that nationality, but she also had no nationality because Larissa was not a *française de souche*, that is, the daughter of French citizens or persons to whom France had given some sort of official migratory status beyond that of students.

The lights of Paris did not translate into an offer of citizenship to a girl who was born there, as a result of the expulsion of Jews from Eastern Europe. This could not have been a very comforting sign, and I imagine that Misha and Noemí understood its message with perfect clarity: their time in Paris was transitory, a passage and not a destination. It was certainly in Paris that Noemí developed her keen sensitivity to the hypocrisy of imperial civilization, with its exalted humanism always blemished by a relentlessly self-serving politics.

Nova Sulitza

The political experience that they had gained with Mariátegui in South America, their involvement with the Institut d'Ethnologie, their socialist and antifascist activism, and their ethnological studies oriented toward a critique of racism must have made Misha and Noemí keenly aware of just how dangerous it was for them to stay in Europe. In 1934, Misha toured Poland. He was in Warsaw and a few other places giving talks against the racial pseudoscience of the Nazis. I don't know the details of that experience, such as where the invitation had come from or even what exact places he visited. All that I do know is that he gave his talks in Yiddish. I imagine that it must have been disquieting to feel Germany's proximity, with Hitler already as its chancellor, and to speak there against "race science" at a time of such virulent anti-Semitic rhetoric.

It is interesting to me that Misha was able so keenly to zero in on the racial problem. My impression is that the Americas provided useful elements for scientifically grounded skepticism with regard to European racism, and Nazi race science in particular, for a number of reasons. First, Misha had experienced treatment as a racial inferior in Romania ("a Jew"), and then as a racial superior ("a European") in Peru and Colombia — he could offer direct testimony on racial myths and their perversions. Second, he had been part of two major racial emancipation movements: the rise of emancipated Jewish modernism, and the reconfiguration of Peruvian nationality, turning on its indigenous society. Finally, he had seen how ethnic groups emerge out of slavery and into freedom: the Chinese in Peru, and Afro-descendants in both Peru and Colombia.

The Nazi movement and anti-Semitic parties in Poland and Romania wanted to intimidate and suppress a people who were legally emancipated, and who had all of the elements needed for collective identification: a language (be it Yiddish or Hebrew), a tradition, a history. They sought to do this on the basis of pseudoscientific ideas concerning race and "natural" hierarchies. Misha's experiences with emancipatory movements in Peru and Eastern Europe were now wedded to formal ethnological training with one of the world's leading critics of racism and "race science," so he decided to take this knowledge to those living close to the heart of the beast, and traveled through Poland in 1934.

After this tour, Misha and Noemí decided to travel with Larissa to Nova Sulitza. Noemí would get a chance to meet her in-laws there, while Misha's parents, Hershel and Leah, would be introduced to their new granddaughter. Above all, the return trip to Nova Sulitza would be an opportunity to try to convince Misha's family to leave Bessarabia for good, and join the young couple in Colombia.

There is little documentation of this interesting moment in their lives — just a couple of photographs, really. According to my mother, Misha devoted the two years that they stayed in Bessarabia to traveling to different villages to try to convince the greatest number of Jews possible to emigrate. I don't know which villages he visited, nor with what organizations he may have tried to work, but going back to Bessarabia like this was certainly both a risky and a daring decision.

The situation for Jews in Romania had gotten considerably worse in the ten years that had passed since Misha left Nova Sulitza in 1924. At the time of his move to Peru, Cuza's anti-Semitic party (the National League of Christian defense, or ANC) had just been formed. Three years later, the Legion of the Archangel Michael (more commonly known as the Iron Guard) was also formed. Both organizations now wedded political propaganda to regular intimidation of Jews in the public schools and universities and agitation among peasants in the countryside. Many of these peasants already felt animosity toward the Jews, who controlled much of the commerce in the region. However, Bessarabia's traditional anti-Semitism, with its religious leanings, received a decidedly genocidal charge thanks to right-wing agitation, which enjoyed the added prestige of coming from Romania's main cities and having the support of activists in the universities.

And the international scene had also changed. At the beginning of the 1920s, the governments of Romania were at least vaguely liberal, and they had a tense relation with fascist parties, even when they tolerated the intimidation and even the murder of Jews. Now Hitler was chancellor of Germany, so within Romania the prestige of Nazism was on the rise and its anti-Semitic parties were finding allies in the government.

The Great Depression had also impacted Romania's exports and, given the Jews' pivotal role in the commercialization of agriculture, it was easy to blame them for the downturn and so to channel peasant unease in their direction. The extent to which Romania's two anti-Semitic political parties were able to convince peasants to dehumanize their Jewish neighbors is shocking. Reporting during the Second World War, barely five years after Noemí and Misha's departure, the Italian journalist Curzio Malaparte described one of the many ways in which these peasants, now soldiers, murdered Jews:

> At times in the riverbed and on the sandy banks that sloped up from it, the reeds and willows would tremble slightly as if, upon hearing a human approaching, some animal had hidden there. Then, shouting, "Mice! Mice!" the soldiers would take up their rifles and fire into the reeds. Women, uncombed girls, men dressed in long coats, and children would then emerge, running and tripping over themselves, falling and then picking themselves up. These were Jews from nearby villages who had escaped and hidden themselves among the reeds and willows.[115]

This process of dehumanization was already well on its way by 1935, when Misha, Noemí, and Larissa returned to Nova Sulitza. Even so, I don't know how successful Misha was in his efforts to save his fellow countrymen. In his own house and family, he only met with mixed success. The decision to leave the village and region where one was born is never easy. Together with the natural reluctance to leave behind one's home, the travel costs were high, and the greater part of Bessarabia's Jewish population was poor. By the mid- and late

1930s countries like Peru were no longer encouraging Jewish emigration either. Bribes were often required in order to gain visas, and even that path was not guaranteed. To these impediments one must add yet another, which came from the town's living memory. During the First World War, the Austrian army came to the town, taking food—which was always abundant in Bessarabia—before going on its way. Nova Sulitza had not been a strategic point of military occupation, nor had any battles been fought there. It is true that after the war there were bandits who set fire to part of the village, but the inhabitants had organized militias that successfully fought them off, and the damage that they inflicted was not lasting.

left: My great-uncle Zuñe (Alfonso), my great-grandmother Leah, and Misha Adler at the family home in Nova Sulitza, c. 1934.
right: Misha, Leah, Noemí, and my great-grandfather Hershel seated on the railing of the Nova Sulitza house, c. 1934.

Hershel and Leah Adler did not face an insurmountable economic impediment to emigration, since they were relatively prosperous, but they didn't want to leave their home and start their lives over on a different continent. They also had a vivid memory of the Great War's low local impact. Even so, they were not completely insensitive to Misha's arguments either, nor were they entirely oblivious to the realities that surrounded them, and so they supported the departure of their children, Misha, Ana, Rebeca, and Zuñe, while deciding themselves to remain.

Hershel and Leah at their home in 1935
with their two granddaughters,
Meri Meilijson (*left*) and Larissa Adler (*right*).

Misha Adler (*standing on the right*), Noemí Milstein
(*at the back of the line*), and Larissa Adler (*in front*).
I'm not sure at whose house this photo was taken,
nor if these friends or relatives survived the Holocaust.

Each one of their children already had a South American connection, in any case. Ana had married Israel ("Susye") Meilijson, from Nova Sulitza, who had worked as a peddler in Cumaná and later emigrated with Ana to Caracas. Their daughter, Meri, then only four years old, appears in a photo taken in Nova Sulitza next to my mother. Rebeca, of whom I also have a photograph from this time, seated on her mother's lap, would marry Simón Vurgait, a friend of Misha's who had emigrated with him to Peru, and who also ended up spending his life in Caracas. For his part, Misha's younger brother Zuñe had also worked as a peddler in Cumaná alongside his future brother-in-law, Susye, back in the 1920s, and both had returned to Nova Sulitza. After Misha and Noemí's visit, Zuñe left for good and established himself in Bogotá, where he opened a shoe store.

Rebeca Adler, with her parents,
Leah and Hershel, c. 1935.

The four siblings left Nova Sulitza together in 1936. They were among the last who were able to leave before the outbreak of the war. Hershel and Leah stayed and died in a concentration camp at Bershad.

CHAPTER TEN

Genocide

Transnistria

What was it like for Leah and Hershel to remain in Nova Sulitza without their children? Maybe they felt a sense of peace knowing that their children would be safe, mixed with sadness at the thought that they might never see them again. Even in the best of cases, transatlantic travel was not a minor undertaking, and world politics made it progressively more difficult for one to acquire the necessary visas for any foreseeable reunion. At the local level, things were just getting worse. Economics professor Alexandru C. Cuza, the founder of the anti-Semitic League of National Christian Defense, had formed an alliance with the National Agrarian Party of Octaviano Goga, and together they created a new fascist party, the National Christian Party, which brought the Goga-Cuza duo to the head of the government. Although the pair lasted only one year in power, official anti-Semitism gained general acceptance, and the way was now well paved for an alliance between Romania and Hitler's Germany.

The Goga-Cuza government promoted regulations that effectively either excluded or restricted the number of Jews in the fields of medicine, law, pharmacology, industry, business, and administration, making it in all cases a requirement to demonstrate Romanian citizenship. In passing these regulations, the government knew very well that the majority of Jews in Bessarabia had been prevented from acquiring Romanian citizenship, despite the laws of 1923. These policies were accompanied by a ferocious media campaign that filled the Jews of Bessarabia with fear, except that by this time, leaving the country was practically impossible.

Energized by Hitler's new power, the anti-Semitic party of Cuza launched a campaign of terror. Nova Sulitzers were worried, because the Goga-Cuza party had carried out pogroms in the nearby villages of Vorsha and Arad, and Jews were being attacked randomly on the trains. The fear increased when Cuza's party set up offices in Nova Sulitza as well is in the neighboring towns. Nova Sulitza's Jews were convinced that they were soon going to be the target of a pogrom, and their feeling of dread was made even more acute after Germany's annexation of Austria and Czechoslovakia. By that point, the people became terrified and began to look for visas in order to emigrate to any country at all, but by this time it was too late.[116]

Instead of people managing to get out, though, something entirely unexpected happened. Hitler and Stalin had signed their nonaggression pact, and among its secret clauses was a provision allowing the Soviet Union once again to take possession of Bessarabia. This indeed took place, and on June 29, 1940, Soviet troops entered Nova Sulitza, with a great deployment of tanks and troops, while the Romanian army was forced to withdraw in humiliation. Given the rising tension with the Romanians, Soviet troops were received as liberators; Nova Sulitzers had been living in a state of terror under the policies of Cuza, and they were expecting a pogrom at any moment. The Romanian army would later exact revenge on Bessarabia's Jewish communities for having so happily received the Soviets, using that as a pretext for murder and pillage.

The first Soviet annexation of Bessarabia lasted only one year (June 1940 to June 1941), and while official Soviet anti-Semitism was much less pronounced than its Romanian counterpart, the local effects of occupation were terrible nonetheless. We know the history of this period thanks to Rabinovici's invaluable book, since communication between Nova Sulitza and its South American diaspora was abruptly cut off after the Soviets occupied the town.

The first effect of the Soviet annexation was that the economy of Nova Sulitza, which had been declining since the 1920s, now entered into a free fall. Bessarabia was now cut off from the West, so all export business came to a grinding halt. Nova Sulitza was a small commercial city, with almost no industry, and without the business of exporting produce to the West, its economy collapsed. The Soviets also outlawed the free movement of people, further asphyxiating commerce and causing the ruin of Jewish businesses. Despite the region's agricultural wealth, there was now hunger and famine. To deal with the problem, the Soviet government forcibly sent a hundred young

Jewish men away to work in Russian coal mines, in conditions of freezing temperatures, hunger, and illness, a move that reduced these young men to being slaves of the state.[117] Bonded labor was back. Those young men never came back, and most of them died in the mines.

The Soviet administration of Bessarabia also instituted a new system of governance, new identity papers, and above all new ways to classify the population according to its loyalty to the regime (real or supposed). An office of the secret police (NKVD) now opened in Nova Sulitza, and it introduced a fear-based system of social control, based on a wide network of informants. The old local leadership was replaced by party cadres from Ukraine or Russia. The Soviets then began to expropriate private homes and force the former owners to share them with other families from within or beyond the village. There is no proof of this, but it seems very likely that Hershel and Leah had to accept other families into their home during this period. Rabinovici explains that the first houses to be expropriated were made of stone, which were those of the wealthiest families, but the wooden homes, such as that owned by my great-grandparents, were expropriated soon thereafter.

Political disappearances also began to take place. A politics of silence was gaining ground in Nova Sulitza. Nobody knew anything, nobody said anything. And it was best to know nothing. The people worked in the jobs to which they were assigned, and they survived as best they could. The economy was so depressed that there was hunger everywhere, and theft became so widespread that each workplace had to employ guards both day and night so that food didn't disappear.[118]

Once all of Nova Sulitza's population had been catalogued by the NKVD, there was a second forced deportation, this time not to the coal mines but to an unspecified place within the Soviet Union. Many of those deported were the owners of houses with their families, that is, the most prominent people of the town. Rabinovici speaks of the impossibility of describing "the atmosphere of fear and horror that took over the village."[119] The decline of Jewish Nova Sulitza, which had begun with a wave of emigration after the First World War and accelerated during the widespread fear of Romanian fascists, now entered into a new phase of displacement and terror under the Soviets. Misha and Noemí would not learn about the experience of Soviet terror and slavery until a couple of years after the end of the Second World War, when they managed to speak with some of the survivors.

The first Soviet occupation of Bessarabia was both disastrous and short-lived; the territory would soon return to Romanian control. During the run-up to the Second World War — the invasion of Czechoslovakia and the annexation of Austria — Romania had remained neutral. Its old elite maintained close ties to France, and the two principal fascist parties — Cuza's National Christians and Codreanu's Iron Guard — had left power. Hitler and Stalin had also signed their nonaggression pact, and as Romania was situated between both countries, there was in principle no one for Romania to fight. With the entrance of the Nazis into Paris, Romania's old Francophone elite lost its luster, and the country had to cede to Nazi pressure and return the region of Dobruja to Bulgaria, northern Transylvania to Hungary, and Bessarabia to the Soviet Union.

The political decline of Romania's Francophone elites opened the door to a new coup d'*état*, which brought Ion Antonescu to power. Field Marshall Antonescu, a Romanian army officer and a supporter of the Nazis, would become prime minister and *conducator* of Romania on September 5, 1940.

Early in 1941, Antonescu signed his own secret accord with Hitler, according to which German troops might cross Romanian territory should they wish to violate their pact with Stalin and invade the Soviet Union through Ukraine. The Hitler-Antonescu pact also stipulated that the Romanian army would participate in the invasion of the Soviet Union on the side of the Germans, and that Romania would in return be permitted to recover Bessarabia and to annex a part of Ukraine that Hitler, who was fond of inventing cartographies to suit his designs, had christened Transnistria (literally, "beyond the Dniester"). The name resonated with "Transylvania" ("beyond the forest"), which Romania had been forced to return to Hungary as part of its agreement with Hitler, so that the Führer would give Romania Transnistria in recompense for having transferred Transylvania back to Germany's old ally, Hungary.

Transnistria was a territory inhabited by approximately three million people, the majority of whom were Ukrainians and Russians. There were also roughly 311,000 Jews, 300,000 Moldovans or Romanians, and 125,000 ethnic Germans. The territory was bounded by the Dniester River in the west and the Bug River to the east, with the Black Sea in the south and the Lyadova River to the north.[120] Its largest city was Odessa, which was an important Yiddish intellectual center at the time. The new territory also included the two towns that the

Milsteins came from — Yaruga and Mogilev — in the district of Podolia. Noemí's sister Shura and her young husband, Shmuel Grossman, were living in Mogilev when the war broke out.

Operation Barbarossa, the code name for the Nazi invasion of the Soviet Union, began on June 22, 1941. The Germans entered freely into Romania, as agreed, and they were joined by the Romanian army in their invasion of the Ukraine. By August 19, Antonescu had established his government in Transnistria, although the city of Odessa resisted until October 16. Antonescu's idea was to transform Transnistria into an agricultural export center, the profits from which would finance Romania's war effort.[121]

Transnistria would also serve as a death camp. The Romanian government sought to carry out a program of ethnic cleansing and to eliminate the Jews, especially in Bessarabia, Bukovina, Banat, and Dobruja, which the country had acquired after the First World War. The extermination policy was systematic. In fact, it preceded the program for the so-called Final Solution agreed upon by the Nazis at the Wannsee conference by around six months.

The widespread murder of Romanian Jews had certain points in common with the Armenian genocide in Turkey. As Matatias Carp explains in his *Black Book*, with support from documents and other materials that he compiled between June 1940 and May 1943:

> The Romanian massacres lacked technological and scientific organization; there were no gas chambers, no crematoria, and no policies to process dead bodies. They also did not use the hair,

teeth, or fat from their victims for industrial ends. Romanian fascism used its own unique methods of extermination, which also differed from traditional methods known since the invention of rope and gunpowder. For example, they would beat people until they succumbed, or they would suffocate them in cars that lacked ventilation. Some victims were sold as slaves. The wealthiest would be shot as they marched in columns, so that the Romanians might sell their clothing. Some Jews were quartered to lubricate the axles of carts with their blood. The list of crimes doesn't stop there.[122]

The forced marches of Jews from Bessarabia to Transnistria were a torture from beginning to end, marked by beatings, murderers, and above all, theft: "the Jews were robbed by those looking to harm them and by those charged with protecting them; they were robbed in order to kill them; and they were killed in order to rob them. They were robbed also because, in any case, they were already dead."[123] In 1940, there were 760,000 Jews in Romania; 400,000 were murdered. In Bessarabia and Bukovina, there were 314,000 Jews in 1940, and in those regions there remained only 19,500 in 1942.[124] This was the context in which Hershel Adler and Leah Altman perished.

Romanian soldiers entered Nova Sulitza on July 7, 1941; they were welcomed by the Christian residents, who waved Romanian flags. A three-day pogrom began that day, during which 975 residents were murdered and roughly half of the Jewish houses in the town were burned down.[125] Sadly, my great-grandparents were not among the first group of victims. Instead, they not only experienced the terror of that pogrom but also suffered deportation to Transnistria and finally died in the midst of winter, at the Bershad ghetto.

After the pogrom in Nova Sulitza, the Jews who survived were held in a factory on the Bukovina side (the Caruso factories), where they remained for three days while Romanian soldiers registered their names one by one. Also held there were Jews from neighboring towns. Once everyone was registered, those whose homes were still standing could provisionally return to them. Rabinovici recalls that upon returning, they found that "everything had been stolen by the Christians, who had carried off everything in carts. My house had also been robbed. My former servants came to the house with their relatives and stole everything with no remorse. With no restraint at all, the Christians mercilessly robbed and killed their former Jewish friends and neighbors, people with whom they had lived in peace for generations."[126]

They remained in the village for about a month, once again in their homes, trying in vain to understand what would become of them. On July 25, there began a rumor that they would all be deported. The Jews of the village put together a collection and managed to scrape together one million *lei* (the Romanian currency) to bribe the local officials to cancel the deportation order. The money was accepted, but the deportation was not canceled. When officials ignore even the moral claims of bribery and move instead to open theft, civilians are placed face to face with the state's most naked form of power, which, in this case, was also a prelude to mass murder.

On July 27, 1941, two days after the bribes, it was announced that all of Nova Sulitza's Jews—young and old, women and children, healthy and ill—should lock up their houses, hand the keys to a police officer, and leave with only what they could carry. They would then begin the long march from Nova Sulitza to Transnistria. This was the last day of Jewish Nova Sulitza.[127] After that, the town persisted only in the memories of a widely scattered network of migrants and refugees.

The murders that the Romanian troops committed upon entering the towns and cities of Bessarabia were extraordinarily cruel. Their hatred had been fired up during almost twenty years of anti-Semitic campaigns. Carp recalls that in the town of Parliti, the murder of Jews was carried out in such a horrifying manner that even the German officials who accompanied Romanian troops lodged a complaint with the Romanian high command.[128]

Malaparte tells a similar story. He had witnessed with horror the pogrom of the provincial city of Iasi, which was the largest of those that took place in Romania, and of special significance given the importance of that city. Sometime later, while in Warsaw, he recounted the experience of that pogrom to the German lawyer Hans Frank, who was the Reich's governor-general of occupied Poland. With respect to the number of those murdered during that riot (seven thousand), Frank responded matter-of-factly: "That's a fairly respectable number, but that wasn't a decent way to achieve it. It's not necessary to do it in that way...The Romanians are not a civilized people." Later, he added, "I share and understand your horror regarding the massacres in Iasi. As a man, as a German, and as the Governor-General of Poland, I disapprove of pogroms...Germany is a country that possesses a superior civilization, and it detests such barbarous methods."[129] After the war, Frank was tried and found guilty of numerous war crimes, for which he was executed by hanging.

To give an idea of the Romanian "methods," I can cite the memoir of Josef Govrin, who recalls the entry of Romanian troops into Edinitz, a town near Nova Sulitza and with many similar characteristics. As in Nova Sulitza, the soldiers and their local allies indulged in a frenzy of murder and pillage that lasted three days, and they then deported the surviving Jews to Transnistria:

> Hundreds of women and children were carried to a nearby forest by Romanian soldiers, who brutally raped them. Only a few survived, and of these many committed suicide. Among them was my ten-year-old classmate, Blimale Mutzelmacher and her two sisters, Ester and Zahava, along with their mother, Sima. They were all raped in the presence of their father or husband. Afterward, the mother and the three sisters committed suicide, hanging themselves, and Mr. Mutzelmacher threw himself down a well near their house. I still remember Blimale's smile on her beautiful and childish face.[130]

In various passages of his reports on the destruction caused by the war in Transnistria and Bessarabia, Malaparte stresses the extent to which Romanian officials tolerated the ferocity with which peasants and villagers attacked Jews. His description of the Iasi pogrom closes with members of the noble Sturdza family passing through the town in their horse-drawn carriage, just hours after the end of the massacre: "With a happy jingling of harness bells, the carriage passed between piles of naked bodies, while on both sides of the road, two rows of people lowered their heads in reverence, their hands filled with the plunder they had taken. The carriage passed by, pulled by two purebred white horses and driven by a eunuch named Grigori, who appeared regal and solemn atop the carriage, hanging before the horses the red tassel of his whip."[131]

My poor great-grandparents and other members of my family—whose names I have never known—were forced to live through these pogroms and later suffer prolonged marches through mud and snow. On July 29, 1941, Romanian troops ordered the Jewish population of Nova Sulitza, 5,357 people in all, to begin moving. According to the record published by Yad Vashem, 1,500 carts were taken for the journey.[132] One of these belonged to my great-grandparents, who began the march with an in-law, Ethia Meilijsohn, and her mother, who was sick and could not walk.[133] The older woman died on the road.

Unlike what occurred with almost all the deportations from Bessarabia and Bukovina, there were no deaths between Nova Sulitza and Ataki, where they were to cross the Dniester into Transnistria. This was because the police officer charged with leading the convoy, whose last name was Yeftudio, made sure that they all arrived alive. For this he was chastised by his superiors. Yeftudio was later recognized by the survivors from Nova Sulitza as one of the Righteous Gentiles.

As the convoy arrived in Ataki, it announced that the Germans in Mogilev, on the other side of the Dniester, would not accept any more deportees. As a result, they were forced to march back to Secureni, and from there to the Codreni forest, which lies between Secureni and Edinetz. Here they were forced to camp for five days. It was also here that people began to die from exhaustion and hunger. Rabinovici states that it took people some time to begin to understand fully what the purpose of all of this was; that is, it took the Jews of Nova Sulitza weeks to understand and accept that what they were facing was a deliberate program of extermination, and not a disorganized process of forced resettlement.

The Christian population of the various towns and villages along the way to Transnistria met Nova Sulitza's Jews with insults, and mobs that were eager to beat and rob them on the banks of the Dniester, but commander Yeftudio prevented these beatings until he was relieved from duty. And it was precisely then, on their first night near that river, that a group of villagers saw hundreds of bodies washed up on the shore. For the first time, they understood that they were facing collective extermination. And yet they had to continue, and even backtrack for a while, since the Germans forbade the crossing of the Dniester at Ataki because of an excess of traffic.[134]

Forced to go back toward Bessarabia, the remaining members of the caravan stopped for a short time in Edinetz, where they were held on a farm with wells that had been intentionally contaminated by the Romanian population. Here the Jews began to die at a rate of approximately six per day until the end of August, when a typhoid epidemic struck and began to kill between twenty and thirty people each day. It was also in Edinetz that Yeftudio was relieved from his command, meaning that the people of Nova Sulitza also lost the little protection they had. They remained in the Edinetz ghetto until October 10, when the worst part of the march began. One portion of the

Jews from Nova Sulitza was sent to Markolesht, and the other was forced back to Ataki and from there to Mogilev Podolsk. Many were murdered on these roads, some shot by soldiers wishing to reduce the number of refugees, and others by peasants wishing to rob them of whatever they still possessed.

On a mountain near Climauți, the Romanian soldiers guarding the caravan abandoned their posts to take refuge from the cold in some nearby houses. Winter had come early that year, and in mid-October there was a terrible storm that brought snow and ice. That first night, groups of local peasants sacked the Jewish caravan, taking even the clothes they were wearing. Many people died there. Rabinovici recalls the scene: people transformed into frozen pillars, running wildly to try to avoid freezing: "The sound of the storm's wind, the cries of people freezing, and the cries of the victims of the attack all mixed together into an incredible and indescribable inferno. The voices will always be with me, along with the images of that horrible night on the Klimotz mountain."[135]

Those who survived this ordeal arrived back at the crossing point in Ataki a few days later and finally crossed the Dniester into Mogilev. Many, such as Rabinovici himself, remained in that city's ghetto. According to the record at Yad Vashem, "the majority of the Jews deported from Nova Sulitza to Mogilev were shot by Romanian police. Those who survived were sent to Bershad and Obodovca."[136]

The story that my mother told us regarding the death of her grandparents Hershel and Leah is that they were attacked on the road to Transnistria by Romanian peasants, who robbed them of everything and killed them with two Shabbat candlesticks that they carried among their things. My mother tells me that this version of the story came to her from her mother, and the scene corresponds to what people from the community experienced in the hills above Climăuți. The other version of the story is that of my uncles Manuel and Mauricio, which came to them from Ethia Meilijsohn. She was with my great-grandparents during the entire journey, and managed to survive the Bershad ghetto. After the war, she emigrated to South America to be reunited with her family. Since she was a direct witness, hers seems to be the most reliable source.

According to Ethia, my great-grandparents Leah and Hershel survived the arduous trip from Markolesht and finally arrived at the concentration camp in Bershad, which was the end point of their march. On the road and in the camps, everything had to be purchased. Hershel bought three spaces in an abandoned stable, where he, Leah, and Ethia could sleep. All of those deported to Bershad slept in abandoned barns or stables. That winter of 1941–42 was especially harsh, with temperatures reaching forty below zero almost constantly. In that abandoned stable, my great-grandparents faced the winter that killed most of the Jews in Bershad. In the end, it would also kill them. There were doctors among the deported, but there was no medicine. In the camps, even simple and curable illnesses usually led to death. Leah died first, of dysentery. Shortly afterward, Hershel died of typhoid.

Each of their bodies was placed in a corner of the stable, until they were taken away to be "buried," although in fact they were just thrown into a mass grave that was then covered with snow. The cold made it too difficult to bury anyone properly, so that my great-grandparents' bodies remained in that ditch, covered with snow, unburied, exposed.

Obituary of Hershel Adler, published
as a headline in the first issue of
the weekly publication *Grancolombia*,
edited by his son, Misha Adler.

CHAPTER ELEVEN

The National Disease

The banality of evil?

In her well-known book on the trial of Adolf Eichmann, Hannah Arendt speaks of the legal and political importance that the denationalization of the Jews had for their extermination. They lost all of their rights of citizenship, usually through laws designed for this purpose, and often they were deported, to be killed in places where they similarly had no claim to nationality.[137] In my research into the fate of my great-grandparents, I was interested to discover that in countries such as Romania, too, Jews residing in recently acquired territories like Bessarabia, whose Romanian nationality was dubious, were killed first and in a more systematic manner than those who were from the old Romanian kingdom. The fact that so many Eastern European Jews were nationless and thus protected by no sovereign state facilitated the genocide.

The state of Israel became an urgent project for a large portion of the international community after the Holocaust, for precisely this reason. Once created, the Jewish state also facilitated the search for and arrest of war criminals such as Adolf Eichmann, since the genocide had been carried out against a people whose cause was now championed by a sovereign state, capable of apprehending and bringing to justice genocidal criminals. The contrast between this case and that of the Roma people is revealing: since there has never been a sovereign Romani state, the Roma were not able to bring their murderers to trial.

Israel's role in bringing former Nazis to justice was important because West German chancellor Konrad Adenauer (1949–63) was not particularly interested in prosecuting war criminals, and Nazi refugees in countries such as Argentina and Paraguay had a cozy relationship with the governments that had received them. Besides, it was too often accepted that many of the Nazis who had executed the program of genocide were following the orders of the Reich, and the German Jews whom they murdered had lost their citizenship prior to being deported, so the German state was no longer legally bound to prosecute on their behalf.

Hannah Arendt recognized all of this, but she still questioned the legitimacy of holding Eichmann's trial in Israel. For Arendt, Eichmann's crime had still not been properly typified, and it was in fact a new type of crime altogether: genocide on a global scale was an attack not only on the Jewish people but also on humanity itself. This new type of crime against humanity, she argued, should be judged by an international tribunal and not in the courts of any one country, not even in Israel. This was Arendt's argument.

It is worth pointing out that there are relevant parallels between Arendt's idea of the crime against Jews as a crime against humanity and José Carlos Mariátegui's ideas concerning the Jewish question. Despite the fact that Mariátegui was writing earlier, in the middle and late 1920s, and so well before the Holocaust, there is a real affinity between his ideas and Arendt's analysis. Mariátegui saw the Jews as the world's first genuinely universal, postnational subjects. The extermination of the Jews — which could not have been foreseen while Mariátegui was alive — was, by extension, an attack on universal subjects with values, and so on humanity itself.

Furthermore, this new genocidal pulsation had been pursued by a new species of nationalist imperialism that projected the legal authority of the nation-state outward onto conquered territories, and so set out to do away with a people on a universal scale, wherever they might be found. One might say that a universal social subject, the Jews, had been persecuted and murdered by a relatively new social formation, the imperial nation-state. The German nation-state had made use of the instruments at its disposal, starting with its own laws, to criminalize these people, deny them legal protection, and then to murder them wherever they might be found.

This new type of crime — genocide on a global scale — also produced a new type of criminal, of which Eichmann was a prime example. Arendt characterized this new criminal type as "banal" because these criminals operated within legally sanctioned bureaucracies, so they could readily argue that they had no malicious intent, but were "just following orders." So, although Eichmann acknowledged having rounded up and deported hundreds of thousands of Jews to their deaths, he nonetheless considered himself to be innocent of any crime.[138] There was no malicious intent in his actions, as he was only a law-abiding officer, following his legally sanctioned orders.

This new type of "banal" criminal was one of Arendt's important discoveries, in particular because people who have done so much harm are always imagined as towering figures of power and even genius, not ordinary petty bureaucrats. Arendt echoes Friedrich Nietzsche's claim that Judeo-Christian culture always imagines evil to be a hyper-powerful force. According to Nietzsche, this is because Christianity and Judaism were in their origins slave religions, and for slaves, evil is rooted in the culture of the masters, whether they be Egyptian pharaohs or Roman patricians. The culture of the master is hyper-powerful for the slave, and when that power is in addition directed toward the oppression of the True Faith, it becomes truly "evil" in the modern sense.

It follows that in the Judeo-Christian tradition, evil has all the trappings of power and prestige, and given that Eichmann's trial was slated to be a cathartic event, meant to give the people of Israel the satisfaction of retribution, Eichmann could not be figured as the small person that he actually was. For the process to have its desired effect, Eichmann had to be driven by powerful demons, and not by such banal pursuits as promotion or garnering credit from his political connections.

This is all true, but the problem with Arendt's formulation of "the banality of evil" is that it has frequently been misread as a general characterization of all crime and all evil in the context of genocide. And of course, this is not at all the case. The by-now quite recognizable image of the typical war criminal as an officious little bureaucrat is just one sort of player in the historical drama of genocide. In the case of Bessarabia, for instance, the peasants who beat and robbed starving and frozen refugees, who raped and killed women, were not bureaucrats looking to climb the organizational ladder, as was the case with Eichmann.

They might have been spurred forward with material incentives — taking possessions from Jews, for instance — or by an ideology of ethno-religious cleansing, but their violence was not the direct result either of following orders or of an ambition to climb a bureaucratic ladder. Rather, their cruelty was often framed in relation to values that were culled from peasant communalism itself, and to practices connected to its protection.

As an example, we might turn once again to Malaparte, who interviewed a group of Romanian peasant soldiers standing before a destroyed Ukrainian village that was very much like their own. In an attempt to justify their actions, the soldiers told Malaparte, "We don't destroy villages or harm the peasants. We only go after the Jews."[139] The separation of the Jewish Other from views of the purity of the peasant village was a way to try to contain their violence within a moral framework that made sense to them, but it also justified violent acts that exceeded bureaucratic aims. So, whereas the rational carrying out of the Final Solution treated Jews as garbage that needed to be "processed" in the most industrialized and antiseptic manner possible, the violence of pogroms always came charged with a level of outrage that outstrips bureaucratic process.

In other words, violence against the Jewish "internal enemy" was in fact carried out by a variety of social types, of which Eichmann represented only one: those who followed the orders of their superiors in a bureaucratically implemented project of genocide. It is perhaps in recognition of the overwhelming multiplication of atrocity that Malaparte decided that the subject of his remarkable book was not the war, but rather *kaputt*, that is, the breakdown of order: "a living and macabre monster" that destroyed Europe. So, in Malaparte's gripping description of what he experienced in Bessarabia and Transnistria in 1941 and 1942, the "engine of history" is both bureaucratic rationality and also its limits and collapse. Bureaucratic rationality is only one aspect of the genocidal frenzy, and the bureaucrat is only one of its criminal types.

Rhinoceroses

In the 1930s and 1940s, Bucharest boasted a small but distinguished intellectual class made up of perhaps two hundred or so figures, who were fond of splitting their leisure between two cafés, Corso and Captsa.[140] This was a world of densely interwoven social connections, but it was also a world of exalted ideologies. Mihail Sebastian, a Jewish playwright, memoirist, and novelist whose original name was Iosef Hechter, was a prominent figure there. He was also a privileged witness of this world's tragic descent, which he recorded in an extraordinary diary that was hidden by his brother after his death in 1945 and published in 1996. The publication of Mihail Sebastian's diary caused a great scandal in Romania, a country that has not been very eager to come to grips with its history of anti-Semitism.[141]

In the 1930s and 1940s, Romanian intellectuals were in their majority anti-Semitic and fascists, and they didn't flinch at the idea of ethnic cleansing (or "purification," as Field Marshall Antonescu called it). And I'm not speaking here of anodyne characters or of mediocre minds like that of Adolf Eichmann. Eugène Ionesco describes the phenomenon in detail, since he was one of comparatively few famous Romanian intellectuals who did not sympathize with the fascist Iron Guard in the 1930s. Ionesco describes the contagious aspect of fascism in a well-known work in which the "normal" characters morph one by one into rhinoceroses.

In his memoir, Ionesco quotes from his Budapest diaries of the 1930s to pinpoint the moment when the idea for his *Rhinoceros* first came to him. The passage from that diary reads as follows:

> I have before me a rhinocerontile slogan, a slogan for the "New Man" that any normal person cannot understand: "All for the State," "All for the Nation," "All for the Race"...But what is the State? What is the Nation? What is Society? They are dehumanizing abstractions, not existential realities but rather putrid, supremely alienating abstractions. Humanity does not exist: there are only people. Society does not exist: there are only friends. It's not the same for a rhinoceros. To me, their state is a phantasm; for them, the person of flesh and blood is the phantasm.[142]

A number of key Romanian intellectuals embraced fascism

and leaned heavily on anti-Semitism for its ideological justification. Like Ionesco's rhinoceroses, they felt that flesh-and-blood humans were of little importance. And they spent the terrible summer of 1941 cheering along the process of ethnic cleansing that was then being launched, and inventing fables to justify it.

On June 24, 1941, for instance, three days after the Nazi invasion of the Soviet Union, Sebastian writes that there appeared all over Bucharest two poster designs painted by Anestin, a celebrated Bucharest graphic artist. One of them portrayed Stalin with bloody hands and read, "The Butcher of Red Square." The other poster "shows a Jewish man in a red robe, long curly sideburns, a religious cap, and a beard, holding a hammer in one hand and a sickle in the other; hidden behind his robe are three Soviet soldiers." Above the image, the poster read, "Who Are the Masters of Bolshevism?"[143]

The following week, Jews were banned from raising the Romanian flag in their homes. Frightened by the intensity of the anti-Semitic radio campaign, the posters on the streets, and the newspapers, Sebastian stopped going out of his apartment. He devoted his time to reading Thucydides and *War and Peace*, trying to think through the war from that vantage point, since he could find nothing but horror in the daily news. It was during that week that the Romanian army entered into Bessarabia and unleashed pogroms in every village.

During those same days, Ionesco received a visit from the writer Eugen Lovinescu, who told him, "The Russians must be defeated and the Germans victorious. If not, we will be governed by Jews and cobblers."[144] A rhinoceros. A few days later, the writer and erstwhile friend of Sebastian, Camil Petrescu, shared a series of predictions regarding what he saw as the inevitable results of the war, with some typically shameful phrases that Sebastian cites verbatim: "Germany will conquer all of Russia, and Hitler will be recognized by everyone as having freed the world from Bolshevism. In the end, some concessions will also be given to the Jews ('things cannot continue like this'); they'll get their own state in Russia, perhaps even in Birobidzhan."[145] Another rhinoceros. And so Bucharest's intelligentsia was steadily engrossed by one, and another, and another.

In those days, Romanian intellectuals played at war, and they indulged all sorts of fantasies of grandeur. They also loudly blamed the Jews for just about everything, though in private they sometimes recognized that the situation in which the Jews now found themselves was a little excessive. Even so, they claimed that everything would calm down once they'd won the war. Apparently, they had so internalized the idea of the "Eternal Jew," that they could not imagine that after the genocidal campaign, there wouldn't be enough survivors for things to "calm down." In the meantime, they took care not to raise their voices in defense of Jews. The aforementioned Petrescu fearfully warned his friend Sebastian not to ask him for any favors should he find himself in trouble. There were limits to interracial solidarity, even among friends.

Around the same time, another celebrated and far from anodyne Romanian "rhinoceros," Mircea Eliade (1907–86), found himself in Portugal serving as a cultural attaché. The day after the Nazi and Romanian invasion of the Soviet Union, Eliade wrote in his diary: "I am overwhelmed by the fury of my love of country and by my incandescent nationalism. I can do no work since Romania entered the war. I cannot write. I have once again abandoned my novel."[146] Interestingly, in this same entry, Eliade laments the mediocrity of the Romanian government—one might say, its colonization by a legion of banal Eichmanns—but his criticism is put forward from a passionately fascist point of view: he speaks of the sacrifices made by the Iron Guard in the 1930s, and mourns his "martyred" coreligionists, because the government of Antonescu has now been populated by hacks:

> All the massacres, all the prison camps, all the humiliations, all the rebellions, all the purifications, all the liberal programs—all of this to end up with Pamfil Seicaru, our eternal Pamfil, who has terrorized us and all our governments, but somehow always lands on his feet. Corneliu Codreanu, dead; Iorga, dead; also dead are Nae Ionesco, Armand, I. G. Duca, Moruzov—all of the Iron Guard bosses are dead, as well as those who executed them—while Pamfil remains alive, active, and patriotic.[147]

This pathetic lamentation was thus triggered by the fact that Romanian fascism had fallen into the hands of hackneyed bureaucrats, true, but even so, the responsibility for genocide does not fall only upon those bureaucrats. While people including my great-grandparents Hershel and Leah were dying of cold and starvation in the Bershad ghetto at the hands of the government that Eliade represented, this intellectual was caught up in the hubris of his own grandeur: "My detachment from the search for glory and wealth will allow me to write works of incontestable value. And I shall begin to write them one of these days."[148]

The logic of Jewish genocide certainly created a new type of criminal, as Arendt argued: rather than towering princes of evil, they were bureaucratic types who were responsible for the execution of mass murder. But genocide is a process that needs to be cultivated over a period of time, it has many moments, and in them different actors play their part. My great-grandparents' death came at the hands of soldiers who followed the orders of commanders who in turn were observing the laws and directives of their government, true. The infamous *Einsatzgruppen* of the SS also participated in the atrocities, insofar as they provided the Romanian army with a murderous example, gunning down Jews in mass executions.

But peasants and neighbors from Nova Sulitza and the other Bessarabian towns also participated in the slaughter and pillage, and their hatred had long been stoked by the very Iron Guard to which Eliade so proudly belonged. Those Iron Guard militants were not following orders, in fact the Iron Guard was for years a clandestine organization. Among those militants, narcissism and an exalted sense of honor were much more salient features than banality, nor were they spurred on by bureaucratic opportunism, but rather by their own delusions of grandeur, and the megalomaniacal fantasy of transforming the destiny of their nation.

It bothers me that Eliade, who would become a widely admired professor of religion and mythology at the University of Chicago, where I later also taught, never paid even the smallest price for his role in these events. When I started to look into what was happening in Bucharest when Jewish Nova Sulitza died, I was struck by Eliade's role. Genocide is not only executed by the bureaucratic machine, it is also narrated into existence by intellectuals and propagandists, myth by myth. This is a form of evil that concerns me very particularly.

Iphigenia *in Bucharest*

Eliade wrote his first drama in the autumn of 1939, and it was performed in the National Theater of Bucharest at the beginning of 1941, just before the Romanian invasion of the Soviet Union. It was a version of Euripides' *Iphigenia in Aulis*, so it dealt with sacrifice.

In the *Iphigenia* of Euripides, Agamemnon has offended the goddess Artemis, who vents her spleen by preventing the Achaean fleet from leaving port. The wind doesn't blow, and the Greek ships can't sail. The Achaeans consult the seer Calchas, who suggests that Agamemnon must sacrifice his daughter, Iphigenia, in order to placate Artemis. In the end, Iphigenia volunteers to be sacrificed, as she prefers to be remembered as a national heroine than to marry and live a long life at the expense of the Achaean people.

Eliade would make use of this legend to write a play dedicated to the sacrifice of Ion Motza and Vasile Marin, two Iron Guard militants who decided to go to Spain to fight on the side of fascism during that country's three-year civil war. They both died on the same day in 1937, fighting to capture Madrid. Motza's and Marin's bodies were repatriated and paraded by train from town to town, on their way to a mass funeral in Bucharest. Crowds gathered at each stop, with the people crying in unison that they would gladly sacrifice themselves for the fatherland to avenge their fallen countrymen.[149]

In the same year as Motza and Marin's funeral, Eliade found himself stripped of his professorship at the University of Bucharest because of his activities in the Iron Guard, which was a clandestine organization then. A year later, he was arrested as part of a government crackdown on the far right that charged him with authoring Iron Guard propaganda. During this tense period, Eliade wrote newspaper articles glorifying Motza and Marin and praising the Iron Guard's founders. When he was released from jail, in November 1938, he immediately set to work on *Iphigenia*.

Eliade's work comfirms Ionesco's complaint: for a fascist, the state is concrete while human beings are immaterial. To Eliade, a mythical character from antiquity like Iphigenia was transcendent, and the martyrs Motza and Marin were transcendent, but the flesh-and-blood humans who were to be sent to die in war in order to follow such "immortal" sacrifices mattered little. What really mattered was the immortality of their gesture, and not the fact that invading the Soviet Union implied sending the Romanian army off to slaughter.

Eliade was also fond of another story that he believed offered a key to understanding the true Romanian essence: the legend of Master Manole. It tells of the construction of a great cathedral, a process that ultimately requires the pious master builder Manole (through a dream vision) to bury his pregnant wife alive in the building's foundation. The story is, in essence, a Christian version of the tale of Iphigenia: the willing sacrifice of what one holds dearest for a higher ideal.

Through all their fixation on sacrificial ecstasy, Romanian fascists never stopped to consider that the Jews perhaps might also form a part of their community, if given a chance. To them, the mass murder of Jews was an act of common prophylaxis. The death of two imbecilic heroes—who went to Spain voluntarily to fight for Franco—moved the country to tears, but the cowardly murder of one, one hundred, or even hundreds of thousands of Jews meant nothing except the "purification of the nation." On the other hand, as the alleged source for all evils undermining the national community, Jews stabilized the fascists' worldview, so anti-Semites might have felt some ambivalence about losing the Jews altogether. Their total absence might leave the surviving community with the melancholy feeling of having annihilated a people while still nursing the social ills for which they had been blamed. Maybe some of these fascists thought that they might bring the Jews back if they ever felt a need for them? If they did secretly hold such hopes, they were disappointed: today in Romania there is only their stark absence.

Years after the war, Eliade published a (strategically redacted) edition of his diaries, where he offered effusive praise for Mihail Sebastian, exclaiming: "How I empathized with his immense efforts, and with all the suffering that came with each page he wrote!...I will never forgive myself for not going back to see him in August 1942, when I returned to Bucharest for a week. I was ashamed of myself at that point—I was a cultural attaché in Lisbon, while he had suffered numerous humiliations for having been born, and for wishing to remain Iosef Hechter. I now agonize over this in vain, as it is too late."[150] Iosef Hechter had taken on the pen name Mihail Sebastian, and insisted in his writing that there was such a thing as a Romanian Jew, that it was possible to be both Jewish and Romanian.

With the publication of these lines about Sebastian having been humiliated for wishing publicly to remain Jewish, Eliade revealed himself to be a rascal and con artist. The affection and admiration that he had for Sebastian were genuine — the two were very close friends — but Eliade was personally responsible for at least a few of the humiliations suffered by Sebastian for "wishing to remain Iosef Hechter," and as an ideologue of the rabidly anti-Semitic Iron Guard, Eliade could hardly expect Sebastian to have had an easy time "remaining Iosef Hechter."

Eliade mentions his shame for not having visited Sebastian in 1942, supposedly provoked by the privileges that he knew he enjoyed as a cultural attaché in fascist Portugal while Sebastian was humiliated for "wishing to be" Jewish in Bucharest. But Sebastian was not being persecuted for "wishing to remain" a Jew; he had been raised Jewish whether he liked it or not, and everyone knew that he was Jewish. Meanwhile, in all his pathetic self-recrimination, Eliade somehow fails to mention that anti-Semitism was part of the very foundation of the Iron Guard, to which he had himself been so committed.

In his discussion of the origin of his image of the rhinoceros, Ionesco clearly identified the pivotal role that anti-Semitism had for Romania's fascists:

> I have witnessed transformations [of people into rhinoceroses]. I've seen people change almost before my very eyes... There is the example of I. He was part of our group... We were young then, so how could we intellectually resist all the specialists who

had converted into fanatics? Sociologists, cultural philosophers, biologists who had found "scientific" reasons to justify racism; writers, journalists...One day, I. showed up and told us that we were right, of course, and that the rest were without a doubt monstrous or stupid. "Nevertheless," he said, "it's strange that at times, at times, they seem to be right on a particular point..." One point out of 10,000..."Such as, for example, they say that the Jew..." At that moment, we all realize that I. has already been trapped by the machine...I gave them between four and six weeks before they succumbed definitively, giving in to the temptation of power...[151]

Anti-Semitism was in fact the original feature of the rhinoceros.

Sebastian, for his part, was an unusual witness to the Jewish genocide in Romania, because he knew it from its gestational period in the 1930s, since he worked and lived alongside the crème de la crème of Bucharest intellectuals. So many of them were leaders of the Iron Guard! Sebastian also witnessed how his old friend Mircea Eliade wrote articles from his post as attaché in Portugal as a kind of Nero, playing the lyre with his fascist panegyrics while the Red Army destroyed the Romanian army at the Battle of Stalingrad. After the war, Eliade covered up his role in the elimination of the Jewish population of Romania, but he and his companions in fact accomplished their mission, as Jews are now largely absent in that country.

Coda: Shura

When Boris, Tania, Noemí, and Pupe first crossed the Dniester, they were forced to leave behind Shura and Revka. Desolate, these two returned to the large house in Mogilev and were never rescued. Revka died when her granddaughter Shura was only six years old. Before her death, she split her large house in two, giving half to Shura and the other to a couple, Nahum and Surka, in exchange for them taking care of the little girl and looking out for her. But Shura once again had bad luck.

Surka let her go hungry and beat her. According to Rita, Shura's daughter, the only days that Surka and Nahum treated her mother well were when packets of food and money arrived from Peru and Colombia (sent by Boris and Tania). On the following day, they would again cut off the supply of what had been sent and continue to starve her as usual. Shura would wander the streets after school, looking for food. As soon as she graduated, she took a job as a salesgirl in a shop, and when she reached adulthood, she sold her share of the house for a loss and went to live in a rented room in order finally to take leave of the couple who had so abused her. In those years, Shura still maintained an occasional correspondence with her parents, although sadly the letters have not survived. Their correspondence was definitely cut off with the outbreak of war.[152]

In 1940, one year before the Nazi invasion, Shura married Shmuel Grossman, who was from Yaruga, the same as Boris. At first the couple lived in Mogilev, but when the war broke out, Shmuel joined the Red Army while Shura, already pregnant, went to live with her in-laws in Yaruga. Shura lived in the same house as her in-laws, Susa and Haim, along with an uncle and his daughters. Shortly after her arrival, the town was bombed, and they sought shelter in the basement. At precisely that moment, Shura's contractions began and her daughter, my aunt Rita, was born in that basement.

Shura Milstein and Shmuel Grossman, recently married, 1940.

Because of the war, there was insufficient food for the baby. Shura drank a lot of water in order to have at least some milk to give her daughter. The little girl cried from hunger. When the Romanian and German troops invaded, the Jewish section of Yaruga was transformed into a ghetto, as had happened in all of the occupied towns of Transnistria. These ghettos were fenced spaces in which Jews were left to eke out a living or die little by little from hunger and thirst or from illnesses. At times, soldiers and police officers would shoot them.

The people living with Shura worked on a collective farm (*kholkhoz*), and they were required to hand over their produce to the Germans and Romanians, leaving them only with food that was bruised or rotten. At times, their Ukrainian neighbors would give them a bit of milk for the baby. At night, they trafficked in contraband. The Romanians had constructed a ghetto in Mogilev that housed more than forty thousand Jews, and Shura would use a boat to sneak twenty-five-liter fuel drums across the Dniester. In Mogilev, she would trade the fuel for bread. It was very dangerous work, and I still don't know where she got the fuel. Maybe she took it from the *kholkhoz*, but I can't be sure. Shura could also occasionally produce small quantities of soap that she knew how to make: she was Boris's daughter, after all.

Naphtoli Rabinovici spent the war in the Mogilev ghetto, and he described the economy of the place. In order to survive, the Jews depended on two things: finding work repairing Romanian and German tanks and war equipment, and getting help from friends or relatives who had remained in the ghettos of Czernowitz or Bucharest. The rest depended on the black market economy, as was the case with Shura. The alternative was dying of hunger or typhoid, as happened to the majority.[153]

Shura, little Rita (born in a Transnistria ghetto in 1941),
and Shmuel, 1949.

Shura managed to survive in the ghetto, but she had no idea
what had become of her husband, Shmuel. During the war,
newspapers didn't circulate much, and there was no radio in
the Yaruga ghetto. Rita, Shura's daughter, remembers the day
when they installed a microphone and loudspeakers in the village, in order to announce the end of the war. Rita would have
been three or four years old at the time.[154]

Shura was finally lucky, too, because Shmuel survived the
war intact. He fought very bravely in the Russian army, was
decorated and promoted to the rank of officer. One benefit of
this was that the family was allowed to move to Czernowitz
(which by then was known by its Russian name, Chernovtsy),
where conditions were better than in Yaruga or Mogilev, and
where many Ukrainian Jews who had survived the Holocaust
took refuge. In Chernovtsy, things improved a bit for the
young couple. They worked in a shop, and were occasionally

able to hawk goods on the black market that was so crucial for the Soviet economy.

Shmuel and Shura later had a son, Marc, who studied medicine. Both Rita and Marc grew up and got married. In the 1970s, Rita and her husband, Yuri Sikirin, requested permission to move to Israel, which was, in the end, granted. In 1977, Shura and Shmuel followed them. Shura died in Nathanya on May 5, 1980. Shmuel survived her by many years. He also died in Nathanya, in 2003. May they rest in peace.

PART THREE

Colombian Refuge

CHAPTER TWELVE

Family Life

Tuluá

In 1936, Misha, Noemí, and Larissa arrived in Tuluá, situated in the Valle del Cauca, Colombia. Noemí arrived pregnant with Manuel, and she gave birth to him in that city. At the time, Tuluá was a town of no more than 12,000 residents, but it had a certain literary fame due to Jorge Isaacs's *María*, considered by many to be the best Latin American novel of the nineteenth century. My grandfather was among the novel's fans, in no small measure because Isaacs's father was Jewish. Misha's work on behalf of the Jewish people made him attentive to the contributions of Jews to cultural life. In the first issue of *Repertorio Hebreo*, Misha had already published a brief essay by the Peruvian poet José María Eguren on Isaacs's genius. In the essay, Eguren speaks openly of the novelist's origins: "Of the Colombian race and of the Hebrew race, of that most creative lineage, which at present counts among its number Albert

Einstein, Henri Bergson, and Waldo Frank at the very pinnacle of knowledge."[155]

(It now seems odd to see the name of Waldo Frank, who has largely been forgotten, being invoked with such conviction and emphasis alongside those of Einstein and Bergson. Frank was a well-known figure in US intellectual and leftist circles, but Latin American intellectuals of the time held him in especially high esteem because he was one of the comparatively few established American figures who engaged in a direct dialogue with South American intellectuals. Before the Cold War there was not much interest in Latin American public opinion, and until the so-called Latin American literary boom of the 1960s and 1970s, even intellectual figures of the stature of Mariátegui, Victoria Ocampo, or Jorge Luis Borges were pretty much unknown to readers of English.)

left to right: Pupe, Tania, Noemí (behind baby Manuel), Larissa (as a child), Boris, Misha. Tuluá, c. 1937. The people in the photo were numbered by hand to point out to Shura who each one was.

Our family arrived in Tuluá because Boris and Tania had settled there, in a large house on Calle 31, number 27-57. When my grandparents and my mother arrived, Boris had already set up a soap mill that resembled the one he had run in Mogilev. The milling of soap had been his family's business for three generations, a fact that might explain Boris's lifelong preoccupation with personal hygiene and neatness. Now, in Tuluá, he had returned to his ancestral occupation.

Advertisement for Boris's marbled soap. *El Mercurio*, 1934.

According to a witness from the time, Boris's marbled soap was "the first blue soap ever sold in Tuluá; before, the people washed their clothes with bleach."[156] The fact that the people of Tuluá used only bleach, and that there was not yet any commercial soap available for clothes, was surely a factor in Boris's decision to settle in such an out-of-the-way place.

According to my uncle Manuel, business was so good that they soon added a third oven to the operation. The mill was located in an annex that was next to the family's home, and one could enter it directly from home through a secure metal door. Following Calle 31 from Boris's house and walking past the soap factory, one reached the Tuluá River. There on the left it was common to find people bathing, and to the right women washing clothes. Upon first arriving at the town, Boris had gone to the river and showed the women how to wash with his marbled blue-and-white soap, a secret formula developed by his family, and he gave away samples.

The innovation was appreciated, and the soap mill grew steadily. Soap was sold by the box, and meticulous records were kept. People came for the boxes with handcarts; the soap was then distributed to the stores in the city and in the surrounding small towns and villages. As a supplementary product, the mill also produced candles, which were sold in three sizes.

I don't know how many employees worked there. Manuel remembers that they were few — maybe around three. One of them had an exceptionally good singing voice. In a characteristic gesture, once my grandfather Misha discovered the man's talent, he took him to a radio station in the region's capital, Cali, so that they might hear him sing. The man quickly left his job at the soap mill and became a full-time singer under the alias "Arnulfo Granados." His greatest radiophonic hit was with the song "Granada," by the great Mexican composer Agustín Lara.

I've tried to imagine the solitude that Misha and Noemí might have felt while living in Tuluá. Colombia had never been especially open to emigration, and it shut its doors to Jewish immigration tightly toward the end of 1938, after Kristallnacht.[157] Perhaps Misha's feeling of orphanhood was mitigated by the beauty of the landscape, which had transcended into literature thanks to Jorge Isaacs, a writer who was even more alone in his Judaism than my grandfather. Isaacs's descriptions of the landscape of Valle del Cauca were already a common-place in the Latin American imagination.

"The sky," Isaacs begins, "the horizons, the pampas, and the peaks of the Cauca move to silence all who contemplate them, as when in a dance hall one encounters the woman that we dreamed of when we were eighteen years old. She burns our forehead with one fleeting glance, and her voice becomes singular, unique. The great beauties of creation cannot be seen and sung at once." The spellbinding power of the landscape motivated and authorized an inchoate flow of emotion that must have been engrossing and soothing at the same time. No need to talk. And now the family found itself precisely in that place. It was from there that Noemí and Misha would strive for the upkeep and education of their young family, but also for the survival of their people and of the world itself. It was from the Colombian provinces that the family would have to piece together its fractured history and develop a stance for itself in the world.

Jorge Isaacs had achieved all of this in his writing, of course, but he had also devoted a lot of his energy to Colombian politics. Although his book begins with bucolic scenes of family love, a plantation home surrounded by the all-embracing foliage, with its main characters surrounded by loyal and adoring slaves, in real life, Jorge Isaacs participated in Colombia's civil wars between Liberals and Conservatives of the 1860s, which left the family's estates in ruins. By the time he finally sat down to write his *María*, he had lost his family's fortune.

Such a combination of idyllic memory, the recognition of a place's utopian possibilities, and the harsh nature of actually experienced social life might well have inspired my grandfather, although I don't know that for sure, because it is also true that Misha's identification with Colombia was in some ways very different from that of Isaacs. George Henry Isaacs, Jorge Isaacs's British father, had acquired Colombian citizenship through the intervention of Simón Bolívar himself, in exchange for his donation of some cows. Later he established two successful plantations in Valle del Cauca: La Manuelita and El Paraíso, which later served as models for the setting of his son Jorge Isaacs's famous novel.

My grandparents, for their part, had no chance of obtaining Colombian nationality, even if they had had a whole herd of cows to offer then-president Alfonso López Pumarejo. Immigration policies in Colombia had already been somewhat restrictive since the 1920s, but by the time my grandparents arrived in 1936, anti-Jewish sentiment was being stirred up by certain sectors of the middle class. These were mostly businessmen who were resentful of the competition from Jewish peddlers and their wholesalers, and they vented their frustration loudly enough to express open sympathy with the Brown Shirts. In Colombia, there were three hundred officially registered members of the Nazi Party at the time, which put that country in second place for Latin American affiliates, after Chile.[158]

When Colombia closed its doors to Jewish immigration, in a law that went into effect in January 1939, it also took the opportunity to deny nationality to any current Jewish residents who lacked it.[159] This law primarily affected German Jews, who had lost their nationality through the Nuremberg Laws (1935). Although my grandparents were technically Romanian, and they may or may not have been carrying a dubiously legal Peruvian passport, they were in reality either stateless or perilously close to statelessness. My mother, for her part, was unambiguously stateless, for she had been born in France to parents who were not permanent residents, and she could not receive Romanian nationality from them for the reasons I've already explained.

Despite these difficulties, though, my grandparents knew that they had political work to do in Colombia. They were needed to participate in the fight against fascism and Hitler, to defend European Jews, and to prepare Colombia's position in the face of a world war that was now imminent.

Perhaps due to the urgency of the Jewish question by 1936, or because my grandparents had now become parents, my grandfather's activity in Colombia was much more attentive to the Jewish community than it had been in Lima. His first journalism job was as an editorial assistant for *Nuestra Tribuna*, a journal published by the Bogotá Jewish community and directed by Jaime Fainboim. I have in my possession only one issue of that paper, from April 1937. The first thing that stands out is that *Nuestra Tribuna* was clearly looking to build excellent relations with the Colombian government. Thus, the issue that I have opens with an obituary for former Colombian president Enrique Olaya Herrera, who had just died in Italy. The piece closes: "It is for this reason that we, the Jewish community of Colombia, linked in numerous ways with bonds that compel us to feel love for this generous land, feel very deeply and weep with the Colombian people over the death of the illustrious man named Enrique Olaya Herrera."[160]

There were good reasons for this expression of loyalty, together with a profession of love for the land. Olaya Herrera had been the president of Colombia from 1930 to 1934, and in those years, he allowed Jews from Eastern Europe to enter the country despite the fact that, as in most other countries on the continent, Colombian immigration policies from the 1920s manifested racist tendencies. For example, Law 48, passed in 1920, prohibited "the entrance into the country of elements who, given their ethnic, organic, or racial conditions, are determined inappropriate for nationality and for the better development of the 'race.'"[161] That law, and a subsequent one passed in 1922, legitimized a policy of Jewish exclusion, should such exclusion ever be deemed desirable.

Even so, a number of Jewish families like the Milsteins arrived in Colombia between the mid-1920s and the mid-1930s. Olaya Herrera's successor, Alfonso López Pumarejo, was also a member of the Liberal Party, nevertheless there was by that time much more resistance to Jewish immigration, as Colombian society began to fracture in the face of Nazism in Germany. Also significant was the effect of the Spanish Civil War, as the conflict's Nationalist faction had stirred the sympathies of the Colombian Conservative Party.

Jewish immigration to Colombia, although numerically insignificant, was nonetheless quite visible. Jewish peddlers were knocking on people's doors. That always makes people visible. But it also mattered that the peddlers subtly disrupted established class lines: tailored suits were important items at the time, indeed it is fair to say that suits were to middle-class status what noble titles had once been for the aristocracy. They certified legitimate inclusion.

Cartoon of the purported role of "Jewish rats"
in Colombian national commerce.

In the South America of the 1920s, the "middle class" was still a relatively recent thing, and a suit was often required attire to navigate its labor market of white-collar employees, schoolteachers, and specialized tradesmen. Making tailored suits available door to door and on credit broadened popular access to the world of middle class aspirations, with significant political and cultural effects. In fact, greater access to urbane clothing was both one condition and one effect of Latin America's first wave of "populism," a set of movements that involved the eruption of upwardly mobile urban dwellers into the up-to-then restricted and aristocratic preserves of political life. This may well be the reason why the wardrobe became such an obsession of revered populist parvenus like Evita Perón, in Argentina, to name the most famous example. In such a context, the work of Jewish peddlers was both a symptom and a harbinger of social disruption and change in the class structure.

Because they resented competition from Jewish peddlers, some merchants espoused anti-Semitism, and allied themselves politically with conservative Catholics, who likely had only superficial interest in the Jewish question per se, but they sympathized with Franco and therefore also looked favorably upon his ally Hitler.

Although President López Pumarejo was a Liberal, his government was by no means immune to the pressures that came from a combination of Catholic Conservatives, the anti-Semitism of some merchants, and political groups that sympathized with the Nazis. So, in 1934 López Pumarejo's minister of foreign relations, Dario Echandía, began to deny entry visas to German Jews, alleging that "Colombia's possibilities, with the exception of the agrarian sector, do not offer a rosy picture for refugees who might come here and establish dangerous levels of competition with the workers of this country."[162]

The foreign minister preferred to mask the anxieties of the merchants that he was protecting behind supposed concern for the interests and well-being of the workers. The workers in Colombia were not threatened by Jewish migration, in part because of its small numbers, and in part because Colombia's low wages, its racial hierarchy, and the comparatively high education of Jews made it unlikely that Jews would become robust competitors for Colombia's industrial workers. Still, it was easier to restrict Jewish immigration with the pretext that it would be harmful to workers than by acknowledging that they ramped up competition for Colombia's privileged merchants.

As a result, Jews had to try to show that they had positive accomplishments that might contribute to Colombian progress in areas other than industrial labor and commerce — in the professions, for instance, or in agriculture. It does not seem unlikely to me that my great-grandfather Boris decided to buy land in Cauca Valley in order to acquire credentials as an agriculturalist, and so strengthen his claim of belonging in Colombia.

Historian Lina María Leal makes it clear that by 1936 there was a lobby of anti-Semites who intervened regularly in Colombia's chambers of commerce, magazines, and newspapers. There had been nothing like that in Lima in the 1920s, when my grandparents arrived there. But now they were compelled to face this wave of racism, given that it manifested itself not only at the local level but above all globally.

In the context of internal class disruptions, and international alliances between the Conservatives and Europe's fascist block, good relations with the Colombian government were very important, even urgent, for Colombian Jews to develop, and that contrasted with the confrontational attitude that Misha and Noemí had struck when they arrived in Peru, ten years earlier. In the police dossier associated with my grandfather's deportation from Peru, he is mentioned as an individual with "disruptive ideas" who, besides being "a confessed communist," had taken part in a movement of unemployed workers and had given political speeches to textile workers.[163]

In Peru, Misha and Noemí felt free to exercise their activism among the working class and university students, even though the Peruvian government viewed those activities as subversive. Oppositional politics would not beckon them so much in Colombia, because the couple's political efforts were directed instead to building or solidifying an alliance between the Jewish community and the government, and against any tendency that might tilt Colombia to the side of fascism.

Education

When my grandparents arrived in Colombia, their main job, beyond what they needed to do to support their family, was to help consolidate Jewish culture in this new country, and fight against fascism. Educational work came naturally to my grandfather. Within the Jewish community, through *Nuestra Tribuna*, he mobilized his Americanist knowledge to expand Jewish interest and identification with Colombia, and with the Americas more broadly. At the same time, he also looked to strengthen Jewish consciousness itself, by promoting Hebrew and Yiddish education.

In the first issue of *Nuestra Tribuna* on which my grandfather worked (April 1937), he translated from Yiddish an article written by a community leader, Simón Guberek, who speaks of the educational situation of the Jewish youth in Colombia and even proposes a role for Misha in it.[164] Guberek begins by saying that the Jewish community of Bogotá had by that time existed for ten years and that there were roughly three hundred children who had no access to a Jewish education. "As a consequence of this, we have a generation completely distanced from our way of being and our national culture."[165] My own grandparents must have been a bit concerned about this specific issue: their daughter Larissa was at that time five years old, spoke only Spanish, and had little access to Jewish traditions outside of the family home. "Luckily for us," Guberek continued, "Dr. Adler occasionally comes to Bogotá from Cali — a man from the world of science and a teacher with special gifts." There was at that time a meeting of community members who adopted the resolution to entrust Adler with the responsibility of forming a Jewish school in Bogotá.

The task would not be easy because, to use Guberek's own words, "it will be necessary to raise donations (even beyond the tuition that parents would pay) because there still does not exist an organized *kehillah* (community)."[166] He then closed his article expressing hope for Dr. Adler's school, though he also offered a sobering warning: "I know that the entire Jewish community will make sure that the current initiative does not suffer the same fate as earlier institutions in Bogotá."[167]

In a separate book, published in Yiddish in Buenos Aires, Guberek wrote about the divisions that existed in Bogotá's small Jewish community during those years before the war. In a nutshell, there was in it a conservative group that fought for the foundation of religious institutions such as the mikvah (a ritual bath required for women by religious authorities), and a leftist group that was fond of alluding to "a new light that comes from the East" (i.e., the Soviet Union).[168] I don't know the details of that conflict, but it surely contributed to the failure of the school my grandfather was asked to direct.

Just a few months after his arrival to Colombia from Bessarabia, Misha established the first Jewish school in Cali, the "Jorge Isaacs," which was soon recognized as the best Jewish school in the country. I am told that the school still exists. From there, Misha moved to Bogotá in 1937 to establish the Colombian-Hebrew school, which he directed until 1938. Possibly due to the already mentioned internal rifts in the Jewish community, the school was not economically sustainable, so the family returned to Cali, and from there moved to Manizales, where Noemí and Misha's third child, Mauricio, was born on October 20, 1941.

The move to Manizales, which was a provincial city of relatively minor importance, made it hard for my grandparents to lead either an intellectual or a political life, and it suggests that the young couple was not making ends meet in Cali. For my grandfather, Manizales implied a return to commercial life and also employment in his father-in-law's business: Boris had just won a large contract as a supplier of railway ties for the railroad that was then being built between Nariño (on the border between Colombia and Ecuador) and Antioquia. The first phase of that work had been completed through a partnership with the sawmill of Boris's neighbor in Tuluá, a Mr. Levy, but the second phase required a new sawmill, in Manizales, which Misha would now manage. Misha, it should be said, was a useful associate, given that he had studied at the university in Lima, and had engaged in political activity there, and thus he could easily build a fluid rapport with contractors, supervisors, and the like.

It had become clear that it wouldn't be possible to support the family on what Misha earned through his intellectual work at that point, but this didn't mean that those ideals were buried. Thus, Misha struck up a friendship with one of Manizales's

priests, Father Bernardo Jaramillo, an enlightened man with a
desire to extend a hand of friendship to the Jewish people. Jaramillo even asked Misha to teach him Hebrew, which he did.
My family still has a letter that Jaramillo wrote to my grandfather in Hebrew, after the family had moved from Manizales
to Medellín.

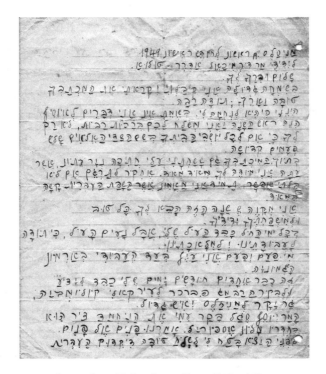

Letter from Father Jaramillo to Misha Adler,
written after a trip to Medellín
during which the priest stayed in my grandparents' house.

In Colombia, my grandfather's educational work was thus
oriented to Jewish education both within and outside of the

community. From this period, we also have a letter from a Colombian senator, the Liberal Armando Solano, written in 1938. In it, Solano defends Jews against persecution and argues that Colombia should allow them to immigrate there. The letter was written only three weeks after Kristallnacht, and it is exactly contemporary with the decision of the Colombian government to close its doors definitively to Jewish immigration.

Solano mentions something in his letter with which surely my grandfather agreed: "It is not true that there is anti-Semitism in Colombia. Special interests, wounded by commercial competition and instigated by political reactionaries, have created that appearance. Our people are traditionally and radically opposed to all exclusion, to all racial hatred. Their hospitality is axiomatic."[169] My own sense is that Solano was to a large degree correct in this — people in South America tended to be both kind and hospitable to strangers, including to the new Jewish immigrants. On the other hand, it is also true that refugees and émigrés such as my grandparents tended always to emphasize this local quality, and to express limitless gratitude for having been taken in and accepted, while minimizing local chauvinist tendencies that also existed and surfaced at times. But the point, at that critical historical juncture, was to emphasize Colombian hospitality, on one hand, and to stress the Jews' potential contributions to national progress.

So, for instance, Senator Solano spoke of the Jews' promise as agricultural colonists, as a way of sidestepping anti-immigrant pressure from wounded special interests in the urban business sector. The senator added that "vast expanses of our territory can and should be colonized by Jewish communities, which have provided good evidence in Palestine and elsewhere of their agricultural capacity and organizing abilities. Colombia is a country of immigrants, and it could easily assimilate thousands of Jews." My grandparents, for their part, highlighted the Jews' diversity of talents — in art, the sciences, literature, philosophy, medicine, manual labor, industry, agriculture, and so on. It was important that not all Jews be seen as merchants and peddlers, and the best way to do this was to showcase the excellent work being done by Jews in a variety of domains. And indeed, even the first great Colombian novel, *María*, had been written by a Jew, during a time when there were practically no Jews in the country. Was this not an auspicious sign for their potential contribution to national society, if they were given the space and opportunity, and if prejudices were set aside?

Family life

It is not easy to reconstruct the life of the Adler family between its arrival in Tuluá in 1936 and its move to Medellín, five years later. My mother, who was the oldest of her siblings, spent her childhood moving from one school to another and from place to place. This circumstance made access to formal schooling complicated when she was ready to start high school.

In 1887, Colombia signed a formal accord with the Vatican, the so-called Concordato, which stipulated, among other things, that the country would not offer mixed-sex education in public schools. That, in turn, meant that there was less access to secondary education for girls than for boys, especially in the provinces. My grandparents found themselves with little choice but to place my mother in a Catholic boarding school, the Instituto Central Feminino, in the city of Tunja, between Bogotá and Sogamoso. One of my childhood memories is Larissa's story about her experience there. She lived in dread of being exposed as Jewish and having her classmates find her strange and reject her, and to avoid that, she went to mass every single day. But her anguish never relented, because of a teacher who watched over their dormitory at night, and took sadistic pleasure in making insinuations that she might expose Larissa's secret to the class.

left to right: Manuel, Mauricio, and Larissa Adler
in Colombia (possibly Medellín).

"Larissa, you were talking in your sleep again," she would say, in front of my mother's schoolmates. "You said such strange things... 'Everyone thinks that I'm —,' you were saying, 'but I'm —'" Every day my mother suffered the suspense that the teacher might at last finish the sentence. "Everyone thinks that

I'm *Catholic*, but I'm *Jewish*." The teachers knew of Larissa's Judaism, because her parents had provided them with that information, ironically with the aim of exempting Larissa from attending mass on Sundays with the other students. But since her classmates had not been told, it had the opposite effect: in order to appear "normal," Larissa attended mass every day.

At the end of the year, the family moved to Medellín, and Noemí and Misha took my mother out of that school and enrolled her in a local private school. The move to Medellín was due to my great-grandmother Tania's cancer diagnosis. There was a hospital in Medellín with specialists better equipped to treat her than what existed in Cali or Tuluá. Also, Boris had opened a sawmill in that city, once again managed by Misha, to provide the railroad ties for the third phase of railway construction, so that the family could stay by Tania's side during her treatment. Except that Tania survived for only a few weeks. She died in March 1942, without ever receiving any news of her daughter Shura. She was buried in Medellín, and Misha, Noemí, and their children stayed in that city for two years.

These were times of enormous anguish. At Hitler's conference in Wannsee (just outside of Berlin) in January 1942 the Nazis decided to move forward with the extermination of the Jews in all of Europe. My grandparents still didn't know what had happened to Hershel, Leah, Shura, and their other relatives who had remained in Nova Sulitza and in Mogilev, Czernowitz, or Odessa, and they followed with anguish the news on the radio of Nazi operations on the Eastern front. The extent to which they communicated these worries to their kids isn't entirely clear to me. I have the impression that Misha and

Noemí made a consistent effort to shield their children from fully undertanding what was at stake.

LA COLONIA HEBREA DE COLOMBIA

Recibió confirmación de fuentes fidedignas de que Hitler ha ordenado la exterminación de todos los judíos en los territorios dominados por Alemania hasta el 31 de diciembre de 1942.

Con este motivo, el día de hoy, 2 de diciembre, será considerado día de luto mundial judío, con ayunos, permaneciendo cerrados todos los establecimientos hebreos y efectuándose ceremonias religiosas en todo el país, a las cuales se invita a toda la colonia.

A las 3 p. m. gran reunión en el Centro Israelita de Bogotá, Calle 24, No. 5-63.

Se invita a todos los simpatizantes.

Bogotá's Jewish community declares a day of mourning in response to Hitler's decision to murder every Jew living in German-occupied lands.

In the midst of the world's difficulties, the family was establishing itself in Colombia. Children were being born — Misha and Noemí now had three. My great-uncle Alfonso ("Zuñe") settled down and had a family in Bogotá. My great-aunt Pupe got married. My mother remembers that in her early childhood, Pupe Milstein had a secret Gentile (Catholic) boyfriend from an important Medellín family, and he wanted to marry her. They sometimes used Larissa as a decoy so that Pupe could go to the movies secretly to meet her boyfriend there.

One day Misha saw them together, and he told Boris. According to my mother, Misha's informing on his young sister-in-law might have been motivated by watchfulness of Larissa's own future. If Pupe married a Christian, the possibility of a marriage within the Jewish community for Larissa diminished, and this may have been something that concerned Misha, because while Boris was a prosperous businessman, Larissa would have no dowry to speak of. That is one possible explanation, but in those years of such uncertainty in Europe, my grandparents might also have seen their situation in Colombia as transitory, and they feared the rootedness that came with assimilation.

Under the Torah ark at Pupe Milstein's wedding, 1944.
In the center, Pupe, and to the right, my grandmother.
To the left, her new sister-in-law, Sara Dargoltz de Perlman.

Whatever the cause, what is known is that Pupe ended things with her boyfriend after they were caught, and was sent to study in Bogotá, where later she would meet and marry Isaac Perlman. I mention the anecdote of Pupe's boyfriend to give a sense of the context in which my family lived in places such as Tuluá, which had almost no other Jewish families. For Boris's generation, or even that of my grandfather, this was a completely novel situation: in Bessarabia, in Czernowitz, or in

Ukraine, Jewish communities were large and geographically concentrated. There was, as well, very strong discrimination against them on the part of the dominant society, which made it pretty easy for people to marry "within the faith." In South America, the situation became blurred as much for demographic reasons as for the relatively high prestige that Jews had in the Americas. In such a context, reproducing the community required explicit effort.

Pupe's wedding occurred during the war, although after Tania's passing, and it suggests something about community life that was taking root in the South American margins of the European disaster.

Tania

Tania Greisser de Milstein died of cancer in Medellín, Colombia, on March 15, 1942. What in reality do we know of her? My mother remembers a lot. She says that every afternoon she would sit on the porch of their house in Tuluá and cry over the loss of her daughter Shura, who, for her part, grew up believing that she had been deliberately abandoned. Shura had no idea how much her parents had suffered for her, and she only learned the truth when my parents traveled to Moscow in 1970 to meet her.

The story that Shura transmitted to her daughter Rita is that when the family was crossing the Dniester River and she started to cry, Tania wished to stay with her, but Boris insisted that they leave her and come back for her later. That is, it became accepted fact that Tania had been forced to leave her daughter behind. For me, Tania is the very figure of loss: crying in the afternoons on the porch of her house on the other side of the world from where her abandoned daughter had been left; using whatever strength she had to hold together what remained of the family; dying young of cancer.

A characteristically matriarchal portrait of Tania,
sent to Shura by her sister Noemí in 1955,
thirteen years after Tania's death.

How old was Tania when she died? I'm not quite sure. Her gravestone doesn't indicate a date of birth, but her oldest daughter, Noemí, was born in 1911. I imagine that Tania must not have been much older than twenty at that time, or perhaps even younger, in which case she would have been born just after 1890 and thus would have died at roughly fifty years of age, which coincides with my mother's own estimates. Although in photos her appearance was always that of the prototypical Ukrainian *matriosha* — a short, round woman of indefinite years — this is more the effect of the style of the times than a reflection of her true age.

Now, writing this book, it strikes me that Tania died in March 1942. If the family had remained in Czernowitz, eternally waiting for Shura's departure from Ukraine, she would have died at roughly the same time, except in a Transnistrian ghetto, like Misha's parents. It is unlikely that she and Boris would have survived the frozen journey through Bessarabia and Ukraine, the violence of the road, the conditions of the ghettos, or the concentration camps. In this, Tania was lucky, and Boris was at least partially right. Tania survived the violence of the revolution and the counterrevolution and managed to see two of her three daughters grow up. She became the matriarch of a flourishing family from her home in Tuluá, and she was able to spend time with three of her grandchildren — Larissa, Manuel, and Mauricio. Tania was the bridgehead for the survival of my mother's family, no more and no less, but despite this, she is, at least in my imagination, a symbol of irreparable loss. Tania is, besides, part of the life experience that most marked my mother, and she doubtless shaped how the latter raised us: a philosophy very much opposed to complaining and that cultivated flexibility and adaptation instead. Shura had been abandoned because she cried, so one mustn't cry. In my house, to be a complainer or whiner was a bad thing. Keep calm and carry on. And behind that calm, maintain a constant vigilance regarding family unity.

Diglossia in America

My great-grandmother Tania was the first member of my family to die in America. There is an interesting feature in the photos that I have of her grave. The first stone, the original, is written in Hebrew, and with the date of her death registered according to the Jewish calendar. The second, however, put in place to freshen up the grave, likely around 1960, carries an inscription in Spanish that reads: "Tania Greisser de Milstein died on March 15, 1942." This linguistic detail warrants some reflection.

left: The original grave of Tania Greisser de Milstein.
right: Tania's grave, ordered redone by Victor Perlman, probably around 1960.
Cemetery of the Union Israelita de Beneficiencia. Medellín, Colombia.

Tania's grave is in the first row of the women's section of the Jewish cemetery of Medellín. It is, as Roberto Esquenazi, the president of the Jewish community of Medellín, has graciously informed me, the fifth oldest grave in the cemetery. That is, Tania was one of the first Jewish women to be buried in Medellín (of course, only if we do not count so-called Marranos from the colonial period). Tania was part of the first generation of Ashkenazim in Colombia. Boris's request to have her gravestone written in Hebrew, even without a date of death according to the Christian calendar, speaks of a generation raised in the diglossia of Russia, where Jewish separation was obligatory, and where communication in Yiddish or Hebrew was a way of unifying Jews, even in far-flung regions that had their own different national languages (Polish, Russian, or German, for example).

Yiddish and Hebrew were also a way for the Old World and the New to communicate, especially given the success of the Yiddish press in New York and Buenos Aires.[170] But how did this linguistic community operate in America? Was it even relevant in places such as Bogotá, Medellín, and Cali, that had such small Jewish communities?

According to my uncle Manuel, his grandfather Boris was a man who liked routines. He woke up every day before five a.m. and after getting himself ready for the day, he sat down in a comfortable and simple armchair. In the room there was a round glass table and another rectangular one next to his chair.

"There he is, seated, smoking his daily tobacco, drinking strong coffee, and reading the Yiddish newspaper that came to his home directly from New York."[171] The newspaper in question was the *Forverts* (Forward), which always arrived a few weeks late, but which Boris read scrupulously, all the way through. With a Social Democrat or socialist slant, the *Forverts* was the only newspaper that Boris read, in spite of the fact that he could read other languages and that the news in Yiddish always arrived a few weeks after the events being covered.

Yiddish in America occupied a place somewhat different from what it had for Boris and Tania in Ukraine. There were Ukrainian and Romanian Jews in the capitals and provincial cities of Colombia, Venezuela, Argentina, Chile, Ecuador, Peru, Bolivia, and Panama, and some even came from the very same villages in Eastern Europe. Nova Sulitza, for example, sent migrants to Lima, Caracas, and Bogotá, but also Cumaná, Cali, Cerro de Pasco, and Huancayo, not to mention Philadelphia and other US destinations. There were people from Czernowitz in all of those places as well. According to what Alvarez Gardeazábal has told me, Tuluá had a market called "Ucrania" (which, to be clear, did not belong to Boris). Such a geographically dispersed but socially connected diaspora still had some intimate uses for Yiddish, even beyond their interest in maintaining connections with the truly large Ashkenazi communities in Buenos Aires or New York, for example.

Within Latin American cities, there were some attempts, usually unsuccessful, to create Yiddish-speaking communities that might have the same vitality that the language had in towns and cities of Eastern Europe. In fact, the work history of my grandfather Misha in Colombia is in part the story of the failure to construct a robust speech community. Misha founded the Jewish school in Cali (the Jorge Isaacs), and he also attempted to found one in Bogotá. Both efforts encountered serious difficulties in the 1930s and 1940s. Why was this so?

In his 1937 call to form a Jewish school in Bogotá that would teach Hebrew and Yiddish, Guberek mentions as a cause of past failures a certain disunity in the community.[172] That may well be, but it is also likely that the small size of the community played a larger part: it was difficult for such a project, which required teachers for all grades, to be economically viable with such a small population.

Besides, there were other reasons for the Jewish community to communicate in Spanish, even internally. The newspaper *Nuestra Tribuna* comes to mind. It was published in Spanish even during the 1930s, when the whole of Colombia's Jewish community still spoke Yiddish and many still spoke broken Spanish. The journal's editors even went to the trouble of translating Yiddish articles into Spanish. Why worry about presenting everything in correct Spanish? Why did the Jewish community of Bogotá not publish something like the *Forverts* in Yiddish?

I think the decision was prompted by two different factors. First, the community was concerned with tightening its bonds with non-Jewish allies. *Nuestra Tribuna* published a fair amount of copy on Colombian topics, learned articles on the history and archaeology of the country, and it adopted a generally patriotic attitude toward Colombia. Indeed, my grandfather's learned Americanism served the community's effort to strengthen these connections very well.

The second factor may have been connected to the difficulty associated with developing a Yiddish education for the younger members of the community who were born or raised in Colombia. There were not the necessary resources to institutionalize a formal Jewish education, which meant that all the young people were being educated in Spanish-speaking schools. My mother, for example, who was among the first generation of Colombian Jews, went to Catholic schools and public high schools in which she was consistently the only non-Catholic in the class. She understood Yiddish, but she didn't speak it, nor did she know how to read it.

In this way, Yiddish became a generational trait and an oral language. The uses of proficiency in Yiddish to mark an "insider" and an "outsider" began to vary substantially, until it finally arrived at cases such as that of my brothers and me, who only know a few words (*mensch*, *chutzpah*, *mishugge*, etc.), a number of which are now even part of regular American English (though not of Spanish). What remains for us are the ruins of my grandparents' native language; words that enrich whatever high prestige language we speak—whether this be Spanish, English, French, or whatever — but, like any ruin, those words also mark a genealogy.

CHAPTER THIRTEEN

The Need for a New World

Nuevo Mundo

One year after the death of my great-grandmother Tania, *Nuevo Mundo* appeared in Medellín, edited and administered by Dr. Miguel Adler (Edificio Jenaro Gutiérrez, Office no. 204; telephone number 175.38). The magazine was part of a larger business owned by my grandparents called Nuevo Mundo (New World), which presented itself as a distributor of books, periodicals, and art objects. They had tried to get it running from Bogotá in 1938, but with no success. Of those first attempts, there is only a 1938 letter written on letterhead that reads,

Nuevo Mundo
Monthly Journal
Director Dr. Miguel Adler
Bogotá, Colombia

and that also states the business address as "Carrera 13-A No. 27-00."

It is thus not entirely clear whether Misha managed to produce anything in Bogotá in 1938 or not, but the magazine that appeared in Medellín is listed as the first issue of the first volume of the journal, and in no place does it say that this is a new series, so I suppose that the project was planned out in 1938 but that it did not manage to materialize until 1942.

The first issue of *Nuevo Mundo*, with a photo on the cover
of Augustín Tisoy Jacanamijoy, and a smaller image
of José Carlos Mariátegui.

On the title page of the first issue, there is an editorial titled "Norms and Purpose," in which *Nuevo Mundo* presents itself as an antifascist publication, and then characterizes itself in the following way: "This is an open forum for all ideas, in accordance with the statement of Saint-Just: 'Freedom for everything and all people, except for the enemies of freedom.'"[173]

The cover of the first issue of the journal partook of the celebrations then taking place in Colombia on April 19 for the "Day of the Indigenous." It has a photo of Agustín Tisoy, a young man from the Putumayo who, "as the son of a free Colombia, as a member of an aboriginal ethnic group, and as a practicing Catholic, knows that the Nazis threaten the independence of all weaker groups, the freedom of races they refer to as 'inferior,' and the sacred right of faith. For this reason, he appears making the Democratic salute of 'V for victory.'"[174]

According to my mother, Agustín Tisoy Jacanamijoy was a young Indian from the jungles of the Putumayo who sold native crafts in the streets of Medellín, and with whom Misha had entered into conversation. One of my grandfather's specialties was talking to all sorts of people, and in that conversation, Agustín mentioned that he wished to become a lawyer in order to defend his people. In a characteristic gesture, Misha brought him to live in his house and put him "under scholarship," that is, he housed and fed Agustín for a year so that he could study. Larissa remembers that she, an eleven-year-old girl, and Agustín, who might have been around eighteen, would sit together at the dining room table to do their homework.

In his introductory editorial, Misha wrote, "In our times, when the outdated nationalist systems of old Europe have capsized in a sea of blood, barbarity, and ignominy, the concept of what should be understood by *New World* (Nuevo Mundo) acquires for all Americans—and for Americanized Europeans who have arrived in this hemisphere in a search for liberty and refuge—a deeper and more transcendent sense than that held by the explorers of the fifteenth and sixteenth centuries."[175]

Misha's Americanism had grown in rich soil: at José Carlos Mariátegui's Red Corner and at the Universidad de San Marcos, at the Institut d'Ethnologie in Paris with Paul Rivet, and especially in his extensive experience of the city and the country in Peru and Colombia. Now his Americanism took on world-historical relevance as an image of a possible collective future, in the face of Europe's self-destruction.

"America," he continued, "is the laboratory in which a modern modality of human coexistence is put to the test. Here the blood of all the races is mixed, and a formidable block of nations is now being formed that will try to make their borders not barriers but rather conduits of exchange." He later closed with:

> As long as there exists the danger that a fascist system will alter the rhythm of general progress, clutching in its claws a Europe that is enslaved by terror and imperialist exploitation, and as long as the already outdated methods of colonial domination exist in the most remote parts of the globe, the young American civilization will not be safe, nor will it advance with the speed and breadth that it might gain in a world where no peoples or persons are deprived of liberty.

The main point of Misha's inaugural essay—and of the publication as a whole—was to "maintain a combative stance in the most noble and elevated sense of the term: serving as an offensive and defensive weapon in the fight that all free people sustain against Nazi-fascist barbarity, and to contribute in this way to the universal triumph of democracy." This was the Americanism of my grandfather in its maximalist expression.

Agustín Tisoy Jacanamijoy

On the third page of the first issue of *Nuevo Mundo*, reserved for advertisements that covered publication costs, there appears an ad for Piel Roja (Redskin) cigarettes, with the slogan, "It attracts us all." No doubt. The pull of the native was strong and widely disseminated in Colombia.

Advertisement in *Nuevo Mundo*, April 1943.

According to a brief story in *Nuevo Mundo*, Agustín Tisoy had enrolled as a freshman in the Universidad de Antioquia, "the first time in this institution that a man of pure native blood has arrived in its classrooms in search of instruction."[176]

The story continues, stating that, after meeting him on the streets of Medellín, Misha helped Agustín to enroll in the university. "This indigenous student embodies the Greek ideal of health: a healthy mind in a healthy body. He is vigorous, intelligent, observant, and unassuming; there is nothing boastful or servile about him; he is free from any inferiority complex. He knows that he can rise through his studies, and he is fully dedicated to his cultural development." Agustín was, in essence, the Americanist (and socialist) ideal of the new man.

Misha Adler, Agustín Tisoy, and two unidentified companions
facing the future, in an Americanist photograph
that imitates the aesthetic of Eisenstein. Medellín, 1943.

Agustín also published a piece in *Nuevo Mundo*, where he tells the story of his village, Santiago, and the region where it is located, the Sibundoy Valley, in the Putumayo. He explains that the indigenous people of the Putumayo River are called "Ingas" and are descendants of Peruvian Incas.[177] The grandeur of the Incas found a refuge in the Colombian Amazon. This way of making the past live in the present is something that brought Misha and Agustín together, because it takes the characteristic form of Jewish messianism.

Each year during Passover, Jews commemorate their liberation from slavery — the departure from Egypt, the leadership of Moses. During Passover dinner, it is customary to explain to children the reasons for the celebration. All the pedagogical emphasis that characterizes Judaism is concentrated in those explanations. At one point in the ritual, the Haggadah presents the questions that four different types of children might be tempted to ask around the Passover feast: these four types are the learned child, the bad child, the foolish child, and the child who does not know how to ask.

The bad child's question is, "Why do you do these things?" And the answer is: "I do it because of what God did for *me* when he freed us from Egypt." For *me* and not for *you*, because if the bad child had been in Egypt, God would not have freed him. That is a good example of messianic time, in which the acts of the past are always powerful, living examples. Redemption in the past is a sign of a redemption that is yet to come.

Agustín Tisoy was an indigenous Inga, from the Sibundoy Valley. The Inga are Quechua speakers, and it is said that they descend from the Inca Huayna Cápac. For my grandfather, this story revived the past in the present, and offered hope for redeeming it. The fact that the Incas' hidden descendants were alive and well provided an opening for a "New World" that would no longer be characterized by colonial exploitation but rather by a mode of coexistence in which "the blood of all the races is mixed," and borders are "not barriers but rather conduits of exchange." In this way, for my grandfather, Agustín Tisoy's wish to study law in order to defend his people was a sign that the search for universal redemption through illumination and translation was well under way. For my grandfather, America was a laboratory in which the language of paradise could be developed, and might well come to life once again.

The second issue

I don't know if my grandparents managed to publish more than the two issues of *Nuevo Mundo* that are still in my family's possession. My mother helped her mother put copies in labeled envelopes and mail them as "exchange" to various contacts in Latin American capitals, but despite their efforts, it is practically impossible to find any trace of the publication in any library today. I couldn't even find *Nuevo Mundo* in WorldCat, the digital library catalog that brings together data from university libraries all across the United States and Europe.

The second issue of *Nuevo Mundo* appeared in June 1943, and we know, through a letter from Agustín Tisoy to my grandfather, that my grandparents had left Medellín before

November of that year. As it was a periodical that was meant to appear three times a year, it is not impossible that there was a third issue, corresponding to September 1943.

Cover of the second issue
of *Nuevo Mundo*, June 1943.

CHAPTER FOURTEEN

The Limits of Adaptation

Colombian-Soviet friendship

Nuevo Mundo was relatively successful, I think. For instance, in Medellín, Misha befriended Adolfo Restrepo, son of a former Colombian president, director of an important textile mill, and a militant anti-Nazi activist. It was perhaps because of this connection that Misha was invited to give a speech before the full Congress of Antioquia, arguing for Colombia's entry into the war.

Despite all this good work, though, my grandparents were compelled to shut down *Nuevo Mundo* in late 1943 and move to Bogotá, where Misha would work as the director of the Institute for Colombian-Soviet Friendship, created to bring these two countries together within the broader context of the Second World War. As a speaker of Russian, an Americanist trained and credentialed in Paris, and the author of a dissertation on Karl Marx, Misha was well qualified to carry out this work. The institute offered Russian lessons, taught by Misha and Noemí, and both of them also did work in translation from Russian to Spanish and vice versa.

When I learned that Misha served as director of the Institute for Colombian-Soviet Friendship, I thought that he must have been a member of the Communist Party, despite my family's strenuous claims to the contrary. There are clues that support my suspicions. In *Repertorio Hebreo*, for example, Misha published defenses of the Soviet Union, as we have seen. My mother also remembers that a number of Colombian communists would come to the house, including a man named Augusto Durán, who (according to her recollection) was married to Dina Chosnik, a Jewish woman and friend of her parents'.[178] Doing a bit of research, I was able to confirm that Durán became secretary-general of the Communist Party of Colombia in 1938.

On the other hand, there is also evidence that supports my family's version of things. My grandparents were *mariateguistas*, and José Carlos Mariátegui had a complicated relationship with the Komintern, a fact that delayed the formation of the Communist Party in Peru.[179] On the other hand, Paul Rivet's example in the French Socialist Party and in an Anti-Fascist Defense League that promoted the formation of a wide front may have offered a more congenial position to Misha, especially in his Colombian circumstances.

In the end, there is one persuasive piece of information that convinced me that Misha and Noemí had not been members of the Colombian Communist Party. This is that in 1937, during the time of Stalin's worst persecutions against Leon Trotsky, *Nuestra Tribuna*, where my grandfather served as an editorial assistant, approvingly published the following note: "In an interview given to a representative of the Jewish Telegraph Agency, Leon Trotsky declared that Jews need their own homeland. In the same interview, Trotsky accused the Soviet government of anti-Semitism."[180]

A positive mention of Trotsky, and an accusation of anti-Semitism against the Soviet Union, published in 1937, is not imaginable from any member of the Communist Party, even though my grandparents supported the Soviet Union in the context of the war and were friends with prominent Colombian communists who were indeed members of the party. I shared this hypothesis with Professor Victor Jeifets of the Russian Academy of Science, a specialist in the history of the Komintern in the Americas and author of a biographical dictionary of relevant figures that includes an entry for "Miguel Adler," and he agreed with my conclusion, although there is still uncertainty in the case, because the Institute for Colombian-Soviet Friendship was destroyed during the Bogotazo riots of 1948.[181]

Party member or not, though, the Soviet embassy felt sufficient confidence in Misha's loyalties to ask that he help consolidate cultural relations with Colombia. And of course Misha was loyal to them. After the end of the Battle of Stalingrad, in February 1943, the Red Army went on the offensive on the Eastern front, and so the Soviets became first and foremost the force of liberation that kept alive Misha's hope of still finding his parents alive.

Birobidzhan

For his work teaching Russian, translating, and other activities, Misha received a salary from the Soviet embassy. From that era, my mother remembered especially an embassy employee, a Mr. Antipov, who was a pleasant man and a friend of the family. But we enter into a blurry and polemical region of my family's history here, because the memories of these times were Larissa's alone — she was the oldest of her siblings — and they refer to an uncertain date. Even so, I think that it must have been right after the end of the war or perhaps a little earlier, maybe the end of 1944, when Ukraine and Romania had already been liberated, but before Misha came to know of the treatment that the people of Nova Sulitza received as subjects of the Soviet Union.

Larissa remembers that her parents had applied for a visa so that the family might return to the Soviet Union.

"What?" (This was my reaction upon hearing the story.) My mother then explained to me that, at a certain point, her parents decided to try to move to Birobidzhan, the "Jewish Republic" that Stalin established near the Soviet border with Manchuria.

I confess that I had to read up on the place, since I had never heard of it until that point. Birobidzhan's history is related on one hand to the complex trajectory that the question of nationalities had in the Soviet Union, and on the other with the anti-Semitism of the Stalin era, the Yiddishism that existed in the Soviet Union, and also the death of millions of Soviet Jews during the war. I'll provide here a thumbnail outline of that story, to explain what was at stake.

After the Russian Revolution, the Soviet Union implemented a genuinely innovative policy regarding nationalities. The historian Terry Martin characterizes it as an "empire of affirmative action," because the Soviet Union was the first case of a republic concerned with providing political, linguistic, and cultural representation to each of the "nationalities" that existed in its vast territory.[182] As we have seen, Lenin considered the emancipation of repressed nationalities to be a necessary step on the path to universal socialist emancipation, and for that reason, the Soviet Union was conceived of as a union of "republics," formed in principle to recognize each one of the nationalities that composed the vast territory of the former Russian Empire. Each republic would be governed as a "Soviet," in other words as a communist council.

In this context, the international borders of the Soviet Union immediately became especially sensitive zones, because there were many communities from a single "nationality" that spread across international borders. This issue was especially difficult in the densely populated western borders of the Soviet Union, where there were Polish speakers on the Soviet and Polish sides of the border, Lithuanians on both sides of the same border, speakers of Ukrainian on the Soviet and Romanian sides, speakers of Yiddish that stretched across the Soviet, Romanian, Lithuanian, and Polish borders, speakers of German on the Soviet and Polish sides of the border, speakers of Armenian on the Turkish and Soviet sides of the border, and so on.

In the 1920s, the communist government used its innovative policy on national minorities as a propaganda tool. Martin summarizes the strategy in the following way: "now on the

Western border the Soviet Union divided the ethnic territory of Finns, Belarusians, Ukrainians, and Romanians. Given this, they had the hope that an ostentatiously generous treatment of these ethnicities within the Soviet Union might attract their compatriots from Poland, Finland, and Romania."[183]

The policy, known as *korenizatsiia*, or "indigenization," had positive results, because of which the Jews of Bessarabia and Bukovina tended to maintain an agnostic and at times a positive attitude toward the Soviet Union, in spite of their fear of communism. In the end, the Soviet Union was the only country whose government financed schools in Yiddish and also economically supported publishing houses, courts, and municipal councils that operated in that language.[184] Indeed, there existed an enormous contrast between the Soviet policy of nationalities and the anti-Semitism that the Polish or Romanian states encouraged.[185] This impacted Misha, who, as we have seen, argued in 1929 that "a true miracle has occurred with the October Revolution with respect to our Jewish problem."[186]

During the 1920s, and taking advantage of the positive results of *korenizatsiia*, the Soviet government asked the League of Nations to allow a plebiscite in Bessarabia to determine if the population preferred to return to the Soviet Union and thus reject Romanian annexation.[187] The Romanian government never permitted such a plebiscite, and it instead projected its anti-Soviet sentiment on the Jews, who were represented as "Russian propagandists capable of anything to harm our state."[188] The belief that Jews were communist agents became a given in Romania.[189] On the other hand, the Romanians had not done much to gain the loyalty of the Jewish population of

Bessarabia, and even those who proudly identified themselves as Romanians of the "Old Kingdom" were the object of skeptical incredulity and not infrequent insults, as we saw in the case of Mihail Sebastian.

The pamphlet "On the Struggle against Anti-Semitism in the Schools,"
published by the Popular Commissariat for the Illumination
of the Socialist and Federal Soviet Republic, 1929.

The Soviet policy against anti-Semitism remained in place throughout the 1920s and, although to a lesser degree, the 1930s. It is certainly true that anti-Semitism — even official anti-Semitism — did not end with the Russian Revolution; but the official critique of anti-Semitism had very palpable effects nonetheless. In her study of the history of anti-Semitism in the border region between Romania and Ukraine, Dumitru shows that the common folk — peasants, artisans, and the people in general — in Bessarabia and Bukovina participated on a massive scale in the robbery, rape, murder, and genocide of the Jewish population, while the Ukrainian population, on the other side of the Soviet border, did not: "there is no evidence of episodes of collective violence against Jews in any of the villages, towns, or cities of Transnistria. Neither the testimony of survivors, nor government records — not even secondary sources — report this sort of event."[190] In other words, the Soviet state's efforts to uproot anti-Semitism had a marked effect, a fact that became quite conspicuous after 1941, during the Nazi occupation, when peasants on either side of the old Soviet border were given a green light to kill and rob Jews.

Even with all of these efforts to recognize and protect national minorities, the question of creating a Jewish republic within the Soviet Union was problematic for Stalin, for various reasons. To begin with, in order to establish a national republic, there had to be a territory associated with that nationality. In the case of the Jews, this presented a serious difficulty, because the Jewish population of the Russian Empire had been concentrated in a Pale of Settlement that stretched across the entire western fringe of the Soviet Union, beginning in the north in Lithuania, passing through the annexed provinces of Poland (Galicia and Belarus), and down to Ukraine and Bessarabia in the south. It was an enormous territory, and of great strategic importance, given that it touched the borders of various other military powers (Finland, Poland, Romania, Bulgaria, Serbia, Greece, Turkey…).

The second problem was that Jews lived in urban areas that were surrounded by peasants who belonged to some other ethnic group: Moldovans, Ukrainians, Belarusians, Poles, Lithuanians, Russians. It would be difficult to empty out the countryside of these nationalities in order to hand over land to the Jews.

The third complication had to do with anti-Semitism, international support for Jews, and Soviet realpolitik. Although Soviet policy condemned anti-Semitism, it was a widespread phenomenon that had been promoted over centuries by the Orthodox Church and the czars, and it continued to be politically useful. Having a ready-made scapegoat at hand is never an easy resource for politicians to abandon, and both Stalin and his successors made use of it. Moreover, because the Jews had defenders beyond Soviet borders — notably in the United Kingdom, France, and the United States — they could be used as a bargaining chip for negotiations on the international stage. In a context of totalitarian oppression, the Jews could be (and sometimes were) treated as hostages when the opportunity arose.

For these reasons, Stalin did not want to establish a republic or *oblast* (administrative province) in Crimea or in any of the other areas of majority Jewish population; instead he declared in 1928 that Birobidzhan would be a Jewish district (*raion*), even though that territory had no Jewish population and was located thousands of miles away from the old Pale of Settlement. In 1934, Stalin granted the territory the status of *oblast*, and from that time forward, Birobidzhan was considered the "Judeo-Soviet homeland," although it never managed to bring together more than thirty thousand Jews to live there, compared with the almost three million who lived in the Soviet

Union before the Second World War, and the approximately one million Jews who survived the war. Robert Weinberg wrote a book about Birobidzhan, a small region on the Chinese border that was far from anything and lacking everything.[191] And yet, at a certain point, my grandparents considered moving there. Why?

Reasons

To be perfectly honest, we will now never know what was behind my family's Birobidzhan pipe dream. My mother says that she and her parents spent four months waiting for the Soviet visa, and that in the end, Antipov came to my grandparents' house to inform them that their application had been denied. Given the friendship between my grandfather and Antipov, it doesn't seem impossible that Antipov secretly decided to save my family the misery of moving to Birobidzhan and simply "forgot" to submit their application. If that is what happened, then may God bless Mr. Antipov!

Weinberg's book provides information about what happened to Jewish intellectuals who supported the move to Birobidzhan.[192] They were, for the most part, Yiddishists who felt a certain ambivalence about reviving Hebrew as a national language, and in the context of the extermination of European Jews, decided to support the formation of a Jewish homeland near the Soviet border with China. The majority of the most prominent of these intellectuals were in the end tried, sentenced, and executed by Stalin. Should they have moved to Birobidzhan, it seems rather likely that my grandfather too would have been marginalized and surveilled as an example of the much criticized "cosmopolitan Jew" (especially given his interest in Hebrew) and finally targeted by one of Stalin's purges.

How could it have occurred to a man who was not even a member of the Communist Party to try his family's luck in such a remote place? Here I have nothing but speculation. Indeed, not even the plan to go to Birobidzhan is verifiable, beyond the memory of my mother. Her brother Manuel, who was nine or ten at the time, neither remembers waiting for the Soviet visa nor believes that such a plan was possible. In the end, he says, Misha was always a Zionist. His plan was to go to Palestine, not the Soviet Union.

Manuel's argument seems reasonable, but Larissa's recollection could not have emerged from nothing. Her memories, although blurry in some aspects, were also very precise: she remembered the names of the communists who visited her parents' house, as well as the name and even the face and gestures of the Soviet official who told them their visa had been denied. She remembered that the idea of a visa was motivated by a projected move to Birobidzhan, which was an improbable and almost unknown place, and so a detail that was difficult to make up.

My own opinion is that the idea of moving to Birobidzhan was very real, and that there was, even if for a brief time, an earnest exploration of the possibility of moving there. But how to explain that such an outlandish idea could have been entertained by a family that was living in Colombia? Let me try my hand at an explanation.

The year must have been 1945 or maybe the end of 1944.

If the war was not yet over, at the very least the advance of the Allies was now clearly unstoppable; or maybe the idea emerged immediately after Hitler's demise, but before the end of the war in the Pacific. I'm not sure, but at that time, Misha and Noemí still had no news at all from Nova Sulitza — they hadn't had direct information from the place since the Soviet annexation, in 1940. So they didn't even know if Misha's parents still lived or had died. They also didn't know whether Shura was still alive. And there were other relatives, too, whose names I may never know, but whose faces remained in photos like this one of Leah and her sisters.

On the left, Leah Altman de Adler. To her right,
three sisters whose names and fates I do not know.
It's not impossible that all of them died in Transnistria.

Besides this, Misha had spent one or two years working as the director of the Institute for Colombian-Soviet Friendship, and during that time he had access to Soviet propaganda and forged friendships with high-ranking members of the Colombian Communist Party, as well as with personnel from the Soviet delegation. Misha and Noemí had no ambivalence at that time with respect to who were the good guys and who were the bad guys in the Great Struggle. It was true that there had been a pact between Stalin and Hitler, but it seemed perhaps justifiable in the face of Hitler's overwhelming military power; and after the war with the Soviet Union finally started, it was the Russians who managed to halt the German advance, something that nobody else had been able to do. The Russians had fought and won savage and devastating battles, like the Siege of Leningrad and the Battle of Stalingrad. The Red Army was a liberating force, there was no two ways about that.

To this, one must add the policy of nationalities that had caught Misha's attention since the last years of his youth. Given that Misha and Noemí both spoke fluent Russian, and the friendship that still prevailed among the Allies, I imagine that they thought that, no matter how remote or inhospitable the place might be, the "Judeo-Soviet homeland" could be a viable place in which to find and reunite their lost family members and then live in a Jewish cultural context.

Agustín Tisoy II

My family has in its possession a letter from Agustín Tisoy, dated December 11, 1943, from Santiago (Sibundoy Valley, in the Putumayo), directed to Dr. Miguel Adler, and written with excellent penmanship, with no lines crossed or words scratched out. It reads as follows:

My dear and most remembered Godfather:

If you are well and together with your family, this fills me with pleasure. I am well.

I am writing to you to express my gratitude for the honorable and complete manner in which you concerned yourself with my studies.

On November 30, I left Medellín to go to Putumayo, and on December 4, I arrived in the Sibundoy Valley, where I was well received. Everybody was so happy and quizzed me about life in the city, and they also asked about you and my godmother, and they all send their regards.

I did very well in my studies at the University of Antioquia; I received an award for my final exams, and I earned excellent grades this year; now some of my neighbors also wish to begin their studies.

I will continue studying at the University of Antioquia; but I also very fondly ask you after some years that you help me to transfer to Bogotá or to the United States.

This coming year I will finish the Ynga grammar, and I'll be very pleased to send it to my godmother Doña Elisa Noemí so that we might publish it.

I need a few copies of *Nuevo Mundo*, should you consider it possible to send them to me — the issue with my picture on the front.

In the name of my tribe, greetings to the entire family, especially to my godmother, and my thoughts and best wishes.

It is my pleasure once again to express my sincere gratitude for all your help.

Yours very truly,
Agustín Tisoy J.

This letter is interesting for a number of reasons. Agustín expresses his desire to continue his studies, which implies emigrating, ideally no longer to Medellín, but to Bogotá or even the United States. He wishes to continue educating himself in order to deepen his study and writing on his people. He mentions the project of developing an Ynga grammar, to be published through Misha. At the same time, he asks for a few copies of the issue of *Nuevo Mundo* that has his picture on the cover.

The letter also reflects the tensions that are associated with cultural mediation that native intellectuals have borne throughout Latin America: it becomes hard to stay in the native village, but also impossible to leave without deepening one's identification with it. Agustín wanted to leave, and he wanted to write Ynga grammars. In the person of an intellectual figure of great stature, like the Peruvian writer José María Arguedas, such tensions brought about the birth of new literary inventions, written in a Spanish that was markedly impacted by Quechua. But this sort of creative leap is very difficult to achieve indeed, and Agustín perhaps did not know how, or maybe he did not wish to make it.

The last news that my family received of Agustín Tisoy was that, thanks to his high level of education, and maybe even bolstered by his capacity to represent his people, demonstrated on the cover and in the pages of *Nuevo Mundo*, Agustín rose to the rank of cacique, and became a local political boss. In that lonely context, he then turned to alcohol. This was the difficult end of the young man who my grandfather believed might represent all of the pent-up potential of the New World.

The final period

In 1945 or 1946, Misha became gravely ill with typhoid fever, and was for a time on the brink of death. He was saved only by the recent discovery of penicillin. Even so, he was bedridden for several months, a situation that the Soviet legation took advantage of to sever its contract with him, without any workers' compensation that might help his family through such a difficult moment. Afterward, Misha's delicate health forced him to leave Bogotá. The family went to live in Sogamoso, a city not far from Medellín, that had the special benefit of being near the curative baths at Paipa, which my grandfather frequented regularly, following the doctors' orders.

My mother says that this episode marked the origin of her anticommunism: the absolute lack of solidarity on the part of the communists with the people who had been loyal to them. She also mentioned a second factor: she did not like the way in which the elite members of the Colombian Communist Party treated their servants. Larissa would have been around thirteen years old at this time: old enough to sniff out the hypocritical distance that existed between grand claims and intimate practice, and also mature enough to understand and suffer the precarious condition in which the Soviet embassy had left her parents.

The family went to Sogamoso, and my grandparents opened up a store in the Central Plaza there, across from the church: the Almacén del Día. This establishment distributed a variety of products, frequently purchased from providers who were friends, and that ranged from knitting wool to ornaments of Mexican onyx. Their real strength, though, was vinyl records, and they also sold RCA-Victor record players. It was thanks to those records, which ranchers from the region purchased, that my mother learned much of the popular music that she sang to us throughout her life.

Advertisement for Almacén del Día
in *Grancolombia*, July 1947.

One difficulty that came with moving out of Bogotá was that Larissa was still in high school, and Sogamoso had no secondary school for girls. The solution was typical of my grandparents, who never had money but always had friends. So Misha spoke to the director of the boys' high school, who was a Liberal, and managed (why not?) to enroll Larissa in his school as its only female student. The memory of this experience was one of my mother's favorite stories: the image of herself at fourteen, on the first day of class at an all-boys' school. The rumor of her entrance had already spread through the entire town. She would have to walk up an ample staircase to the school's second floor, which allowed the boys, who gathered in the patio to witness and comment on her entrance, to see her legs.

As the story went, the teachers gave Larissa the key to their bathroom, so that she didn't have to share that with her classmates. And the faculty soon noticed that the boys started to behave better than usual, because a young lady was present, and they felt grateful for the positive effect that my mother's presence had on the other students. Larissa soon became Miss Popularity at her high school, and she was even presented as the school's candidate for Queen of Spring.

This is a story that I heard since my childhood, including its more or less predictable denouement: Colombia still had its agreement with the Vatican that prohibited mixed education in public schools, and someone from one of the "good families" of Sogamoso complained about the presence of a young girl at the school. Since the director defended his decision to admit her — with support, besides, from teachers and students — the case went to the Ministry of Education. The government at that time was Liberal, so the file made its way up to the desk of the minister of education himself, who, in spite of his own best instincts, found himself compelled to comply with the terms of the Vatican accord.

Larissa thus had to leave Sogamozo for Bogotá at the start of the following school year. The American School in Bogotá was mixed-sex, and so an adequate place for Larissa's education.

By 1947, my grandfather's romance with the Soviet Union had ended, because news of Stalin's purges had finally reached him, and also because of his own experience with the embassy, but above all due to the accounts of people from Nova Sulitza who had survived the war. Totalitarianism could not be defended by a libertarian like my grandfather, who cited Saint-Just to justify his work on *Nuevo Mundo*. Together with the Soviet Union, the Americans had also been the great rescuers of Europe and of European Jewry. My grandparents thus had a positive attitude toward the United States, making it acceptable for Larissa to study at the American School.

My grandmother went to the capital and dropped off her only daughter, who was fifteen years old, at the house of a woman who had survived the Holocaust and who had arrived recently in Bogotá alone and very traumatized. The woman almost didn't speak at all, but she rented out a room to my mother. Before leaving her, Noemí told Larissa that she would never leave her alone in Bogotá if she did not believe Larissa to be an extraordinarily mature and responsible young woman. I think that this sense of premature responsibility, forged in a context of chronic precariousness, was also very present in my own upbringing.

Like her father when he arrived in Lima, Larissa dealt with her situation by making friends, and she ended up finding two excellent ones: Marcos Tychbrocher and Gerardo Gunsburger. They picked her up every day in the morning on the way to school and walked her home every afternoon. They went to the movies together. The three were inseparable.

Larissa with Gerardo Gunsburger,
in a signed farewell photo. Bogotá, c. 1949.

Grancolombia

In July 1947, a date that was selected to coincide with Colombian independence, my grandfather launched yet another weekly periodical printed on newspaper stock that was titled *Grancolombia*. It was a publication that supported "the solidarity and the culture of the neighboring countries of Colombia, Venezuela, Ecuador, and Panama." It was also "the authentic voice of the Jewish community of [Colombia], in the service of Jews around the world, of peace, of universal brotherhood, and justice toward every human."[193]

Grancolombia sought to create its own special niche: there was at that time no periodical in Colombia focused on Jewish culture, and I'm not sure if there were any in the other countries included in its scope. My grandfather had the recognition and the personal connections required to attract Jewish and non-Jewish intellectuals from all of these countries, as well as collaborations from other South American countries, notably Peru, Argentina, Uruguay, and Chile. *Grancolombia* wanted to be a collaborative space for Jewish and non-Jewish intellectuals. In this regard, it continued the spirit and idea that my grandfather had nursed since the publication of *Repertorio Hebreo*, and which he summarized in his opening editorial, stating that "our publication is an open tribune. The thought of free people will be favorably welcomed and respected in our pages... We wish to approach with great warmth the youth of these countries, and for them, Jews and non-Jews, we offer this journal, *Grancolombia*."[194]

The effort to create a medium of dialogue between Jews and non-Jews was carried forth from various different angles. In social terms, it mattered that *Grancolombia* stepped into a recognizable intellectual space, and not just any member of the Jewish community of Bogotá could have achieved this. In the first issue of the periodical, Misha situates himself in the local intellectual field: "Upon entering the family of American journalists," he writes, "I aspire to continue my defense of the democratic cause as I have done in Europe and also in this country from the space of my intellectual activities."[195] And he continued from here to name his intellectual associates and partners, from the cities of Medellín, Bogotá, and Caracas: Abel Naranjo Villegas, Otto Morales Benítez, Julio César Arroyave, Fernando González, Baldomero Sanín Cano, Luis Vidales, Armando Solano... The list is long, and with the exception of two names (Germán Arciniegas and Rómulo Gallegos), it was completely unknown to me, as I know little of Colombia. So I showed it to my friend María Victoria Uribe, a distinguished Colombian anthropologist, who did me the favor of identifying each one of the people mentioned. She later characterized the list as a whole in the following terms: "Your grandfather associated with the best-known Colombian intellectuals of the time, many of them Liberals, some freethinkers, and others communists."[196] This was the network of friends that Misha wanted to attract and bring into the pages of *Grancolombia*.

Bogotazo

On April 9, 1948, Jorge Eliécer Gaitán, the Liberal Party presidential candidate and champion of the downtrodden, was murdered. This assassination produced expressions of collective grief and distress that are reminiscent in some ways of the murder of Martin Luther King Jr. and they sparked a day of enraged rioting, looting, and destruction — known as the Bogotazo — that was followed by the nation's descent into a ten-year spiral of violence, known as La Violencia, ostensibly between Gaitán's peasant supporters and their opponents in the Conservative Party. Gaitán was a popular leader whose platform converged with that of the Mexican Revolution — agrarian reform, anti-imperialism, defense of the workers. His assassination fractured Colombian political life for decades, maybe even into the present. For this reason, Colombians still think of the Bogotazo as a turning point in the nation's history, a moment that left a very deep mark.

My mother was at school that day, but when Gaitán was murdered it was immediately closed and all the children were sent home. Accompanied as always by Marcos and Gerardo, Larissa witnessed looting and the closing of the city firsthand. She then had the presence of mind to go with her friends to a radio station that was sending news to the people of Bogotá and to their relatives in the provinces. Telephone lines had been cut and transportation was interrupted. For all intents and purposes, the capital had been cut off from the world, so that only the radio remained to let family in the provinces know that you were safe. My mother sent a message to Tuluá saying that she was fine.

Some of Boris's neighbors heard the news, and they went over to his house to tell everyone. Misha, for some reason, had set off for Bogotá precisely on April 9, but he got stuck on the way. Meanwhile, my mother went to the building in which her uncle Zuñe (Misha's brother) and her aunt Pupe (Noemí's sister) lived. For reasons that I still don't understand, neither of them was especially concerned about her situation, and they let Larissa return to the place where she was staying. Walking along the streets of Bogotá, my mother ran into a naval officer who knew the family from Sogamoso; he greeted her affectionately, and expressed concern that she was alone in the city. She explained to him that she was trying to get to Tuluá, and he accompanied her to the airport and arranged air transport to Cali. From there, my mother took the train to Tuluá, and arrived at her grandfather's house safe and sound and without further trouble.

This is the history that I have about my family during the Bogotazo. A trivial anecdote maybe, and thankfully one without any great consequences. Nevertheless, the Bogotazo and the endemic violence that followed it is part of the backdrop for my family's history during its final years in Colombia.

Why emigrate?

From the time of the *Repertorio Hebreo*, my grandparents' work had a Zionist element, but it accelerated strongly after the end of the war and with the chaos in which it left both the Jewish world and Europe. In this sense, their decision to leave for Israel immediately after receiving the news of its independence seems perfectly consequential. The attraction of Eretz Israel, the idea of having one's own place, one's own language, a history and a culture that could be upheld common; the idea of being able to construct a fully Jewish version of modernity and to regenerate the people after the implacable destruction to which it had been submitted, was a magnet that must have been attractive.

Nova Sulitza no longer existed except as a network that was scattered throughout the world. Misha's family members who had remained there were all dead. That entire world was gone. Shura was alive, but the family didn't know this yet, and in any case, the possibility of returning to the Soviet Union made no sense and no longer held any attraction, besides the fact that their one attempt to gain a visa to go there had failed. Israel truly presented itself as the promised land where the family might establish itself and finally gain some stability.

Even so, I believe that a decision to emigrate cannot be understood well if one doesn't consider the dynamics between the place to which one is drawn and the one being left behind. What were my grandparents' perspectives with regard to this migration out of America? What were they leaving behind? What horizons might now be opened to them? Those are hard questions to answer.

The existence of the journal *Grancolombia* in itself indicates at least some ambivalence with respect to the idea of emigrating. It was an ambitious editorial project that looked to the future and was not just a pamphlet designed to convince people to move to Israel. Its ambitions were to open up a discussion in the countries of "Greater Colombia," in other words, my grandfather developed *Grancolombia* within a properly South American sphere. As part of the project, *Grancolombia* announced that its parent company, Ediciones Nuevomundo, would also publish historical monographs on each one of the countries of Greater Colombia. This clearly implied a project extending beyond the short term.

An ad for Ediciones Nuevomundo,
directed by Misha Adler.

In that same vein (i.e., that of a possible Colombian future), the first issue of *Grancolombia* announces that beginning in October 1947, the *Revista Nuevomundo* would now be relaunched, and would now appear on a monthly basis. *Grancolombia* also loudly announced its section editors and contributors: the journalist Carlos Delgado Nieto; the writer Salomón Brainsky; the historian Gustavo Jiménez Cohen; the artist Antonio Valencia Mejía; Bernardo Jipkevish and Isaac Brener, of the new generation of Colombian Jews; León Klar to edit a section devoted to chess; the writers Enrique Buenaventura, Manuel González Martínez, and Alejandro Vallejo; and the journalists Rafael Rash and Pablo Balcázar, among others.[197] My grandfather would hardly have gone to such lengths to gather such a well-regarded crew and announce their collective commitment to the future of *Grancolombia* had he already taken a firm decision to emigrate. On the contrary, it seems clear that in 1947, when the independence of Israel was already imminent, emigration was not yet a part of my grandfather's plans.

One of the factors that may have weighed in favor of emigration was their children's Jewish education. My grandfather could no longer live in Bogotá, which was at the end of the day the center of the Colombian Jewish community. Larissa had not been able to attend a Jewish school even for one year of her education. There also certainly existed the idea that Jewish children should come to know Israel and develop within an environment that would make them strong. Ilya, the youngest of the family, had been born in August 1945, barely three months after Germany's surrender. In him, there was new life that needed to be nurtured much more urgently than any impulse to tarry too long over the dead. It was necessary to look to the future. Perhaps the desire to congregate, aggregate, and strengthen oneself is irresistible in a moment like that.

I don't think there was a very clear idea of what the economic implications of moving to Israel might have been. Starting over is always hard, and in Colombia, my grandparents had many friends. And while Misha and Noemí weren't doing very well economically, they at least had a modest survival more or less secure, given their high level of education, the support they could receive from Boris in times of emergency, and the network of relatives and friends that was already successfully established in Bogotá. In Israel, it was possible that this might not be the case. There would be the old friends that they might find from the Romanian Hashomer Hatzair network as well as from South America, obviously, but beyond this there were no guarantees. From an economic perspective, leaving for Israel was a risky decision for a middle-aged couple that had four children to care for.

Another thing that may have influenced their decision was the violence that began to spread to the Cauca region right after the assassination of Gaitán and the Bogotazo. There were signs and events that may well have worried them. First, diplomatic relations with the Soviet Union were cut after the assassination of Gaitán, because of the initial rumor, fed by the right, that both the murder and the riots were the result of a communist plot. The Institute for Colombian-Soviet Friendship was burned down during the riots, and although by 1948 my grandparents were disillusioned with the Soviet Union, they may have felt vulnerable in the face of a rising anticommunist wave. Moreover, some prominent leaders of the Conservative Party were characterizing the Liberal uprising after the Gaitán assassination as a "Judeo-Masonic plot."[198] Misha and Noemí had already left Peru because of that sort of talk. They may not have wanted to continue living in such an environment.

Also, at the time of the Bogotazo, the family was living in Cali, and there was a Liberal uprising in that city after Gaitán's assassination that left twenty-five people dead and more than a hundred injured. This was countered in 1949 by the systematic persecution and murder of many members of the Liberal Party.[199] My grandparents may have been afraid that this polarization would reduce their possibilities of employment. Or maybe they lost someone they knew. In the end, what political guarantees did they have in Colombia?

My grandfather's sense of pride may also have influenced their decision to leave. Over the years, Misha had been forced to ask for help on different occasions. In Peru, in the wake of the Leguía coup, his old shipmates, young "Romanians" like him, had bailed him out. I'm sure that it didn't pain him especially to receive their help, but in Colombia Misha had been forced more than once to rely on his father-in-law's largesse. Boris had not been supportive of his beautiful and brilliant oldest daughter's marriage to a figure as quixotic as my grandfather, nor did he sympathize with the latter's relatively favorable opinion of the Soviet Union, since Boris and Tania had lost a daughter and several relatives fleeing that regime.

I can't imagine that it was easy for Misha to ask his father-in-law for help, even if only occasionally. With the breakout of La Violencia and the accompanying surge of Conservative power in Valle del Cauca, it likely crossed my grandfather's mind that if the situation in Cali got worse, it might become necessary once again to seek employment through Boris. Leaving for Israel would allow my grandparents to frame the entire Colombian experience as an extended parenthesis, conditioned by war and exile, and it offered that intrepid couple the imagined possibility of a new beginning.

I enter once again the terrain of speculation here. What I now write isn't supported by any hard evidence except that it follows a certain logic. In proceeding in this way, I'm well aware that I may be wholly mistaken. In spite of those risks, though, I still would like to offer an interpretation.

My grandparents were both Zionists from their childhood in Eastern Europe. Nevertheless, because of questions of age and the politics of the time, my grandfather didn't manage to emigrate to Palestine as a young man, and my grandmother was still quite young when her family left for Peru. Although the couple kept alive their Zionist sympathies while they resided in Lima, their time and energy there were spent waging a universal battle, of which Judaism formed but a part. Nevertheless, the death of Mariátegui, imprisonment, and their expulsion from Peru was a blow from which the young couple could not recover easily, in spite of the formal course of study that Misha had been able to undertake in Paris.

The reason for this is tough to evaluate. It is possible that Misha didn't have the necessary drive or talent to become a successful intellectual or writer, but such an explanation will always be hard to believe or accept for a grandson who loved him and admired him as much as I did. I think, rather, that circumstances complicated everything for Misha. First, from Paris he had decided to go to Nova Sulitza, where he spent two years trying to get people out. It was an urgent decision, but surely it had a professional cost. Afterward, in emigrating to Colombia, he knew how important it was for Noemí to remain close to her parents, and this is why they settled in Cali rather than Bogotá. Then there was the urgency of establishing Jewish education for the community and the difficulty of setting this up. And, as ever, his antifascist activism. But, above all, their Colombian residency coincided with the years during which they had their children, and Misha and Noemí were obligated to focus on supporting their family. The combination of all of these factors shaped their decision to leave for Israel. The decision represented for them a new beginning, in a land where they would be fully accepted, and where they could and would obtain citizenship. Besides this, perhaps Israel would allow Misha to take up once again the intellectual career that had been interrupted at each step by more practical matters.

There is, as a matter of fact, a small bit of evidence that supports this interpretation, and it is the letter that Misha wrote to Paul Rivet from Israel in 1953, in which he tells his former teacher that he still hopes to form a Center for American Ethnological Investigation in Israel. The letter begins: "Although I have not lost the hope completely to free myself one day from the hard struggle for my family's material existence, and to apply yet the energy, curiosity, and limited intellectual capacity that I possess to the Science of Man and the mutual comprehension between the races and peoples of the world."[200]

It is likely that Misha had lost any hope of being able to realize such a project in Colombia, and that his thinking now was that with a bit of luck he might yet be able to straighten out the path that the war had bent and overcome the setbacks he had encountered first in Peru and later in Colombia.

CHAPTER FIFTEEN

The Limits of Translation

Boris's associates

With Tania's death, Noemí's father, Boris, returned to Tuluá. He was a hard worker, and he labored from sunup to sundown. He was not one to stir up trouble, nor did he tend to have problems with others. He was, on the contrary, a man who loved his routine. One time, worried about Boris's health, my uncle Manuel asked his grandfather why he didn't stop drinking strong coffee and smoking his cigar each morning. Annoyed by the question, Boris gave him a terse response: "I've had this routine my entire life, and I'm not going to change it. End of discussion."[201]

I wonder if a zeal for routine was also behind Boris's decision to remarry. Roughly two years after Tania's death, Boris married a Jewish widow who was also a Yiddish speaker and the owner of a farm in Palmira. Her name was Luisa Blanc or Blank. But the marriage got off to a rocky start, and they divorced after two years. Shortly afterward, Boris married a different woman, also a widow from the community, a Dora Gutt de Finvarb, and that marriage did last.

I've already said that Boris's soap mill was essentially a copy of the one that he had run in Mogilev. This in itself can be read as a testament to Boris's interest in routine, but we could also say, to be more exact, that Boris was intrigued by translation; that is, he was interested in accomplishing in America what he had done in Ukraine. He wanted to change while staying the same. He wanted to run a soap mill and engage in the manufacture and sale of railroad ties in Tuluá as he had in Mogilev; both were small cities that presented no competition for the soap mill, and neither was too far from an important urban center: Odessa in the case of Mogilev, and Cali in the case of Tuluá.

Of course, there were also opportunities in America that did not exist for Jews in Ukraine, such as owning agricultural land. In fact, once Boris's Tuluá businesses were set up, he acquired a farm in the nearby town of Río Frío, next to the Fenicia River, that was called Tesorito (Little Treasure). He also provided capital for the first transport company between Fenicia and Tuluá, which he and his partners called Transportes Fenicia.

Who were Boris's local contacts? There was, in this too, something of the transfer of his Ukrainian experience to the Colombian context. According to family lore, Boris was known to "have a drink with the goyim" in Ukraine, which is a way of saying that he had formed alliances with non-Jewish Ukrainians and Russians. In Tuluá, too, Boris had solid connections outside of the Jewish community. For example, he bought his house on Calle 31 as well as the lot next to it (on which he built his soap mill and a wood storage facility) from a neighbor, José Obdulio Acevedo. Boris's Tesorito farm was next to La Graciela, a property also owned by Obdulio Acevedo, and both were partners in Transportes Fenicia, which was created by a small group of partners from Tuluá when the road to Río Frío was built. Boris's relationship with Obdulio Acevedo would be of great importance during the final years of his life.

Boris also maintained relationships with the small Jewish communities that had taken root in Tuluá, Buga, Palmira, and Cali. I know very little about these communities (when they arrived, etc.), but according to the information that Alvarez Gardeazábal has provided, there were Jewish families in Tuluá from at least the 1930s or 1940s: the Alcalays, the Nagys, the Chapavals, the Translateurs, and the Suttons. There was also the Levy family, who were Boris's neighbors. Adolfo Levy was the owner of a sawmill, and Boris met him through his railroad tie business. As I've mentioned, Boris also had sawmills in Manizales and Medellín.

I'm not sure to what extent the Jewish community was economically important for Boris's business activities. It may not have been all that important; according to one version, he was not very close to the other Jewish families of Tuluá. The impression one gets is that the Jewish community was important to Boris mostly for emotional support and familial relations—he remarried twice within the community, for example. Boris also had at least one partner (Levy) and some providers or buyers from the community, but non-Jews also filled some of those same roles.

Violence in Tuluá

Gaitán was killed on April 9, 1948. Larissa witnessed the violence that followed this murder, the Bogotazo, but without a real understanding of its significance. When I asked my uncle Manuel if the violence affected Boris's business, he replied that he felt that it may have affected the ranch a bit, given the banditry that took place shortly afterward, but not the soap business, the transports, or the railroad tie operation. He remembered that near Fenicia, where the ranch was, there was a place known as the ravine of the dead, down to which the authorities would venture on Mondays to recover bodies and try to identify them. Later they would be buried, usually in a mass grave.

Despite this macabre memory, Manuel doubted that the violence had affected Tuluá's economy or Boris to any great degree. The unidentified bodies that the authorities buried in the common graves had been deliberately thrown into the ravine, and they were not the bodies of locals. Nevertheless, I think that Boris, and perhaps also Misha and Noemí, made a conscious decision to protect the family from the fear caused by La Violencia, because Gaitán's murder unleashed a brutal wave of violence in the region of Tuluá, where a Conservative militia worked to cleanse the countryside of Liberals. Gardeazábal's powerful novel tells how each night the bodies of the dead would flow down the Cauca River:

> *El Siglo* says that they were Conservatives, and *El Tiempo* that they were Liberals, but in La Virginia, where they pulled them

out with their bellies about to burst, their faces chewed up by fish, and their limbs almost always fractured by beatings, none of the dead carried identification papers; and since it was difficult to carry them anywhere in that state of putrefaction, they simply took them from the river and buried them among the other unnamed dead, whose presence steadily grew in the cemeteries of Colombia.[202]

The unnamed dead appeared daily in Tuluá between 1949 and 1953. Their anonymity provoked all manner of rumors, both with respect to who they were and to why they died. Little by little, killing became contagious and its causes evolved from political assassinations to personal vendettas, land grabs, and even the murder of neutral parties simply because they had stubbornly remained neutral. Those thought to be traitors were murdered, and then eventually those who just dared to speak out. Thousands of people were killed in the region around Tuluá during the first four years of La Violencia.

Sectarian violence must have affected Boris one way or another. He had lived in Ukraine during the First World War, the Russian Revolution, the civil wars that followed it, and also the ferocious pogroms carried out by Ukrainian nationalists against Jews in the region in that same period. Boris had remained steadfast through all of that. He milled soap and defended himself and his family, until the day came when he was threatened directly and forced to flee, losing his daughter and his mother-in-law along the way, and living always after with his wife, Tania, grieving over a daughter who might have remained alive and completely unprotected.

Boris would have had no taste for the ideological polarization between Liberals and Conservatives that had now escalated to a level of hatred he knew all too well. I don't know if my great-grandfather was a supporter of Gaitán. He read the *Forverts* and had a daughter and son-in-law who were leftists, so he may have been a supporter, but the similarities between Gaitán's oratory and the Russian agitation from his past may have bothered him, so I'm not sure. On the other hand, it was not easy for Boris to identify himself as a *Godo* (Conservative) either: he wasn't Catholic, and his daughter and son-in-law were both Marxists. Regardless of his ideological sympathies, I'm certain that Boris looked with great concern as the society that had taken him in split in two.

Gardeazábal's novel explains how Tuluá was taken by Conservative forces. When Gaitán was murdered, a throng of Liberal peasants entered the town and burned down the Angel Theater, looted the main store, passed around liquor, hanged a Conservative from the bell tower, and tried to set fire to the Salesian school. The reaction of the local Conservative elite, allied with that of Cali and Buga, was to enlist a local cheese vendor from the market — a man who was at once known to be very brave, ignorant, and fanatically devoted to the Church and the Conservative Party — to arm a local militia to defend the city "from the extermination of all Conservatives, of all religious communities, and above all the Christian faith."[203]

The leader of that militia was known as "The Condor," and his militiamen came to be referred to as his "birds" (*pájaros*). They made their rounds in blue automobiles, in a campaign designed to "cleanse" all of the surrounding countryside of Liberals. Gardeazábal calculates that there were upwards of 3,500 murders in the Tuluá region during the first four years of La Violencia, the great majority of the victims either Liberals or neutral parties. Toward the end of The Condor's reign of terror, he also began to kill a few select members of the old Liberal political elite — high-profile figures from some of Tuluá's oldest leading families. After one of these murders, against which even a local priest lodged a protest, "everyone closed up shop, put everything up for sale, or just left it all to the grace of God before escaping on the first train or the last regional bus that still stopped in the city."[204] Thus, in the years just before his death, Boris again faced the kind of political polarization he had left behind in Ukraine, and also saw his businesses suffer on account of the violence.

Still, there were factors that protected him. First, since he was Jewish and a foreigner, he could not be identified as either Liberal or Conservative. In the countryside, they referred to Boris as "el Míster," and his foreignness mitigated the danger he might otherwise have faced. Boris was also Obdulio Acevedo's neighbor and partner, and the latter was one of the organizers of the local Conservative militia; that is, he was the head of a group of "birds." Because of this, Boris almost certainly enjoyed the protection of the faction that controlled Tuluá. Finally, some of Boris's businesses were shielded from the violence: his sawmills in Tuluá and Manizales suffered very little, because the construction of Colombian railroads wasn't interrupted by the violence, and the government was his main client. The milling of soap likewise went on pretty much as usual, as this product usually enjoys steady demand. It is certain that his finca suffered greatly, but I don't know whether his transport business likewise suffered some adverse effect. In short, the violence did not ruin Boris, although it may have affected his finances to some degree.

It is nonetheless quite likely that the image of calm, routine, and serenity that Manuel remembers from 1953, a few months before Boris's death, was kept up despite a violent situation that affected everything around him. It occurs to me that Boris's calm and his unshakable insistence on routine were both, from the beginning, powerful coping mechanisms in a life that had been so deeply marked by violence. Boris had no desire to change his way of life because of some new upheaval. A life of work and routine were, in the end, his way of confronting uncertainty.

Boris's two deaths

My great-grandfather, Boris Milstein, died of a heart attack in Tuluá on January 11, 1954. This was his second heart attack. After the first, he traveled to the famous Mayo Clinic in the United States to be evaluated by the doctors there. A short time afterward, my uncle Manuel, who was then seventeen years old, visited him in Tuluá and spent some time with him before going on to Bogotá. Manuel found him to be as he ever was, with his unchanging daily routine, and so on.

Later that spring, Manuel received news of his beloved grandfather's death. He wasn't able to attend the funeral, at the Jewish cemetery in Cali, because of the religious practice of burying the dead within twenty-four hours of their passing. However, Manuel did eventually see Isaac Perlman, Dora Gutt, and several of Boris's friends who were by then in Bogotá, and he confirmed to the family that "there was never any reason to question the certified cause of death: myocardial infarction."[205]

This is the same version of events known by my mother and all the other members of my family to whom I have spoken. I believe that story. Still, I am a historian, and that compels me to weigh diverging sources, when these appear; and there exists, in this case, a second version of Boris's death, the source of which is Inés Acevedo, the daughter of José Obdulio Acevedo, Boris's neighbor and business partner.

At the beginning of June 2017, as one of Gustavo Alvarez Gardeazábal's many priceless acts of generosity, he decided to investigate some of the details related in this book. This involved interviewing the remaining old-timers who might remember Boris, and so Gustavo went to Río Frío, where Boris's ranch had been, to interview Señora Acevedo, who was then eighty-nine years old but still perfectly lucid. Inés remembered Boris and his family perfectly. She even cried when Gustavo showed her a photo of them that I had sent him. Inés remembered the story of their escape from Ukraine, the loss of a daughter on the journey, and many other important details. She also had information on Boris's farm, which was adjacent to that of her family. She remembered that they had bought it from Juvenal Villa, who belonged to a family from Santa Rosa del Cabal. All of her memories checked out, except one: Inés affirmed that Boris had died from a cerebral hemorrhage caused by a blow to the head. In other words, Boris died as the result of an attack.

His killer was a certain Carlos Arbeláez, who hit him over the head with the butt of his pistol in the offices of Boris's transport business, Transportes Fenicia, the company in which Inés's father, Obdulio Acevedo, was a partner. Roughly two years after Boris's death, Carlos Arbeláez was himself killed, just as he was planning to murder Inés's husband. Upon hearing the news, Inés told Gustavo Alvarez that she felt that "Divine Justice had made him pay for what he had done to Don Boris."[206]

Neither of the two versions of Boris's death has any eyewitnesses left for corroboration, and there are no police records for Boris's or Carlos Arbeláez's deaths, something that is common for murders during that time in that place, since there were thousands being murdered. One can suspect motives for distorting the truth in each of the two versions of Boris's death. In the case of my family's version, there are no survivors from my grandmother's generation to interview; and it is certainly possible that the members of this generation decided to cover up any news of an attack as cause of death.

The possible motives for hiding this could have been that death by murder was considered shameful, most particularly in the Jewish community, since it might imply that the victim was quarrelsome or had enemies, or else that he or she did not lead an honest life. Moreover, my mother's generation had already suffered enough: the loss of Shura, the murder of Misha's parents, and those other, uncountable murders that had taken place both in Nova Sulitza and in Mogilev. There is, moreover, a document from the period, though a very ambiguous one, that leaves open the possibility of a family cover-up with respect to the true cause of Boris's death. It is the first letter that Shura sent, from the Soviet Union, to my grandmother Noemí about a year after Boris' death, in 1955.

Shura

I don't know the exact channel—if it was through the Red Cross or through some Jewish organization—but some years after the end of the war, maybe around 1948, my grandparents received news about Shura. She had survived the war! Still, the investigative letters sent by Boris and Noemí took almost seven years to reach Shura's hands, due to the displacements caused by the war and the general conditions of the region in those years. For this reason, the first letter that Shura sent to her older sister Noemí is from 1955, around a year after Boris's death. It begins like this: "Hello my dear Lisa, Misha, and children. After seven years, I finally received a letter saying that some of you are alive." And farther down she writes: "For many years, my heart has told me that father was dead, and I understand that the last two letters I sent arrived in Tuluá, and that they have given them to you."

If I correctly understand what is implied in this opening— which carries a strong emotional charge according to Xenia Cherkaev, the young colleague and friend who did me the favor of translating Shura's letters from Russian to English—the identity of the person who first contacted Shura remains a little ambiguous. It seems like the first letter that she got came from an organization, rather than directly from her father or sister, since Shura says: "I finally received the letter saying that some of you are alive." She then says that she sent two letters to Tuluá, which finally arrived in Noemí's hands. Noemí answered those letters directly, informing Shura, among other things, that their father had died. This is the sequence of events that is implicit in Shura's opening lines.

The envelope of the first letter sent from Shura to Noemí,
sent to the family's address in Cali (Calle 25 Norte 5-46).

It is also understood that the two letters that Shura had sent earlier, when she was contacted by the Red Cross or some other organization, did not reach Boris, and that Shura, in turn, never received a letter from her father. The letter that she was now answering would thus have come from Noemí, and it would have been written from Cali, rather than from Tuluá. It must have been a long letter, in which Noemí told Shura of her marriage to Misha, of their children, of how their sister Pupe was doing, of Tania's death, which had occurred thirteen years earlier, and finally of Boris's recent passing.

Shura later asks for more information, including about a couple of family members whom I've never heard of (Lisa and Yasha), and she explains that she has a husband and two children, and that they are all well. Shura points out that of their family, "very few have survived, and we must maintain a close correspondence," adding later that she would like very much to see Noemí, because her story is like a novel. She then adds the following sentence: "All my hope of seeing you has evaporated."

The entire letter is heartbreaking and a bit disheveled, written in a sharp emotional pitch.

Sheet from the first letter that Shura
sent to her sister Noemí, 1955.

At the beginning of the letter, Shura says something that makes me suspect the possibility that there was indeed something secretive or hidden in Boris's manner of death. She says: "I ask you, my dear sister, that you tell me, precisely and with complete openness, the truth regarding everything that happened to Father: what and how it happened, who now lives in his house, and where Pupe is..." And then, at the end of the letter, Shura again insists: "Write in detail about Father, and what and how it happened to him."

For me, these phrases leave open the possibility that there was indeed something delicate to explain with respect to the circumstances of Boris's death, that it was not just a heart attack, which was a common cause of death during that time and presumably required little explanation. Maybe Shura was simply asking Noemí for further details about their father's final moments, but the fact that she asks her for "openness" suggests that there was something more mysterious in the story that my grandmother had written to her sister, when she let her know of their father's death. Shura's letter thus requires us to leave open the hypothesis that Boris was attacked and that he died from to a blow delivered by Carlos Arbeláez.

CHAPTER SIXTEEN

Dialectic of Silence

Column

In my family's history, there is a type of figure. Or maybe it is best described as a syndrome rather than as a subject or a kind of person. Let's call it the *column syndrome*. The column props up, buffers, protects, and endures. Of the Roman temples there mostly survive only the bases and columns as enduring vestiges. Boris had this syndrome, as did his daughter Noemí. My mother and Manuel had it, and they passed it on to me.

Boris was the support for his family in Yaruga and Mogilev. A column. He served as a local representative in Yaruga. Column. Patron. Column. He pulled his family out of the Soviet Union during their moment of greatest danger. Column. He made the decision to leave Shura and Revka behind. Column. He was his family's provider in Colombia. Column.

His oldest daughter, my grandmother Noemí, was, if this is possible, an even stronger column than Boris. Noemí was easily annoyed by anything that smacked of whining or self-pity. Unlike her husband, Misha, she also viewed *indigenismo* with some suspicion, and for a reason that was at once aesthetic and moral: she was repulsed by "the lament of the Indian." I remember her explaining to me, in her apartment in San Bernardino (Caracas), that she was couldn't stand "Andean lamentations," and she added: "I like the culture of the blacks. Nobody has suffered more than them. They were slaves, they have been discriminated against, and they are poor. But they celebrate life and emphasize joyfulness."

In the same way, and for analogous reasons, my grandmother favorably compared the new Venezuelan folklore with its Chilean and Argentinian counterparts. She and Misha had been neighbors and friends of composer and singer Violeta Parra in Santiago, at the beginning of the 1960s. This circumstance filled me with admiration, because Violeta was at that time like a religion to me. Except that to my horror, my grandmother said in a matter-of-fact way that Violeta was crazy, and that she irritated her with so much fussing and whining. Noemí then finished by saying that she preferred to listen to the Venezuelan groups Quinteto Contrapunto and Serenata Guayanesa, which were joyful rather than so very mournful. It was a horrible thought for me at the time, but I now think that maybe she had a point.

My grandmother's impatience with sentimentalism and her respect for use value extended to many other domains. Noemí hated the aristocracy both as a class and as an aspiration, and everything that she considered decadent. She hated antiques, too, and she loved the modern, the new. For the same reasons, she also felt a generalized antipathy for Europe, and for England most especially. On the contrary, she loved all of America, including the United States, which was a beacon of modernity. I can't remember which English writer said that the United States lacked two things: souls and antiques. My grandmother would have taken that as a good thing. At times she exaggerated a bit with all of this. The Beatles, for instance, irritated her. One time, I was listening to "I Wanna Hold Your Hand!" and my grandmother muttered, "English. Decadent."

Silence

Maybe the column metaphor isn't exact, because the work done by family members who serve as columns is not only to prop up, but also to buffer or cushion. The blows that the world inflicted on my grandparents' generation were simply too violent for the family to emerge unscathed. There were always irreparable losses.

Boris "saved the family," true, but he also lost his daughter. Despite having run the considerable risk of returning to Bessarabia during the mid-1930s, Misha failed to get his parents out of Nova Sulitza. There isn't a column made that can withstand such magnitudes of disaster, and part of the work of the column quickly becomes to absorb the blows and attenuate them for others so that they don't lose hope. Hope and serenity. This means that the role of column comes with a communicative function — to be a source of practical wisdom, to be sure, but also to temper or soften news so that fear doesn't spin into vertigo and paralysis, so that depression doesn't become overwhelming, and blows don't prove fatal.

To understand how this works, it is useful to reconsider our two versions of Boris's death. As I've already said, there were good motives to hide the fact that Boris had been attacked, if this was in fact the case. There is the anguish of picturing Boris, an old man living alone with his elderly wife, conducting business in a context of widespread violence, being brutally attacked without anyone in place to defend him. There is a frustrated desire to protect the protector. There is also the ameliorating fact that even if Arbeláez did attack Boris as Inés Acevedo said, his blow was not Boris's immediate cause of death. Acevedo herself remembers it that way. According to her version of the events, Boris died about a month after the attack. Mentioning the attacker would in this case only serve to diminish Boris's life and aggrandize an insignificant figure (Arbeláez). It was more faithful to the character and person that Boris had been to narrate his death as a case of natural causes; or if not this, then to describe it as an accident. And this, indeed, is what Shura ended up doing for her daughter, Rita. According to what Rita told me (through her daughter, Ilana), her mother had told her that Boris had died in a car accident.[207]

There is also the not inconsequential issue of how guilty a child can feel upon learning of a parent's death when they are far away. The guilt of not having been there, or of having been doing something pleasant or even just something normal at the precise time that their loved one was suffering. Visiting a friend, maybe. Eating with the family. Beginning a new endeavor...

If Boris was attacked and the family was far away, the family was unable to protect him, just as he had been unable to protect Shura. And by the mid-1950s, when Boris died, the war was over, and one might well understand if the family just wanted some peace. It wished to move on to another generation and to another moment. Following this logic, it was thus maybe easier to blunt the pain of this unexpected blow, which was now brought on by Colombian violence. If this is in fact what happened, then Boris's three daughters, Noemí, Shura, and Pupe, had all agreed to form a column among themselves.

Concerns

The third characteristic of columns is that they feel compelled to care for others: they even express worries and concerns that they never felt with regard to themselves. The most characteristic expression of my grandfather Misha, whose life was filled not only with adventures but also with very risky decisions, was "Dangerous!" Misha was constantly watching out for anything that might be dangerous for others. An open window: "Dangerous!" A child playing six feet away from that same open window: "*Mamash* [truly] dangerous!"

He was a column, a buffer, and a sentinel in a world of unmanageable dangers.

And Boris died in a hospital bed. Probably from a heart attack.

PART FOUR

National Liberation

Israel

The family left from Puerto Aventura (Colombia) for Israel in 1949, just a year after independence. Misha, for his part, took a more circuitous route. According to my mother, the US government had denied him a visa because of his earlier association with the Soviet Union (the Cold War had begun by then), and the plan was for the family to sail to Israel by way of New York. According to Manuel, my mother was wrong, and their father accompanied them as far as New York, and then went his separate way. According to Mauricio, their father traveled to Marseilles instead of Haifa, to help Eastern European refugees who were still leaving that region make their way toward Israel. I haven't been able to corroborate any of this, each version is certainly possible, and whatever the case, it is certain that Misha arrived in Israel about three months after the rest of the family.

The family sailed first from Puerto de Buenaventura, Colombia, to New York. While in Manhattan, they stayed at the Greystone Hotel, which is not far from where I now live, and from New York they sailed to Israel. The ship itself was a liberating experience for Larissa, who found herself surrounded by Jewish teenagers for the first time, and many of them shared the same socialist ideals as her family. For a girl who had spent her life passing as Catholic, or saying that her name was "Alicia" because her real name sounded perhaps too "Polish," this was an altogether new sensation.

When they arrived in Israel, Noemí tried to place the family in a kibbutz run by the Hashomer Hatzair. They showed up there one night with no prior warning, but the members of the kibbutz couldn't accept them because those were difficult times and of the five family members, only my grandmother and my mother were old enough to work. The kibbutz was not in a position to feed the three younger children. As a result, they were taken to a *Beit Olim* — a refugee camp — in Lod.

Once at the camp, Noemí, who was always very resourceful, offered up her services as a translator for the refugees, since she spoke German, Russian, Yiddish, Hebrew, Romanian, Spanish, and French, as well as some English. Her offer was accepted, and the family was given a house whose former occupants had left it as part of the large Palestinian exodus of 1948, a phenomenon Palestinians refer to as the *Nakba* (Disaster). I will never know how my grandmother felt about that. The creation of national states that were being carved out from the old British Empire was then generating ethnic and religious violence and displacement in a number of regions; the formation of a Jewish national state had sparked a war, created a new diaspora, and was turning the Palestinian people into a "minority" in lands that had for the most part been theirs. Even so, my family felt that the Jewish people had legitimate claims in Palestine, and that national recognition for the Jewish people was an indispensable achievement that offered the family a place where they might be relieved from the constant strain of assimilation and resistance, preserved from the constant threat of persecution, and finally live freely among themselves.

Misha (*right*) with a Dr. Zapler, upon his arrival
in Netanya, Israel, November 1949.

When Misha arrived in Israel, the family moved to the Sha'ar ha-Amakim kibbutz, in the north of Israel. It was inhabited mainly by Serbian and Romanian Jews, and there were even some folks from Nova Sulitza there. Misha worked in construction as an engineer's assistant in that kibbutz. He didn't have much talent for this work, though, so he got a job as a teacher outside of the kibbutz, in the city of Petah Tikva.

The family (minus Larissa) in front of the house in Petah Tikvah (Shikun Fedya, B.84). It is an iconic depiction of the idea of Eretz Israel — a land where one could live free and modestly, cultivating the land and remaining in harmony with the body.

Misha worked as a Hebrew teacher, first in a school associated with a moshav (a kind of agricultural collective), and finally in a more prestigious secondary school, Seminar le-Morim, in Ein Shemer. Neither of those places was close to their home, so Misha had a substantial commute. Meanwhile, my grandfather's intellectual aspirations were still very much in place; thus, at that time he wrote to his former teacher, Paul Rivet, that he had not completely lost "the hope of freeing myself one day from the hard struggle for the material existence of my family, to apply the rest of my energy, curiosity, and the meager intellectual capacity that remains, to the Science of Man."[208]

Misha with his students in a moshav near Petah Tikva.

According to my mother, my grandfather's pride prevented him from asking favors from old friends who were already well established in Israel when they got there. Hannah Lamdan, for instance, had been part of Misha's same *kvutzah* in Nova Sulitza, and she went on to become the director of the leftist party Mapai and a member of the Knesset. There was also Yitzhak Ben-Aharon, who had introduced Misha to Noemí, and who was also a member of the Knesset. But Misha refused to bother either of them even to ask the favor of being transferred to a different school. My mother remembered all of this very well, and I believe that my grandfather was in fact a proud man, and that pride may have exacerbated the difficulties that he faced while trying to establish himself in Israel.

Misha tells Rivet that he had begun "serious and insistent efforts in support of cultural relations between Israel and the countries of Ibero-America." Misha also says that he had obtained an audience with the recently elected president of Israel, Isaac Ben-Zvi, whom he characterized as an exceptional man and "one of the few people still working in the abandoned field of Jewish ethnology," to propose a project focused on strengthening cultural relations between Israel and Ibero-America. Ben-Zvi, who was originally a Ukrainian Jew, founded an institute dedicated to the study of Middle Eastern Jewish history and culture, and Misha evidently felt some empathy with Ben-Zvi's effort to expand the European, Ashkenazi-centered view of the Jewish historical experience. And I don't know what the upshot of their meeting was. Clearly, Misha tried all means at his disposal to get his project up and running, but he simply did not succeed in finding a way forward.

Larissa and Cinna

Let's go back to the story of my mother. Upon arriving in Israel, Noemí sought to place Larissa on a kibbutz; the refugee camp in which they had been placed was dangerous for a teenage girl. Larissa was accepted in a kibbutz that had been created by sabras (Jews born in Israel, whose maternal language is Hebrew), in the north of the country, though she still did not speak Hebrew. She had to learn it as she went along. Larissa was later moved to another kibbutz, also made up of sabras, called Sarid. There she met a boy named Uri, a sabra painter who was "very handsome, with the face of a biblical character." They had a romance that was a bit different from what she was used to in Bogotá, living as they did without parental supervision: Uri built her a tree house; they walked through the mountains, visited biblical sites.

It was in all an experience of freedom and discovery that had little in common with the constricted ways of Tuluá, Sogamoso, or Tunja. Larissa had always been an optimist, and this penchant found even more expression in Israel, where she enjoyed the security of knowing she could provide for herself, with manual labor, and the freedom of not needing to find her place in the rigid class hierarchy of Colombia. While still living on the Sarid kibbutz, my mother got married for the first time. It was a sham marriage: a friend of hers wanted to avoid serving in the army, and he could do that if he was married. This marriage didn't please my grandfather at all, but that's how things were at that time. He couldn't do much about it. My mother divorced her friend when the threat of military service had passed for him, as they had agreed.

One day Noemí and Manuel were on their way to visit Larissa, and on the bus with them was a Chilean doctor, Marcos Kaufman, who wrote for the Hashomer Hatzair newspapers. Upon hearing them speaking Spanish, he struck up a conversation. He was from a nearby kibbutz called Ramot Menashe, which had been founded by South American Jews, mostly Chileans and Argentinians, and he extended an invitation for Larissa to come see him so that he might lend her books in

Spanish. Larissa made some friends on that kibbutz, and then decided to move there. Her Hebrew was still rudimentary, and it made her happy to be among other Latin Americans.

While living in Ramot Menashe, Larissa met Cinna Lomnitz, my father. He had come to talk with her about a common friend who had committed suicide. With his characteristic black humor, my father told me that the conversation about the friend was just a pretext, that he had heard about my mother and he wanted to meet her all along. The beginning of the conversation, seated in the dining room of the kibbutz, was very much my father. He took a piece of bread from the table, pulled out a crumb and put it in front of my mother, and said, *"Te presento a una miga"* (Allow me to introduce you to a crumb) — a play on the Spanish words *amiga* (friend) and *miga* (crumb). They fell in love, and they got married while still living on the kibbutz.

Cinna and Larissa around the time that they met, c. 1950.
Kibbutz Ramot Menashe, Israel.

My father had a more ideologically motivated entry into kibbutz life than my mother, since he had been a member of Hashomer Hatzair in Santiago, and had moved to Israel by himself rather than with his family, with the expressed desire of living on a kibbutz. His full range of motivations for this move had not been so clear to me until very recently, when an aunt discovered a five-page autobiography written by Cinna's mother, my grandmother Bronis, that was penned in the early sixties, shortly after my grandfather's death.

Cinna had been a loner in Chile and this worried his mother, so she introduced him to a German Jewish neighbor who had recently founded the Kidma in Santiago, a Zionist socialist organization that later affiliated itself with the Hashomer Hatzair. Although my father was not particularly enthusiastic about Judaism, and even less about clubs of any sort, he finally accepted an invitation to attend one of the organization's meetings. Cinna immediately loved the people there — especially a tightly knit group of proletarian, rough-and-tumble Czech Jews, with whom he formed a deep and lasting friendship. Cinna joined the movement and remained in it for roughly seven years.

The year of Cinna's introduction to the Kidma was 1943, and thanks to my grandmother's autobiographical notes, I now realize that the experience of living in Chile during these years of the Second World War also played a part in his decision. My grandmother wrote how, one day, my father's brother Eric came home from the French school saying that he was being called a dirty Jew (*"sale juif"*), and that he didn't want to go back there. He wanted to be baptized and become a Catholic, and live just like everybody else. My grandmother understood what was beginning to happen in Chile:

> I knew already, [she wrote,] I closed my eyes, I did not want to see, but the poison was already working. The German Colony, for generations in this country and not knowing any differences, closed their clubs, their schools to the Jews. Their propaganda, managed by skillful agents, had its effect already on the Chileans. They began to ask, to doubt, to suspect us. How is it possible that the Germans with their culture, their knowledge could do all these things—did they really do it, and if so, why? Is it not the Jews' fault? How could we explain, we who did not understand ourselves—how tired we were to argue, to fight, to claim?[209]

Further on she writes: "And then one evening our older son tells us that he had joined the movement to go to Israel. 'I will help to build a home for us all,' he said this, 'even in this distant end of the world [Chile] we are strangers, tolerated.'"[210] Cinna, who was seven years older than my mother, experienced the anxieties that Misha and Noemí had known in Colombia during those same war years, fanned by sectors of Latin America's urban middle classes that either flirted with or openly embraced Nazism. Jews who were fleeing Europe could not take these tendencies lightly, and I believe that, even though it was not yet majoritarian, the local anti-Semitic threat stymied Cinna's self-identification as a Chilean during those years, and led him to embrace Zionism.

My mother's situation was a bit different from my father's. As opposed to Cinna's parents, Misha and Noemí had long been committed to Jewish culture as such, and to the formation of Israel, but Larissa had grown up in the Colombian provinces and far from any Jewish organization. Because she was still a child during the war, and had no direct European life experience the way Cinna did, perhaps Larissa did not feel as deeply threatened by local anti-Semitism, highly unpleasant though it always is. As a result, Larissa did not leave Colombia for Israel as the result of personal conviction. Rather, she moved there with her family, and found herself living alone in a kibbutz because it was safer for her there than in a refugee camp, whereas Cinna had arrived in Israel well prepared for the life of the kibbutz.

In a memoir that he wrote in 1987, Cinna recalled the movement's ideology with a jaded distance: "In those communities, one practiced rigorous collectivism. The collective's authorities were designated and removed in egalitarian assemblies. The kibbutz committee assigned each member their place to live, their place of work, and their functions. Clothing was distributed each Friday and remained the property of the collective: there existed no personal clothing, nor any personal objects. When members decided to leave the collective, they were given a shirt, a pair of pants, a change of underwear, a pair of shoes, and five pounds in cash."[211]

My parents' wedding pictures give an idea of the stark environmental, ideological, and material differences between life on the kibbutz and in a Latin American city, especially if we compare them with the photos taken at my aunt Pupe's wedding in Bogotá, nine years earlier.

Cinna and Larissa's wedding, Petah Tikva, 1952. Seated at the center
are my parents. Behind them and framing the photo, two of their friends
hold flower vases that seem to have been taken from the table.
There is no special wedding attire, just clean clothes.*

The wedding of Pupe Milstein and Isaac Perlman in Bogotá, 1944.
from the left: Misha, Boris, Isaac Perlman, Pupe Milstein de Perlman,
Noemí, Larissa, and Manuel Adler.

I continue quoting from my father:

We aspired to this life that we glorified as if it were the realization of a millenarian dream. To be free in our own land! To be workers! To grow our own food! We wanted to create our own form of life, our own culture, our own sense of morality based on the rejection of all forms of exploitation. To prepare ourselves for this, we cultivated spartan habits. From the simplicity of our manner of dress to the rejection of "bourgeois" forms of life (such as smoking, drinking, wearing makeup, growing mustaches, going to dances and flirting)...[212]

I don't know the details of how or why, but my parents grew tired of life on the kibbutz. I do know that there were ideological conflicts as well as practical ones. My father's 1987 memoir includes a number of friendly but critical comments with regard to Zionism and what happened in the kibbutz movement that he had belonged to. Although Cinna did not explain the specific events that led him and Larissa to leave the kibbutz (and, soon enough, Israel), he did at least suggest what some of his own reasoning may have been.

With regard to Zionism, my father wrote that "Zionism bases its enormous emotional magnetism in the Jew's desire to be normal, to be integrated in the community of nations

---

* The man holding the flower vase on the right is Bernardo (Beco) Baytelman, and next to him is Eliana Albala. Beco and Eliana moved to Mexico from Chile in 1973, after the coup d'état that brought Augusto Pinochet to power. Beco managed to create an extraordinary garden of medicinal plants cultivated by the rural peasants of Morelos, and he left it as a living legacy. It is located in the garden of the Emperor Maximilian's summer house in Cuernavaca.

like one more member, neither better nor worse than any of the others. We shall see how this desire for normality was, to a certain degree, frustrated by its success, but that dialectic was still very distant in 1943, when I joined the Kidma movement."[213]

That movement was deeply ideological, and not so different from what we saw in Misha and Noemí's early formation, decades earlier: "The Marxism that we professed was European and, one might say, a little antiquated. We were anti-Stalinists, we read Trotsky, Bakunin, Saint-Simon, and Fourier, and of course Marx and Engels and their numerous interpreters...You couldn't continue living and working in the Movement unless you renounced all private property and joined an agricultural collective."

But practical realities of Israel and the kibbutzim ended up producing a feeling of disillusion that Cinna explained as follows: "When the ideals are great, the causes for disillusion are often menial. There have been great socialists who have not been able to stand the smell of a proletarian concentration, and fervent revolutionaries who were unable to accept the chicanery of their own bureaucracy. When the State of Israel surged into the world of international politics in 1948 many changes ensued, both positive and negative, that had lethal effects on our juvenile idealism."

Some of these effects stemmed from the everyday realities of living on the kibbutz — the loneliness of that work and the overbearing quality of collective decision making — others from the engagement of wage labor on the kibbutz, and its implications for such spartan and dogmatic collectivist ideals as those that Cinna's movement had cultivated while in Chile. Finally, there was also concern about the longer-term prospects for equality that were being held out by Jewish nationalism, given Israel's beleaguered entry into the community of nations: "Like good socialists, we recognized the rights of the Arab working class and of the Arab nation, and we aspired to a binational state, similar perhaps to Belgium, Canada, or Switzerland (which is trinational), or to many others. We felt that there could only be a Jewish nation in possession of its land if it shared it with an Arab nation that might achieve equal development, with equal opportunities."[214]

However, after 1948, when the movement that Cinna belonged to became a political party, the MAPAM (United Workers' Party), this position was no longer judged to be tenable from an electoral point of view.[215] Whether one, two, or all of these sources of frustration sparked my parents' actual decision to leave the kibbutz, I don't know.

In the end, though, they left the kibbutz as my father described: with a change of clothing in their suitcases and a five-pound note in their pockets. They moved to a new city, Beer Sheva, that was being built up in the Negev desert. My father was an engineer; he had graduated from the Universidad de Chile and had gone on to study for a master's degree in soil mechanics at Harvard, under the supervision of Karl von Terzaghi, who is considered to be the father of geotechnical engineering. Cinna's training had been somewhat underutilized on the kibbutz, where he had worked in kitchens, stables, and orchards, lifting rocks or driving a tractor. At least now he worked on a dam project as an engineer.

The dam zone, near Beer Sheva, c. 1953.

A triumphant Larissa with Jorge.
Beer Sheva, 1954.

When Cinna's boss met my mother, he asked her if she too needed a job. Larissa said that she did, and when he asked her what she knew how to do, she candidly responded with the truth: "I know how to wash dishes." This unpresumptuous (and honest) response pleased my dad's boss, and he then placed her in an administrative position rather than in the kitchen. It was also in Beer Sheba that my brother Jorge was born, on March 23, 1954. Around that same time my father decided to apply for a fellowship for doctoral research, and so for their young family to leave Israel permanently. Cinna was awarded a scholarship to pursue his doctorate in geophysics at Cal Tech, in Pasadena, and the young couple left Israel for California when Jorge was still just a baby.

Return to Colombia

For the rest of the Adlers, life in Israel, while liberating in a number of respects, was nonetheless also not that easy. Misha and Noemí were maybe a bit too old to adapt to agricultural life on the kibbutz, and Misha's possibilities in the intellectual field reached a ceiling, due mostly to the economic pressures that he faced as the head of a family, I think. Manuel was studying at a boarding school in Petah Tikva, but he suffered a serious accident when he was sixteen that broke bones in his face and made it impossible for him to engage in any aerobic exercise. After that, he left the boarding school and returned to live with his parents.

In the afternoons, he went door to door selling books, until he moved to Tel Aviv to work and continue with his studies. There he was admitted into the prestigious Cameri Theater school. Here he was a student of writer Sholem Aleichem's granddaughter, who recommended that Manuel continue his studies in Pasadena, where Larissa and Cinna were soon to go. But Manuel went first instead to Colombia, to complete his recovery and save up a bit of money, selling shoes for his uncle Zuñe. Boris died while Manuel was there, and Noemí traveled to Cali and Tuluá, accompanied by little Ilya, to sign notary papers and receive her part of the inheritance.

Letter from Misha (in Petah Tikva) to Noemí (in Tuluá), 1955.

Misha and Mauricio now found themselves alone in Israel. First Manuel had left, then Noemí and Ilya, and finally Larissa and Cinna. It seems to have been during this separation, by way of letters that came and went, and after seeing what Noemí had received as her inheritance (a sum that would allow them to buy a house), that the couple decided that life in America would be better for them.

My uncle Mauricio thinks that his parents decided to move back to Colombia because they identified more with the Latin American way of life. According to Manuel, it was because two of their four children had already definitively returned to America, so there wasn't much point in staying. According to my mother, my grandparents led a physically trying life in Israel, particularly given my grandfather's bad health. It also must have weighed heavily on Misha that he could not develop his Americanism in Israel, since as Misha told Paul Rivet: "I continue wholly enamored of Indo-Latin-Americans and of the marvelous cultural forms created by the 'autochthonous' and creoles in the (poorly named) Ibero- or Latin American countries."[216] Nostalgia, the closing off of possibilities, economic straits, family division...All of these reasons together shaped the decision, because without renouncing either his Israeli nationality or identity, nor his passion for Jewish culture, Misha finally opted to continue his life in the diaspora, and Noemí, Mauricio, Ilya, and Misha returned to live in Cali.

Misha and Manuel Adler, carrying Jorge (still a baby), and Larissa, visiting the home of Jorge Isaacs, Valle del Cauca, 1956. Cinna is the invisible photographer.

How the marginalized survive

My mother began to study for her bachelor's degree at Berkeley, California, when she was thirty-two years old and had three young sons and a daughter on the way. I was eight years old then. My brothers and I greeted her decision to study with enthusiasm, as did my father, who supported her a great deal in this.

Tania, the blessing of a daughter after three sons,
with a parakeet. Berkeley, California, 1965.

My mother began her studies enthusiastically, and with modest aspirations. For her, everything was a win, so Larissa devoted herself to her studies with an intense immediacy that led her eventually to become a recognized figure in her field. Her doctoral thesis, which was written after the family had moved to Mexico, was published in 1976 by Siglo XXI Press in Mexico City, with the title *¿Cómo sobreviven los marginados?* (How Do the Marginalized Survive?). It is considered a classic in Latin American urban studies, and as I write these lines, the book is in its seventeenth edition. That book was also a factor when she was bestowed Mexico's National Science Award and gained membership as foreign correspondent in the American Academy of Arts and Sciences.

Larissa studying. California, c. 1967.

Larissa's book asks a simple question: How do the people who work in the so-called informal economy manage to survive in the face of chronic employment instability and the lack of any unemployment insurance? Her thesis answered this question descriptively, as a by-product of multiple conversations and observations. In these interactions, Larissa tracked and mapped out the fundamental importance of mutual support, not only in microlevel forms of assistance — in child care, small loans of money, or sharing food — but also in the history of migration itself, in residential patterns, and in work specialization. She documented how people's decisions to migrate were usually conditioned by the fact that they had a relative or friend who invited them to move, who was willing to receive them, or who helped place them in the labor market. For these reasons, people from the same villages and towns frequently settled in the city as neighbors, at least initially. From these primary relationships, they went about expanding their circles of exchange and support. This study situated Larissa in the pioneering generations of anthropological researchers dedicated to the study of "social networks."

If we look at her work from the perspective of my own family, though, I think that my mother discovered her own history refracted in the Cerrada del Cóndor (Mexico City) shantytown that she studied in such detail. How did the Adlers and Milsteins survive? In my grandparents' generation, their patterns of migration, friendships, and matrimonial alliances often revolved around a network of immigrants who came from Bessarabia or Bukovina, and even from Nova Sulitza itself. In fact, it is likely that the experience of Nova Sulitza was somewhere in the back of my mother's mind as she developed her ideas about networks, migrations, mutual help, exchange of favors, patron-client relations, and so forth.

For my family, Nova Sulitza was a kind of Eastern European counterpart of Colombian novelist Gabriel García Márquez's fictive town, Macondo. I've always thought of it like that, but with a difference: Nova Sulitza ceased to be a Jewish place in 1941, and it persisted only through the networks of its exiles, who found one another in places like Lima, Bogotá, Tel Aviv, Philadelphia, Cali, and Caracas. Nova Sulitza existed only in relationships between in-laws, or in the commercial networks of peddlers who knocked on doors throughout much of South America, or in competitive parental bragging over their children's achievements as they advanced in different fields, in Colombia, Israel, the United States, Peru, or wherever. García Márquez's Macondo was figured as a transcendental place that lives on in Latin America's unending history of eccentricity, while extinct Nova Sulitza became a horizon of reference and interpretative key only for a generation or two, because Jewish Nova Sulitza was forever extinguished. It could only be reenacted in social relations, as a more or less tenuously shared memory.

When I was looking for information to write this book, I had an exchange with Victor Perlman, the son of my aunt Pupe, whose father had come from Hotin, a town very near Nova Sulitza. In an email, Victor made the following comment: "Niusic Coifman, the son of Aunt Sara, visited Hotin a few years ago. There's nothing there."[217] "There's nothing there" means that there are no Jews there. For families like ours, Nova Sulitza or Hotin became ghost towns, abandoned cemeteries.

How did the Jews who were marginalized, oppressed, and expelled manage to survive? They survived by developing relationships and knowing how to find themselves in others, and also finding others in themselves. This explains my mother's and my grandparents' remarkable ability to make friends. Her capacity to find herself in others required a mimetic faculty that was so powerful that it was practically an illness, as in Woody Allen's famous character Zelig. There was also understanding and communication in this identification, and not just camouflage. Even when it appears as a reflex, blending in is in fact never effortless. It requires careful observation, and observation produces understanding and is wedded to it. When you understand someone, you can interact, and when you interact, you have real material effects in social intercourse.

Presence and encounter. A photo in which my grandfather
(*center*) seems to be both with and not with scientist
and scholar Alejandro Lipschutz (*to his left*) and
poet Pablo Neruda (*to his right*). Santiago de Chile, 1960.

My grandfather's life was suffused with moments spent with famous figures. There were elective affinities among them, and they tended to understand one another very well. Looking back at the material traces that Misha left behind — photos, journals — he sometimes appeared to me almost as a kind of Zelig, with Mariátegui here, corresponding with Freud there, pleading for support from the president of Israel, corresponding with former Venezuelan president Rómulo Gallegos or Nobel laureate Gabriela Mistral, or living next door to Chilean folk composer Violeta Parra. My grandfather was a "minor figure" because he never had any permanence anywhere, nor did he enjoy material conditions that might have allowed him to lay down roots, but those encounters that he did have with so many friends and acquaintances were not merely adaptations on his part. They were genuine interactions that involved mutual influence, and not just mimesis.

My nationality

At some point during my adolescence, I began to rebel against assimilation. I started to feel proud about feeling rejected, and began to feel grateful that the Mexico where I came of age was not a country of assimilation, so that my foreignness would be with me forever. Unlike Misha, I didn't think of Jewish nationality as a form of emancipation, because I never lived Judaism as an intensely communitarian experience the way he did. Nova Sulitza was too far removed. For me, being Jewish was a sensibility, a turn of mind and a family tradition. And, unlike my father, who later in his life tried to assimilate as a Mexican, I was not so attracted to an identity that I knew to be conditional, and from which I might be excluded at a whim.

Almost unconsciously, I took in the experience of my paternal grandfather, Ricardo (Lomnitz), who was stripped of German citizenship even though he was a decorated war veteran. And also the story of Misha's Romania, where Jews were compelled formally to request citizenship, even though they had lived there for generations, and where these requests were nonetheless routinely deferred or else flatly denied. I also took in the anticolonial nationalism of the Mexican Revolution, with its hoarse cry of "Mexico for the Mexicans," and decided that it was not worth the trouble to invest in my own nationality. Instead, I happily held on to my Chilean passport, even though I had left my country of birth when I was just eleven. Unlike the Romanian Jews of my grandfather's generation, I still have a Chilean nationality just because I was born there. And, unlike what happened with Germany's Jews, Chilean nationality always has been unrenounceable, to which I say, like any and all good Chileans, *Viva Chile, mierda!*

My anti-assimilationism also led me to nurse or at least not to expunge all remnants of my Chilean accent, although I've never had the remotest intention of returning to Chile. I was born there and I spent my childhood there, and that's it. Neither have I tried to eliminate the other Spanish intonations that I've acquired during my travels, or through the sonorous influence of my friends. I have come to realize and accept that I am "alingual" rather than bi- or multilingual: linguistically insecure. Jewish, I suppose. When I was in my twenties, I also accepted the German nationality that was bestowed on my father and my brothers, reverting to the Nuremberg Laws of 1935 that had originally taken it away. Decades later, I took United States citizenship, due to a set of practical considerations — I'd been living there for more than twenty years by then. And so, I voted for the first time. I voted for Obama. Still, I have never fully accepted the yoke of assimilation. Upon taking US nationality, I lost my German passport, without ever having used it. I had been German without speaking any German. Now that I am no longer German, I speak it a bit.

Little by little, I developed an attitude that we might call Zapatista with regard to the topics of both family and nationality: "Family Is for Those Who Work It." Similarly, nationality is for those who work it. Mexican anarchist and revolutionary Ricardo Flores Magón felt that way, too, so that if a foreigner fought for the Mexican Revolution, his party granted him Mexican nationality, end of story. I have long felt, for that very reason, that I am Mexican, not only because I have loved Mexico, but because of how much I have studied it. In May 2017, thanks to the intervention of some dear friends, I finally received Mexican nationality with a presidential waiver, because, due to my job in the United States, I no longer met the ordinary residency requirements. I am proud of having it, because I "worked" in and on Mexico long before I received that recognition. In this case, which is unique for me, my passport certifies a status that I actually earned.

PART FIVE

Childhood as a Collective Achievement

God's face

In the Bible, there are two points where Moses oversteps his bounds. The first comes after the flight from Egypt, when God orders Moses to strike a desert rock with his cane to provide water for the Israelites. Moses does that and enacts the miracle, except that his performance appears to leave open the possibility that the power of miracle was his to wield, rather than God's. So God punishes Moses for that, and he bars him from entering the Promised Land, and in doing so demonstrates, while he is at it, that God disapproves of the idolatry that is implicit in hero worship.

Moses's second transgression is even more interesting. In a moment of sublime ecstasy, he asks God to let him see his face. Instead, God responds by asking Moses to turn his back to him, and lets him know that he will only reveal himself indirectly, through the effects of his acts. Neither Moses nor anyone else may see the face of God (Exodus 33:20). We humans are expected to find God enciphered in the ways of the world.

In the story of Noah, this was pretty much Ham's sin, too: to have dared to look upon his naked father (Noah), and then make some wisecrack about him to his brothers. In doing this, Ham violated a taboo, for sure, but the biblical scene also conjures up a primal fantasy, namely, that we are actually capable of seeing our parents in their full nakedness. When they realized that their drunken father had inadvertently exposed himself, Noah's other two sons, Shem and Japheth, picked up his tunic, walked with their backs turned toward their father averting their eyes, and covered him up. Japheth and Shem thus respected the taboo, and avoided contemplating their father's nudity. In so doing, they also dodged Noah's curse, which fell solely on Ham and on his descendants.

I think that within Judaism, Ham's transgression is a bit more severe than it would have been for polytheists. Ham violated a prohibition — seeing his naked father without averting his eyes — and he is punished for that. Up to here, the Jewish taboo operates pretty much in the same way as what one might expect among polytheists. In monotheism, however, there is an additional sin at stake, idolatry, because by judging his naked father, Ham has put himself in God's position, and God must always be resolutely one. A son can never see his father whole, and pretending to do this is pretending to be God, which, I think, is why Noah's curse is extended to Ham's descendants. Like Moses, Ham wished to look upon his father as an equal, directly to his face.

Something like this takes place between parents and their children. Children are born out of a moment of intimacy to which they can never have access, and about which they can only project one fantasy or another. Parents have lived experiences of which their children can never know. What our parents are to us is only a part of who they are, and to presume that we might see them in their naked wholeness not only humiliates them but also involves raising our own selves up as gods.

Geology of Machu Picchu

My father liked to translate. In fact, translation for us is a family-wide propensity, a kind of occupational hazard. This is because displacement requires translation, and it brings with it the joy of hearing the same thing being said by way of such different sounds, and also discovering the absurd in so many literal translations... or identifying "false friends" between languages with the kind of satisfaction that one might gain from spotting a counterfeit. All of this becomes an obsessive compulsion. "Between, and drink a chair" is a literal translation of "*Entre, y tome asiento,*" which actually means "Come in and take a seat." In my house, we sometimes invited one another to "between and drink a chair," and I've always remained fond of false etymologies and ridiculous translations.

But it was my father who really had a gift for that sort of thing. For him, movement between languages was not only a necessary tactic to achieve social acceptance, it was also a habit that produced clarity and even induced the occasional epiphany. Translation was for Cinna both a pastime and a fascination.

He oftentimes translated texts that caught his eye, usually into Spanish or English. His most ambitious project, I think, was to translate Pablo Neruda's *Las alturas de Machu Picchu* into English, in a version that ended up pleasing Neruda himself.

Unfortunately, I don't have a copy of my father's translation of that long and difficult poem, but I think that I understand why Cinna obsessed over those verses in particular: they are suffused with petrified love. Thus, in one of the poem's sections, Neruda invokes Machu Picchu:

Cuando la mano de color de arcilla
Se convirtió en arcilla, y cuando los pequeños párpados se cerraron
Llenos de ásperos muros, poblados de castillos,
Y cuando todo el hombre se enredó en su agujero,
Quedó la exactitud enarbolada:
El alto sitio de la aurora humana:
La más alta vasija que contuvo el silencio:
Una vida de piedra después de tantas vidas.

When the clay-colored hand
Turned into clay, and when the little eyelids were shut
Full of rasping walls, teeming with castles
And when the whole of man got entangled in his lair,
Exactness remained there, unfurled:
The perch of humanity's dawn:
The highest vessel that contained the silence:
A life of stone after so many lives.[218]

A life of stone after so many lives. Petrification and stillness as relief. And the infinite longing of the Andes as primeval origin. The life of rocks, their history: geology. "Most young people," my father wrote regarding his youth, "are attracted by the world's enormous multiform complexity. I was attracted by its simplicity and its immutable laws. Like Heraclitus, I saw life as a river in which no one bathes twice."[219] My father used to say, as I mentioned at the start of this book, that it was hard to live peacefully near the Andes, that everything was too dramatic, too young. I think that he meant to say not only that the Andes were geologically young, but that they also were a painful reminder of humanity's infancy, as Neruda had said of Machu Picchu:

> *Madre de piedra, espuma de los cóndores.*
> *Alto arrecife de la aurora humana.*
> *Pala perdida en la primera arena.*

> *Mother of stone, foam of condors.*
> *Lofty reef of humanity's dawn.*
> *A lost spade in the primeval sand.*

My father understood the untimely life of rocks, because he loved stillness and oblivion. He knew how to find the poetry of life in what is frozen, unmovable, or petrified, because without that stillness, mimesis finds no relief and it just spins around in an unstoppable vertigo of translation.

In his memoir, Cinna writes about an epiphany that he had about himself when he was fifteen years old or so. He was like a piece of wood, floating downstream.

This metaphoric conception of life was exclusively mine: I hadn't read it anywhere. I realized even then that it was essentially religious, but I wasn't interested in knowing what religion it came from or with which religion it harmonized the best. Probably in those years I thought that it was a kind of pantheism. It wasn't. Neither was it a form of resignation or passivity in the face of existence. Simply put, my attitude consisted in a great modesty in the face of the world, and in a wish to be light, and to go with the flow of existence.[220]

Sina and Cinna

The more I investigate the history of my family, the more I understand the achievement that was our childhood. It is true that, even as children, we had at least some idea of our family's past tragedies; I remember the convulsion that images of concentration camps and the Holocaust provoked in me when I first saw them, at the age of ten or so. People didn't take as much pleasure in violent images back then. When I was a boy, I found movies like *Dracula* and *Frankenstein* absolutely terrifying, and the war scenes from *Gone with the Wind*, which I saw as a child in Berkeley, made me run to the bathroom to vomit, dizzied by the nausea of horror. And so those photos of living human skeletons wandering around Bergen-Belsen or Auschwitz, and of piles of dead bodies surrounded by soldiers, were unassimilable and simply beyond belief.

But it is also true that we had the means to distance ourselves from those images. Speaking of the past repetitively and out loud served to domesticate it, to separate it from us even as we learned to live with it. Even so, this sort of distancing was made a lot easier because, when I saw those pictures, nobody accented their impact by telling me that the parents of my beloved grandfather Misha had died pretty much in that way. Neither did my father tell us of the many aunts, uncles, and cousins that he had lost in precisely those camps. In fact, Cinna never told me about that, and when I asked him just a few years ago for information about the family members that he had lost before and during the war, he could not retrieve a single name. Maybe by that point he truly had blocked all recollection, I'm not sure.

The war left my father with a very small family and, with the exception of our strong connection to my grandmother, we didn't grow up very close to them. After Cinna died, however, I contacted one of his nieces on his mother's side, on the Aronsfrau side, Vivianne, who provided me with a detailed genealogy of that family, from the mid-nineteenth century forward. I see in it a number of relatives who were killed during the war: Chaskel Aronsfrau (died in Paris, 1944); Leib Aronsfrau and his wife, Eva Holander (Auschwitz, 1943), as well as their daughter, Leonore Aronsfrau (Auschwitz, 1943); Chane Aronsfrau (Bochnia, Poland, 1943) and her husband, Israel Fallman (Lacko, Poland, 1942); Frieda Langenauer (wife of Jakob Aronsfrau, Auschwitz, 1942) and her daughters, Fanny and Monique Aronsfrau (Auschwitz, 1942); Leon Aronsfrau (Brussels, 1944). All of these people were close relatives of my grandmother Bronislawa; some were brothers, sisters, brothers-in-law, or sisters-in-law, and some were nieces.

The Lomnitz family, 1937, minus my grandparents and Aunt Wally, who had already emigrated: (*top, from left*) Walter, Leska, Gunther, Ferdinand Margulies, Augusta, Sydney; (*bottom*) Oma Betty, Opa Siegfried, Lieselotte, Magda.

And yet, when I asked my father for the names of the relatives who died during the Holocaust, he seemed not to remember. He couldn't identify a single one by name. And this troubled me, because he had known many — and probably all — of those who had died then: Cinna left Germany when he was already eight years old and he lived in Brussels until he was thirteen, but most of the family had also moved there. It was from Brussels that the Nazis deported those who died in Auschwitz. Others had been shot there, or else in Paris, where a few managed to hide and survive the entire war. These were my father's aunts, uncles, and cousins. Was my father's blocked memory an expression of trauma? Remorse? Desire to protect his children from fear and powerlessness, as he himself had been protected? I'm not sure.

When I pushed Cinna a bit more on this subject, he responded:

> My parents didn't tell us anything, because they were overprotective; they didn't want us to suffer anxiety. Sure, my brother Eric and I knew that there were some evildoers out there named "Hitler" and "Goering," but what had they done? Why were they so bad? Who knew? Eric and I liked to look at animal pictures in Brehm's *Life of Animals*,[221] and when we came across some ugly toads, we named them "Hitler" or "Goering." There was never any talk of the relatives who had stayed behind, nor of anything that might be traumatic. My father was by nature discreet and reserved, and my mother knew all about the psychological complexes that were so fashionable then, and she had read Freud.[222]

On the Lomnitz side of the family, my grandfather Kurt's brother Sydney was killed at Auschwitz together with his wife, Magda, and their two children, Lieselotte and Klaus, and so were his sister Augusta and her husband, Ferdinand Margulies.

Still, I think that my father remembered more than he let on. Maybe his parents had been able to hide less from him than he cared to admit, or else he found things out that he had later suppressed, forgotten, and did not wish to tell me about.

One moving thing about writing this book is that it has gifted me with information that I lacked when I had those frustrating conversations with Cinna. Writing is a transformative art that provides writers with space and time for reflection — this is well known — but I had thought less about how writing also mobilizes friends, fellow travelers, and loved ones who may reach out to help in whatever ways they can.

Just a few weeks before this book entered production, my aunt Barbara, who is the widow of my uncle Eric and so my father's sister-in-law, and who lives in London, found and sent me my grandmother Bronis's autobiography. This manuscript, though very brief, is especially precious because silence was such a cardinal fact in her and my father's lives. Its five pages made me understand that my grandmother Bronis was a much more formidable character than I had given her credit for, and it also offered information that I had long thought was irretrievable.

My grandmother Bronis in a dress reminiscent of the Viennese style painted by Klimt, with Cinna (*right*) and Eric (*left*). Santiago de Chile, c. 1940.

For instance, Bronis writes a few lines about how she and my grandfather heard of the plight of their families back in Belgium while they were already safe in Santiago. That is, about their experience of some of the facts Cinna seemed to have forgotten:

> We had escaped — but there they are, our brothers and sisters who had not believed in the threat and the danger. The news are had — the visas we had sent, they came too late. The countries had closed their doors — even our friendly, hospitable Chile. The letters which came in the beginning now they don't come any more. New words like deportation, camps, extermination, Auschwitz are daily heard in our community — and there is silence . . .
>
> I should feel guilty. There they were dying, our whole family, millions. Here we are closing our eyes, our minds, and enjoying selfishly every minute of the children's lives…A big garden, full of flowers and trees, big enough for the children to play, to have animals, to invite friends.[223]

I think that Cinna's somewhat sarcastic reference to Freud as the source of his mother's overprotectiveness is a kind of obfuscation, because if concern with trauma was once an intellectual fashion, this didn't mean that my father and his parents didn't suffer from it. And of course Cinna knew this, and indeed Freud's exploration of repression might have helped him better to decipher his father's silence and his mother's overprotective impulses.

After Cinna's death, while I was still engaged in basic research for this book, I wrote to Barbara, and I asked her for information on Lomnitz family history. She is a relative by marriage rather than by blood, of course, but there appeared to be no one else left to ask, and although Barbara didn't know all that much about the family, she did tell me one thing that I was surprised not to have known about before, and this was that my grandmother Bronis's father had been murdered. According to Barbara, he had been killed by an employee who wanted to steal from him. She didn't know anything else about the case, though. She didn't even know the man's name, though he was her late husband's grandfather, and the father of a mother-in-law who had lived very close to her for a couple of decades, suggesting that neither Bronis nor Eric had said much about it.

I then asked my mother if she had heard this story, and much to my surprise she had. My grandmother Bronis had confided to my mother in secret that her father had been murdered, and that the deed had been the work of the Nazis, very early in their movement. My mother likewise couldn't remember my great-grandfather's name. Cinna, for his part, never mentioned him to me or to any of my siblings, and he was now dead, so I could no longer ask him about it.

The few discussions that I did try to have with Cinna about his family had often ended up frustrating us both. I was especially irritated by one of his answers in an email exchange on the subject of our family's losses: "It was extremely useful to me to read Ernst Jünger's war diary," he wrote, "because it's a single thread of memory. Jünger writes at one point that life is like one of those Gobelin tapestries with lace made from a single thread. Our history is like that. I lived through the Holocaust as Jünger did: through distant, sporadic, and disconnected news that nonetheless formed a single thread."[224]

Distant and disconnected news? Apparently, the Nazis had killed his maternal grandfather for being Jewish, years before the war had even begun! The family then left Germany just months after Hitler's election. Some emigrated to Belgium and others to France, and they were then murdered in concentration camps or on the street. Cinna, his brother Eric, and their parents managed to find their way to Chile. Where did Cinna's sense of distance and disconnection come from, if not from that cloud of obfuscation that Cinna chalked up to Freud's influence on his mother, rather than to trauma itself?

Sina Aronsfrau

My grandmother Bronislawa's father died in the city of Mannheim on May 22, 1922. His name was Sina Aronsfrau. In other words, my great-grandfather had the same name as my father, although my father had a Latinized version of it bestowed on him ("Cinna" in place of "Sina" or "Zyna"). Equipped just with this information about the person of my great-grandfather — his name and date of death — I began to look for more details: it was likely that I would find at least some news about a prosperous merchant who had been murdered in Mannheim in 1922. I figured that I would need to delve into local newspapers, but to my astonishment, a simple Google search yielded some results!

According to Wikipedia, the murder of Sina Aronsfrau is attributed to a group of men including Hermann Willibald Fischer, who was a member of an extreme-right (Freikorps) terrorist group called Organisation Consul. This group operated between 1919 and 1923, and it had close connections to the Nazi Party (NSDAP), which was formed around the same time. The mission of Organisation Consul was, in its own words, "to cultivate and disseminate nationalist thought; to wage war against all antinationalists and internationalists; the just war against Jews, social democracy, and leftist radicalism; and to foment internal unrest so as to overthrow the antinationalist Weimar Constitution..."[225] Fischer, who according to Wikipedia was somehow involved in my great-grandfather's assassination, became famous for having been one of the three men responsible for murdering Walther Rathenau, the German minister of foreign relations and (not inconsequentially) an assimilated Jew. Rathenau was murdered barely two months after my great-grandfather, on June 24, 1922,[226] and in fact it was the investigation into his murder that led officials to discover that Organisation Consul was also implicated in the assassination of my father's grandfather.

Wikipedia's source for this information is a book on Rathenau's murder written by Humboldt University historian Martin Sabrow, I wrote to Professor Sabrow asking for further information, and he responded with many more details. (Like the Tennessee Williams character Blanche Dubois, this book has "always depended on the kindness of strangers.")

The police never credibly solved the murder, Sabrow wrote, but there is no doubt that it was a political killing, because nothing was stolen. During the police investigation into the Rathenau murder, several witnesses mentioned the murder of Sina Aronsfrau, implicating the writer and nationalist extremist Ernst von Salomon as well. The young men who formed Organisation Consul were all from "good fami-lies" — well-educated and ideologically motivated radicals. The idea to orchestrate political killings took shape during night discussions, and it produced a long hit list that, according to Salomon, had some names scratched out and others added. Many of the people on that list seem to have been put there for reasons that were not transparent to all members of the group. Salomon actually saw the hit list in the room of another one of Rathenau's assassins, and one of the leading ideologues of the movement, Edwin Kern: "It was, in fact, a single dirty sheet of paper with names scribbled all over it in pencil, some crossed out, some written in again. Many of the names meant abso-lutely nothing to me, and I had to take a lot of trouble to find out who the people were...I remember thinking that there were a lot of Jewish names."[227]

Professor Sabrow shared information from the Rathenau murder investigation with me. The detective Waldemar Nie-drig testified that Salomon had confessed to him his involve-ment in Sina Aronsfrau's assassination: "Salomon himself told me that all three of them had [approached] Sina Aronsfrau in his Mannheim office and asked him if he was Sinai Aronsfrau. In response to his affirmative, they said: 'We were just looking for you,' and immediately fired the shot."[228]

Niedrig's testimony was corroborated by a second witness, Theodor Bruedigam, who said that he had heard from a member of the Organisation Consul that Sina Aronsfrau's assassination had been carried out by Karl Tillessen and two other members of the organization, one of whom was probably Ernst von Salo-mon, who himself, twenty years later, published a protracted

"Questionnaire"/confession, in which he acknowledged that, beyond his role in the Rathenau assassination, he had also taken part in several other crimes during those years.[229]

The murders carried out by Organisation Consul were executions that seem generally to have been decided by a council modeled on medieval Vehmic tribunals, which judged the person to be killed in absentia and then ordered the hit. It was not immediately clear why they targeted Sina Aronsfrau, who, though Jewish and reasonably wealthy, was not a prominent public figure in Mannheim.

The gravesite of Sina Aronsfrau,
in the Jewish cemetery of Mannheim.*

My brothers and I grew up with the feeling that Nazi violence and the Holocaust were not so very immediate, because our family had escaped. In reality, though, it had been a horror that had struck home even before the rise of Hitler, but that was then rendered distant by careful and deliberate omission. Even my grandmother's brief autobiographical notes skip over it. And my own father was so confused by his mother's false clues that he was unable to tell me, even when he was eighty-four years old, of his mother's suffering over the murder of her father, which happened when she was almost thirty and barely three years before my father's birth.

Cinna was also not told that his mother's singing career had been cut short by racial persecution. Bronis had her stage debut while still at Munich, where she had studied singing, in a concert that was conducted by Bruno Walter, who afterward said of her that she had a voice of rare beauty. As a result of this success, Bronis received her first regular contract as a performer, but in the end the contract was not signed because she was Jewish. She was nevertheless able to get a promising concert career going, after an acclaimed performance at Cologne's famous Guerzenich Concert Hall, followed by a national tour: "I make the tour across the country and feel already the uncertainty,

---

* The inscription in Hebrew reads: "Memorial for a beloved soul / Like a beautiful flower planted between streams but later ripped from the earth by a fetid wind, an assassin pulled from the world of the living and carried away the distinguished Sina Bar-Yakov Shimon Hakohen, on the fortieth day of Sfirat Ha-Omer (counted from Passover) in the Hebrew year of 5682. His fate was to live 63 years performing good acts with true generosity and charity. He was a pious and learned man, and Torah and wisdom were intertwined in his person. His sons and daughters will cry bitterly for him. May his soul remain tied to the bonds of life." Translation by Elisheva Shaul.

the fear. The conductors ask about my "race," they themselves ashamed, afraid. And the sickness in my body from my remote youth — here it was again."[230]

The sickness of her youth that she refers to is the dread that she felt when her family fled Poland, for Germany, in 1901. The depth of Bronis's losses is hard to reconstruct, because she was always so private about all of this, but she did write about what Germany had meant for her, after Poland:

> How I love this country, how I love the people, I adore everything which comes from there. My mother knows poems from Heine, Goethe, she sings Lieder, German lieder, she has a beautiful voice and people say that one day I will sing like her. One day I will be a singer, an opera singer, I will be famous and I will sing German Lieder and show my country how proud I am to be a part of it...I study Bach, and Haendel and Mozart and in my conscience is always one idea: to show how I am part of this my country, how deep I feel their music and now I can express it. It is like an obsession.

My father, who grew up hiding his connection to Germany — both in Belgium and in Chile — had an imprecise idea of the depth of his mother's attachment to German culture, and does not seem to have been told that racial hatred had denied his mother a singing career, along with all of her passionately cultivated feelings of belonging. Instead, Cinna was led to believe that my grandmother's father had denied her a stage career.

Nor did he know the connection between his grandfather's assassination and the speed with which his parents decided to leave Germany, just a few months after Hitler's election, in 1933. True, they had left thanks to my grandfather's prompting, very shortly after a Nazi-organized public humiliation of Cologne's Jewish lawyers, who were paraded through the city in a garbage truck. But I now realize that Sina Aronsfrau's assassination by the Nazis probably helped my grandfather convince his wife and her family to leave Germany so early.

Most troubling for me, Cinna couldn't seem to put himself in his mother's shoes, a woman who had lost her father, siblings, and nephews, her national identification, and her career because of anti-Semitism, as he tried to explain the silences that he had assimilated during his "overprotected" childhood. Maternal protection took the form of hiding the truth.

What's in a name?

There is a Jewish tradition of naming a child after a deceased relative. In the case of my family, there are several cousins of my daughter's generation named Lisa (or Elisa) and also a Noemí, in honor of my grandmother, Lisa Noemí. There are two Mishas ("Miguel" and "Michael"), and two Ricardos, after my maternal and paternal grandfathers. Sometimes only the first letter of a name is used to honor the deceased, or the person is honored by way of the child's middle name. My middle name, for example, is Walter, in honor of my great-uncle, Walter Lomnitz, whom I never met. My brother Jorge, may he rest in peace, had Simon as a middle name, to honor our uncle Simon, my grandmother Bronis's older brother. My sister is named for her great-grandmother Tania.

My grandmother Bronis's eldest brother, Simon, on April 22, 1916.*

There are two other Jewish naming traditions worth mentioning: to give the baby the name of a favorite biblical figure (Abraham, Isaac, Esther, Miriam, etc.) or, in lieu of using an identifiably Jewish name, to use one liked by the parents and that identifies the child with the culture of the place where they are born. My paternal grandfather's family, for example, who were assimilated Jews, all had German names: Siegfried, Richard ("Kurt"), Walter, and Günther, for instance. My grandmother's family was different, though, because they had emigrated from Poland.

---

* The wealthiest man in the family, he moved to Belgium two years after his father's assassination, where he gambled away most of his fortune. Simon died in Antwerp in 1930.

Sina Aronsfrau.

My great-grandfather Sina was born in Witznitz (Bukovina, Austro-Hungarian Empire), and so not very far from Nova Sulitza, but he moved from there to Bochnia (Galicia, Poland), where his children were born. My grandmother Bronislawa, who was born in 1892, and her parents and siblings moved from Bochnia to Mannheim in 1901. The exact circumstances of the family's departure from Poland aren't clear, but it was undoubtedly influenced by anti-Semitic violence. Indeed, my grandmother's memoir practically begins with traumatic memories from that specific episode:

> My mother holds me in her arms; I am crying, it seems to me,
> that this endless going, going will never stop, this sickness in my
> body will never end. The beautiful voice of my mother calms my

tears: "Soon we will be there, in a wonderful country, nobody will hurt us any more, we will be happy, free."...I am looking at my brother—how strange he looks with his broken nose. I see still the boys running after him, throwing stones, chasing him. We kept it a secret, not wanting to upset my parents—and so his nose became crooked.[231]

Germany was to be, for the Aronsfrau family, a wonderful country "where to be a Jew will be natural, without danger." And it was in Germany that the family made a generationally inflected transition to taking on Christian names. But my great-grandfather, Sina, who was already forty-two when he arrived to Germany, didn't make that much of an effort to "pass" or assimilate as German.

Rather, he kept his Jewish name, Zyne—pronounced "Tsineh"—or Sina, and chose not to use a German cognate, whereas Simon, his eldest son, who arrived in Germany at age sixteen, did get a Christian name, as did all the rest of his siblings. Although Mannheim had a Jewish community since the town's foundation, in the early seventeenth century, Sina identified with Mannheim's Eastern European Jewish émigrés; and at the time of his murder he and his wife, Malka, were on the board of the Ahawas Scholem Club, which was an affiliate of the East Jewish Association. And although Sina dressed both modernly and elegantly—as befitted a prosperous haberdasher—he did not relinquish a certain Eastern Jewish air, the way that his children did. This can be ascertained in the only remaining photo that we have of Sina (above), in contrast with his children's assimilation to German society.

Photo of the Aronsfrau siblings taken on the day of my grandmother's wedding
(with the groom, my grandfather, in the top row on the right) in 1924,
two years after Sina Aronsfrau's assassination.

There is a clue here as to why my father received the rather
unusual name of Cinna. It is a homonym for Sina, of course,
but with a spelling that is Latin rather than Jewish. Cinna, a
secondary figure in Roman history, appears as a conspirator in
William Shakespeare's *Julius Caesar*, and is also the protagonist
in a play by Pierre Corneille. I was always told that the name
ran in the family, but there are no other Cinnas in an Aronsfrau family tree that dates back to the mid-nineteenth century.

Rather than family tradition, there was in fact a lot of fear
encrypted in my father's name. My grandmother gave her firstborn a Latinized version of her own murdered father's name.

Her father, though, had been killed because he was Jewish, so that my father's Jewishness was at least made a little more discreet in his given name. Sina Aronsfrau was murdered in 1922, and Cinna Lomnitz was born in 1925, but the real reasons for Sina's murder were a great secret that was forever kept from both my father and his brother. Indeed, in a fragmentary memoir that my father wrote in 1987, which we only discovered after his death, Cinna does mention that his grandfather had been murdered (a fact that he had never shared with us), but then he attributes the murder to a thief, and not a Nazi or proto-Nazi hate crime.

I believe that Cinna had a secret identity. He grew up, as he told me, overprotected by his mother, and to an extreme degree. It seems to me that his mother obsessively shielded her little "Cinnalein" because she had been so unable to protect her father. She even hid from my father his true identity as the grandson of a murder victim, and specifically as the victim of a hate crime. He was told that his name came from a Hebrew word that means "strong man," but as Israeli friends have confirmed, there is no variant of "Sina" or "Tsina" or "Sinai" that quite suggests this interpretation. A strong man is what my grandparents wished him to be, due to the extreme vulnerability that was encoded in his name.

As my father told me, he and his brother Eric played as children looking at the rich illustrations of animals in Brehm's nature book; and when they encountered "ugly toads," they named them "Hitler" and "Goering." They knew that there was something ugly there, and that it was very close, but they couldn't quite identify it from their bourgeois house in Brussels, where they were pampered and surrounded by nannies and protected from the horror that had already claimed the life of their grandfather and would soon decimate the rest of the family.

The wedding of my grandparents Kurt Lomnitz and Bronislawa Aronsfrau, in Wiesbaden, 1924. In the back row, to the left, is Walther Lomnitz, and in the center is Günther Lomnitz. In the second row, Wally and Leska Lomnitz. The rest are Bronislawa's siblings.

Cinna and Eric spoke in French to each other. They were afraid of being identified as Germans (*Boches*) in Belgium, but their eagerness for assimilation had also been fostered by their mother, who encouraged them to identify with Belgium, much as her own mother had urged her to embrace German identity:

Before me is the picture of my mother holding me in her arms and talking to me about this new homeland — Germany. Like her I have tried to give my children the same feeling everywhere we land. I tried to convince them that this is the end of our wandering. Poor children — how perfect they spoke French, trying to forget German as I wanted to forget Polish many years ago. How their room in Brussels was adorned with the pictures of the King and his family. How they knew the words of the national anthem and how proudly they used to sing it.

She then tried the same thing in Chile, though by that point, the incentives for assimilation were guided less by hope than by fear. In the case of my father, though, his propensity to adapt and go with the current had been hardwired by virtue of his very name.

Names, like passports, often contain a trace of fear. Mine is Claudio. It is a name that was quite popular in Chile when I was born. It was chosen so that I might blend and be Chilean. However, Claudio also carries hidden behind it a second, not especially Latin, name, Walter, which comes from a deceased uncle on the Lomnitz side. And even a third, unregistered, Hebrew name, Dov, which I have very rarely had the occasion or temptation to use, but it exists. My grandfather Misha, on the other hand, imbued with a strong sense of Jewish nationalism, decided at a certain point to try to forgo Adler, a last name that suggested desire to assimilate into the Austro-Hungarian Empire, in favor of the Hebrew Ben Tzvi, which means "Son of Tzvi" (which was Hershel's Hebrew name). In doing this, Misha attempted what many other founders of

Israel and members of his generation had done, some of whom became Ben-Aharon, Ben-Gurion, or Ben-Dayan, for instance. The recognition that the Adler name was a result of collective oppression prompted a gesture of fearlessness and the adoption of a new name. There is fear there too, I think, and a determination to overcome it.

My father's name, however, is the most secretly painful of all the names I know. It points to an absent grandfather whose cause of death his mother couldn't and wouldn't share even with her own son. The overprotection that Cinna so suffered stemmed not only from my grandmother's mortal fear, but also from the impossibility of defending or even crying openly for her father. And my father never really understood the full implications of his own name.

The Aronsfrau murder

About a month ago I received an email from a Karen Strobel, who introduced herself as a researcher in the Mannheim City Archives, working in the section that is dedicated to the documentation of the National Socialism period. Together with a retired history teacher, Brigitte Zwerger, Karen has been doing research and writing on the assassination of Sina Aronsfrau.[232] The case came to their attention because of Martin Sabrow's book on the Rathenau murder, and it rang some bells for them because Karen and Brigitte have worked to uncover the history of national socialism in Mannheim, a city that prides itself — not unjustly — on the strength of its socialist and communist past, but that has tended to forget the Nazi agitation that also flourished there. Karen Strobel heard that I was a descendant of Sina, and that I had published information on the case in Spanish. She was contacting me for that reason, and also to share her research findings.

Karen Strobel's first email included Sina's (or Zyne's) death certificate and much information that I ignored. We then initiated an intense correspondence that is still ongoing, because Karen and Brigitte's research uncovered very much that I had not known or understood. The case of Sina Aronsfrau's murder is still partly unsolved and too intricate to explain fully here, but there are some elements of the story that have implications for my own psychological makeup, though I need to backtrack a bit in order to show why.

When I first learned that Sina Aronsfrau was murdered by anti-Semitic nationalist terrorists, a couple of years ago, I was at a loss to explain the cause of the assassination. The people who Professor Sabrow showed were responsible for killing Sina had previously murdered Matthias Erzberger, tried to murder Philipp Schiedemann, and then later killed Walther Rathenau. My problem was that these three people were very famous indeed: Erzberger had spoken out against the war in 1917 and signed the German armistice with the Allies in 1918, Schiedemann had been the Weimar Republic's first chancellor, and Rathenau was foreign minister. Why would a terrorist outfit that was so ambitious in its political aims go after my great-grandfather?

The truth is, I wasn't sure. Before Karen Strobel approached me, I did not know very much about Sina Aronsfrau. According to family lore, his son Simon, my grandmother's oldest brother, was extraordinarily rich. They said that he owned his own private airplane in the 1920s, and that he had given my grandmother a department store, the Köln Kaufhaus, as a wedding gift. So the family story went. I wasn't sure whether it was true, but it struck me that if Sina Aronsfrau owned a department store in Mannheim, he might have been targeted for that very reason.

The corner building in this 1930s photo still has the
Aronsfrau name on the second floor, where Sina's business was.
The *H* is for Hermann Aronsfrau, Sina's second son.

I knew from reading a book by Paul Lerner that the Nazis decried Jewish-owned department stores as especially pernicious institutions, and also that Germany's Jewish department store owners were universally of Polish origin, like Sina.[233] So maybe Sina was a major tycoon, an owner of a chain of department stores, who had been singled out by the Organisation Consul for that reason, since they tended to go after big targets.

But these conjectures proved to be false. Paul Lerner's book lists the Tietz family as the owners of the Frankfurt and Köln department stores that had supposedly belonged to my family. It is possible that Simon might have given his sister some shares for her wedding—these were joint stock companies by the 1920s—but neither she nor Simon owned anything approaching a partner's stake. Karen Strobel and Brigitte Zwerger's research has identified Sina's and Simon's businesses, and their places of residence, and the story is a bit different from what I had conjectured.

My family lore had it that my grandmother, Bronislawa Aronsfrau, was a German Jew of Polish origin, from a wealthy family, while my grandfather, Kurt Lomnitz, was a true *yeque*, that is a Jew of old German stock that had established itself in the Rhineland since the seventeenth century. Thus, the Lomnitzes, who were lawyers and doctors, were from an upper-middle-class family that had less money but more cultural capital than the Aronsfraus. That part of the equation is true to a certain extent, but my grandmother's Polish origin was in fact less remote than I'd been led to believe: Bronis was actually born in Bochnia (Galicia, Poland), and emigrated to Mannheim when she was already nine years old. Her brother Simon, who was the eldest of the siblings, was sixteen when the family moved to Germany. The family's move from Poland to Mannheim had been prompted by violence, and they embraced Germany as "a country where we need not be afraid anymore, where to be a Jew will be natural, without danger."[234]

Also, the Aronsfraus were more deeply educated than I had been led to believe. Sina and his sons worked very hard from their arrival to Mannheim, and they prospered quite a bit.

Simon and his brothers moved up the social ranks. Bronislawa, for her part, took a teaching degree and graduated first in her entire school. Unlike the men in my Lomnitz family, though, the Aronsfrau brothers did not fight in the First World War. Maybe they were too old to be drafted at the outbreak of the war, and it is unclear whether they were even considered German citizens in 1914. Sina, for his part, was active in Mannheim's Eastern European Jewish community, and so remained unassimilated. In short, the Aronsfraus represented something that German *Völkisch* and anti-Semitic fanatics hated most particularly: foreign Jews who prospered while the Germans fought the war.

This two-family corner building in Mannheim (M2, 17) is where Sina Aronsfrau and his family lived.

And there is more still. Founded in the early seventeenth century, Mannheim never had a Jewish ghetto. Jews had always been free to live anywhere in the city. For their part, Sina and his eldest son Simon took up residence near the Rathaus (city hall), in a very nice upper-middle-class neighborhood. Living there must have been a proud achievement for them, but Karen Strobel and Brigitte Zwerger's meticulous research also shows that the Aronsfraus were pretty much surrounded by Nazis. Sina's next-door neighbor, Heinrich Tillessen, was the uncle of Karl and Heinrich Tillessen, who had murdered Matthias Erzberger a month before Sina's assassination.

Karl Tillessen was the head of a department within Organisation Consul entrusted specifically with terrorist attacks. He was also the person who ordered Fischer and Stern's attempt on Walther Rathenau's life, and orchestrated Ernst von Salomon's participation in it. In other words, my great-grandfather's next-door neighbors were implicated in the plot to murder him. Sina Aronsfrau was neither an accidental target nor a major public figure. Rather, he was well known to his assassins, or at least to the people who ordered the killing.

There may well have been some rivalry between these neighboring families. One of the Tillessen daughters was an opera singer, like my grandmother. Maybe there was some envy or competition there, or coming from another cousin, Bruno Tillessen, who was an actor and opera singer in Munich, which is where my grandmother studied and earned the favor of Bruno Walter. Walter, who was also Jewish and a close collaborator of Gustav Mahler, was at that point director of the Bavarian State Opera, and so was also the pivotal leader for authentic Wagner performances in Germany, since Bayreuth had closed during the First World War. There may have been jealousy or frustration there, as well. But beyond this baseless speculation, it is certain that some of the Tillessens were down-wardly mobile in the postwar years, while Simon, Sina's eldest, opened two new branches of their business in 1919, one in Essen and the other in Gelsenkirchen.

And the Tillessens weren't the Aronsfraus' only Nazi neighbors, either. A couple of houses down the street from Sina Aronsfrau and the Tillessens lived Richard Cordier, who was chairman of the local NSDAP (Nazi Party) in Mannheim. Cordier instigated an assault on young Jewish merchants at the Strohmarkt on January 7, 1922, a few months before Sina's assassination. Simon Aronsfrau, for his part, lived in a very nice nearby building, but after the first war a Dr. Hermann Eckard moved into the downstairs apartment, and Eckard was one of Mannheim's most active Nazi Party members. In short, Sina, the Polish Jew who prospered, and whose children deeply identified with Germany high culture, was living in the midst of the upper crust of the local Nazi Party.

Simon Aronsfrau and his family occupied the third floor
of this Mannheim building (M6, 9).

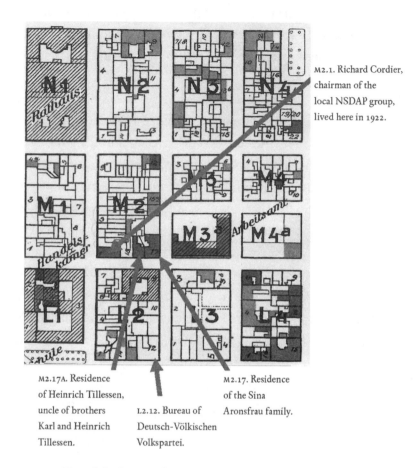

M2.1. Richard Cordier, chairman of the local NSDAP group, lived here in 1922.

M2.17A. Residence of Heinrich Tillessen, uncle of brothers Karl and Heinrich Tillessen.

L2.12. Bureau of Deutsch-Völkischen Volkspartei.

M2.17. Residence of the Sina Aronsfrau family.

Map of the district of Mannheim where Sina Aronsfrau lived, one block from the Rathaus, or city hall.

Sina's assassination also happened at a time of steep inflation and unemployment in postwar Germany, and this provided a good opportunity for upper-middle-class Nazi leaders, like the Tillessens and the Cordiers, to recruit followers among the working classes. The price of bread had risen 75 percent in the months prior to Sina's assassination. There were rail strikes, and a number of shrill and at least mildly violent anti-Semitic incidents in Mannheim during those months, all orchestrated by the newly formed Nazi Party. All orchestrated by Sina's neighbors, in other words.

The day that Sina was murdered, thirty-five new members enlisted in Mannheim's NSDAP, which was the single largest spike in enrollments in the local party up to that point. Strobel and Zwerger's research thus suggests that the Sina Aronsfrau murder may have been used to channel local anxieties, caused by hyperinflation and lack of work, against Jews and toward enlistment in the party. A prosperous, overtly Polish Jew who had thrived during and after the war was a very useful target.

Envy

My father was never told the true story of his grandfather's murder, but his mother and father certainly knew it. In fact, they knew it despite Nazi efforts to obfuscate the case, which I will not get into here, except to say that it involved coaxing two Nazi minors, Max Josef Über and Eduard Däumling, to confess to having accidentally shot and killed Sina Aronsfrau in an effort to rob him. Däumling and Über were tried and convicted for attempted robbery, and let go after a short prison term, after which they went on to good careers under National Socialism. Later (1967), Max Josef Über reached the position of CEO of the German Ford Company (no less!).

Still, despite these youths' confession, after the investigation of the Rathenau murder unfolded and was made public,

Organisation Consul's participation in Sina Aronsfrau's murder was also known. Clearly my grandmother herself believed that it was the Nazis who had killed her father, and not a disgruntled employee who wanted to rob him, since that is what she confidentially told my mother. Moreover, Bronis knew the Tillessens, and had lived in Mannheim when the anti-Semitic riots started there; she knew that Cordier was head of the local Nazi branch, and that her brother Simon's downstairs neighbor was a prominent Nazi. Still, she preferred to keep her two sons in the dark about all of that, confiding the information only to one of her daughters-in-law, my mother.

Cinna himself did not understand the depth of his connection to Sina, or the full reason for his mother's protectiveness. And yet, at some deep level, he did understand at least something of all of this, for I have never met anyone as aware — as dreadfully aware — of the power of envy as my father. He could smell it a mile away. Cinna was attentive even to the possibility of envy, and was always at pains to avoid it, and to keep triumph, accomplishment, and luck as discreet and inconspicuous as possible.

This fear of envy is also a Jewish thing, I think. Certainly for those generations, though I myself was raised with a bit of that too. My great-grandfather Boris was attentive to and concerned about envy, and so was my mother. But my father was sensitive to an extreme degree: for him mimesis was not only about fitting in, it was also about not standing out. It was a form of self-effacement, and dread of hubris. His grandfather had been murdered because of it, and his uncle Simon then squandered his money at the race tracks. Bronis protected her son Cinna from her father Sina's fate, by leading him to believe that her father had been murdered while being robbed. She wanted him to understand that envy could easily turn to murder, and so it needed to be recognized and deflected in time.

Poor Cinna

Dead Rose
An icy breeze silences your rustling, your dormant warmth

Jar of Anguish
My opening cries for you
Because you will receive from me my overflowing, my deaf yearning

Beginning of Autumn
I wonder that today time stops in my hands and my
head rests on the knees of the infinite.

These are among the few poems that I have by my father. Almost nothing. I don't know the exact date of their creation — probably near the end of the 1940s. They are lines that he wrote for a composition by his friend, the musician Leon Schidlowsky, who used them in his work "Five Poems for Contralto and Piano." It is likely that the contralto for whom these musical settings were composed was my grandmother Bronis, who gave classes in operatic singing from her house in Santiago. They are vitalist poems, despite their quiet melancholy, and they were written during an engaged and open young adulthood that followed my father's prolonged reclusion during his high school years.

Cinna may have written the poems in Israel, as they seem at least at one point to allude to the physical transformation that came with life on a kibbutz. This is suggested in the final poem that Cinna wrote for Schidlowsky: "My hands, I offer my hands to the moon / Hands covered by the resin of work and oblivion."

Throughout my childhood, my father was for me a figure of admiration and beauty. Cinna was soft-spoken, and had a delicate sense of irony as well as an encompassing intelligence, with vast knowledge that he never showed off, but which one could call on when necessary. When I was born, Cinna was already an established scientist. He founded the Institute of Geophysics at the Universidad de Chile. We later went to Berkeley, and from there to Mexico City, and in each of those places he was well regarded professionally. And then there was also something that for me had all of the panache of a nobility title, the Lomnitz law — which was an equation proposed by Cinna in his doctoral thesis on the torsion of rocks, which later became canonized as scientific law by Sir Harold Geffreys, a celebrated geophysicist at the University of Cambridge. More recently, my father's equation has been generalized as a relevant principle for all of fluid physics.[235]

From my perspective, Cinna was not someone to be pitied particularly; on the contrary, he was in almost every sense admirable. He was tall, handsome, professionally successful, and admired by his many friends. He had the magnanimity to support his wife, my mother, in her meteoric career. He was the head of my family. Nevertheless, his mother, my grandmother Bronis, at times referred to him as "poor Cinna." Where did that come from?

In the memoir draft that I've mentioned, Cinna speaks of his mother: "Like the woman of great character that she was, she struggled continually with God and destiny to anticipate all of the misfortunes that might materialize and that her fertile imagination presented to her as plausible."[236] He goes on to say: "She knew what adversity and misfortune were. Her father, a peaceful old man with a gray beard (this is how I saw him in an old photograph) had been murdered in his store by thieves. Soon afterward, her venerated mother, an energetic and brilliant woman, died prematurely from a serious illness. Life for her was a balancing act, a tightrope walk over the abyss."[237]

My grandmother Bronis in a studio photo
from the late 1930s or early 1940s.

Overprotection of her children and a deep fear of the poor were the net result of this anxiety. In his memoir, Cinna recounts how one day his mother looked for him high and low and jerked him away terrified when she finally found him at the funeral cortège of a well-known fisherman on the Knokke beach in Belgium, where they spent their summers. Cinna began to cry over the injustice of his mother's rage. "Upon seeing my reaction, my mother immediately calmed down and began to explain to me, as a teacher might, that it could be dangerous for a boy to hang around with 'poor people,' because they could have all manner of contagious diseases."[238]

According to my father, it was at that moment that he began a prolonged rebellion against his mother. "The townspeople, and in this case, the town of Knokke, were *my* people…"[239] I think that it is truer to say that my father's rebellion manifested itself principally in a kind of self-destructive isolation. In the process, he allowed his mother to wrap him up in her angst, something that in the end may have been a self-sacrificial way of protecting her.

"What I wouldn't give, my beautiful mother, to once again caress your golden hair and take refuge next to you, as I did when I was a boy! Who might bring you back now from the infinite expanse of time and death, with your soft eyes and white skin!"

In this elegiac tone, Cinna invokes his mother and begins to piece together his fragile memoirs. I think that Cinna's supposed weakness was feigned as a concession to his mother's need to protect him but it in fact reflected his worries about protecting her. And this is interesting to me, because we have already seen how the column figure, a role of stoic strength, was in my mother's family a form of intergenerational protection. In the case of my father, whose childhood took place in times of Nazism, to accept the outward role of the weakling, or at least that of the introvert, was in some deeply self-destructive fashion a way of protecting his mother, at least up to a point.

It is impossible to imagine that my grandmother didn't often think of her father when pronouncing the name of her son, but as there was much to fear around the subject of Sina Aronsfrau's murder, the story that she told was deliberately altered. My father was already sixty years old when he sat down to write his memoir; still, he tells the story in the following way: "A peaceful old man with a gray beard (this is how I saw him in an old portrait) had been murdered in his store by thieves."[240] There is in this story a strong example of displacement: the Nazi becomes a common thief, and a murder motivated by racial hatred from competitors is turned into a murder motivated by an employee's envy.

Despite police versions to the contrary, my grandmother knew that her father's murder was never the result of a common robbery. A central element of that murder's mystery, which might have been deliberately unresolved by members of a police force that sympathized increasingly with nascent fascism, was precisely that there had been no robbery at all. The report published in the *Frankfurter Zeitung* at the time states: "Last night, the merchant Sina Aronsfrau was murdered in his home, from where he ran a wholesale textile business. Nothing at all was taken."[241] Such murders, with no associated robbery, were characteristic of the political executions carried out by the Organisation Consul.

Nevertheless, Bronis was content to allow her children to believe that a murder that had been motivated by class and racial hatred had been nothing but a common robbery gone awry. Maybe this was my grandmother's way of displacing the horror of Nazism by turning it into a more diffuse fear of the lower classes, with their "dangerous infections." Her father had been murdered by his neighbors. One should beware of one's neighbors. My father rebelled against his mother's dread of the poor, but he did not have the heart to force her to speak out loud of the terror she felt as a result of Nazi violence. He needed to protect her from that.

My grandmother was forced to live with fear during my father's entire childhood. Probably even my grandfather felt it. Given the rapid spread of Nazism during the 1920s and 1930s, it was wise to be secretive about Sina Aronsfrau's murder and, if it was ever necessary to speak of it, to endorse the official story that it had been a common crime, a theft gone awry rather than a political execution. The assassins of the Organisation Consul were heroes of the Nazi Party long before Hitler's electoral triumph, a fact that was recognized in the months immediately following his election. Thus, in July 1933, the new regime had the "martyrs" who had killed Rathenau reburied, and dedicated a new memorial stone to Fischer and Kern that reads:

> *Do what you must*
> *Triumph or Die*
> *And leave the decision*
> *to God*

The commemorative speech that was delivered on that solemn occasion was delivered by SA chief of staff Ernst Röhm (who would be executed by Hitler a year later), and it recognized those assassins in the following terms: "Your spirit, Kern and Fischer, is the spirit of the SS, the black-uniformed soldiers of Hitler…"[242] That same Fischer, "der Geist der SS," was among my great-grandfather's killers. It was safer to pretend that he had been murdered by common thieves.

My grandmother then placed a veil over both the cause of Sina Aronsfrau's death and her dedication of her son to her murdered father's memory, by claiming that "Cinna" was a traditional family name, rather than a distorted version of her father's name. It is understandable that my grandfather let her do this. My grandmother's overprotection of Cinna — her "poor Cinna" — also allowed her to perform the protection that she had not been able to extend to her father, her siblings, or her nephews. Overprotecting Cinna helped her to forget her own impotence.

A sketchbook drawing by Cinna presented as a gift to his father on his birthday, the first celebrated in Chile, on February 16, 1939, with a melancholic photograph of Bronis.

I think that Cinna, who was very sensitive, understood this, and allowed himself to be "poor Cinna" during his childhood and adolescence, and maybe even until he began his socialist and Zionist activism and moved to Israel. Until that moment, at least, Cinna carried out a passive rebellion, which consisted in taking what his mother asked of him to the extreme: isolation. But alongside his rebellion, he always protected his mother. Cinna understood that, despite its extraordinary personal cost, vulnerability was something that his mother needed from him.

The author of my days

Parents no longer have the authority they once did. In what sense is a father the "author of his son's days"? Today, the patriarch Abraham would be in jail for attempted infanticide, and it seems nothing short of grotesque to imagine one's father as a sovereign who can deal with his children as he sees fit. This figure of authorship seems especially inept in the case of my soft-spoken father, who was so punctiliously respectful and also so painfully reserved. Was Cinna in any sense "the author of my days"?

Given the inadequacy of this idea of paternal authorship, let us weigh one "minimalist" alternative. Perhaps I might consider my father as "the author of my days" because he was my *genitor* — that is, he had the faith to procreate as a conscious act. In this there could indeed be authorship, since the decision to reproduce can be a deliberate act, like the creative action of an author. Nevertheless, this image of authorship dissipates at the very moment a father meets his new child.

A father is inevitably surprised by his children, because he will always find in them something of what Freud called *unheimliche*, which can be translated as "sinister" or "uncanny," although it refers most precisely to the discovery or recognition of something profoundly known in what is apparently unfamiliar. More than anything, a father is surprised by his child, who is someone radically new, a stranger, but who then immediately begins to manifest a second order of strangeness that stems not from difference but from similarity. This eruption of deep familiarity in the child offers instants in which the father recognizes himself as author; but such moments are in fact movements in a dance of continual separation and encounter, of identification and radical differentiation.

This dialectic between the unknown and the known can incite a father to try to mold his children in his image, to "straighten them out." Because the father recognizes so much of himself in his child, he can feel tempted to use his power to make the child resemble him. This is the father as master, as a monster who wants his child to live up to the narcissistic image he has of himself. The opposite alternative is also monstrous — the absent or negligent father, who doesn't even try to have a connection with his children.

The education that my father gave me avoided these extremes. Cinna's maternal language was German, but the indelible trauma of Nazism caused him not to teach it to us. In this sense, Cinna did not reproduce himself in us, not even in this fundamental way: we do not share his mother tongue. Neither did he make us study piano, which he — as the son of a musician — had been compelled to learn. At times I resented

Cinna's negligence, since it fostered a kind of intergenerational impoverishment: my father spoke six languages, and I only speak four. And while I do have musical inclinations, I never learned to play piano or read music well.

Still, I also intuited that there was in all of this a desire to protect us from the monstrosity of his unspoken past; of the pain of survival, and of the difficulties that accompany holding on to customs in exile. Cinna tried to teach me to live both with emigration and assimilation. He wanted to show me also how to be like a stone, a part of the landscape. But there was also in all of this an inclination to respect the individual personalities of his children, and to allow us to flourish in the New World.

Cinna forced neither German nor piano on us, and since we weren't made to study, we never learned them. But in exchange he raised us in a free environment, filled with conversation and lived experiences, and he didn't get in the way of each one of his children developing according to his inclinations. There was in this an idea of the overwhelming greatness of the world; a deep recognition that the world exceeded him; and in a place like that, it was better that each one of us exercised our own imagination. In the end, our fathers are never capable of rescuing us from what the world sets before us. In his educational stance with respect to his children, my father always emphasized this limitation.

Bigger but smaller

With the war now a distant memory, and with strong doses of intergenerational amnesia fully administered, my brothers and

I were able to enjoy a dreamlike childhood, full of trips and adventures.

I remember so much beauty from my Chilean childhood! All of those places outside of Santiago and the day trips to the country with the families of my parents' friends. We called them all "uncles" and "aunts," and we had in this way an enormous family: Uncle Chago and Aunt Ruth, Uncle Peter and Aunt Rebeca, Uncle Daniel and Aunt Chofi, Aunt Choli and Uncle Hans... We kids would disappear among the rocks at Cajón del Maipo, exploring its secret caves and scaling its granite boulders. We felt like heroes, and we never complained. We went wherever they took us, we slept wherever we had to sleep, and ate whatever there was to eat, having the time of our lives.

Those places are still so powerful for me that just to say their names invokes them with absolute efficacy: El Cajón del Maipo, El Quisco, Tongoy, Concón, Villa Rica, Vichuquén, Tatalafquén... The plot that my parents bought and then sold for a loss in Los Domínicos. It was then surrounded by countryside and was attached to the house owned by the writer José Donoso, who still wasn't that famous back then. Their other piece of land, also sold for a pittance, on the beach at Cachagua... And the trip to Peru that made such a mark on me. Machu Picchu wrapped for moments in mist and everything wet with the tiny drops, empty, practically empty, for my brothers and me to run through it and lose ourselves among its stone houses. The floating islands of the Uro Indians on Lake Titicaca. The train down the narrow bed of the Urubamba River, with the steps of the Inca terrace farms descending from the hills.

I always thought I came from the perfect family. I loved it so much! We had true freedom. Few rules, and the ones that were there seemed mainly to guarantee safety and respect. Authority was what it was supposed to be: legitimate power. There was openness to curiosity and there was liberality. There was respect for women and an unusual degree of support for my mother on my father's part.

Claudio and Jorge.

My brother Jorge, who was a scientist from the time he was very young, always needed accomplices for his projects: how to distinguish a drone (which doesn't sting) from a worker bee (which does), for example. There were experiments in physics and entomology, and if you made a mistake there were consequences. The bee would sting you, for example. During my childhood, I was stung by no fewer than twenty-three different bees. Counting the stings was as important as if they were scars earned in a duel of honor. As in every scientific matter, honor was important.

Another experiment of Jorge's: to make homemade gunpowder. He bought sulfur at the hardware store (I'm not sure why they sold it), he stole saltpeter from one garden or another, since in Chile it was still used as fertilizer, and so managed to generate toxic yellow clouds, though they never achieved the explosive effect we were looking for. I flourished in this environment, which was at the same time so free and also so silently protected.

In John Steinbeck's *Of Mice and Men*, there is a character named Lennie, a mentally disabled giant who loves the softness of animal fur but ends up crushing the little animals that he tries to hold and caress. My brother Jorge used to say that I was like Lennie. I've always loved blindly, crushing and smothering.

Alberto's laughter.

When I was nine or ten years old, in Berkeley, I invented a battle cry that I let out every time I was overtaken by one of these uncontrollable attacks of crushing love and suffocation, and I repeated it as I chased after Jorge or Alberto to tackle them, smother them, and lick their faces. Lennie.

"Cusi!" That's how my shout began, and upon hearing it, poor Alberto ran like a terrified hare, while I bounded after him, completing the invocation: "Simi bubis cuaxi fatso hashi simi brain!" And then I fell upon him, while the poor kid struggled and kicked, desperate.

I was happy being a giant Lennie, the faithful wingman for any proposal that came from my older brother, although the complicated effects of being big for my age, a "babysaurus," as my dear friend Juan Pérez would have put it, increased once I started school.

Claudio at the Alliance Française. Santiago de Chile, 1963.

My parents placed me in the French school when I was five years old. Even so, I was taller than the majority of my classmates, who generally started first grade at six. Bigger but smaller. Later, when we moved to California, I skipped a year and entered third grade when I was seven. Capable, maybe, but discreetly small in the end. Free, but discreetly protected. Curious and awake, but secretly ignorant. Today I understand the immensity of that hard-won freedom and protection, and what it cost my grandparents and my parents, who are all gone, and I salute them from here.

Mesohippus

My family moved to Berkeley when I was seven years old. It was 1964. As a boy, I caught a glimpse of the Free Speech Movement and later on the flowering of the hippie movement. The arrival of Bob Dylan and rock music. The golden age of Telegraph Avenue, with its throngs of beautiful dropouts, in long skirts or flared jeans, their long hair flowing freely. The black light on phosphorescent posters announcing Jimi Hendrix concerts at the Filmore. The arrival of the Hare Krishnas and incense. Leopold's Records and Moe's Books. I've always loved Berkeley.

In December 1964, while my brothers and I were busy discovering the infinite pleasures of color television — nonexistent in Chile at that time — on a gorgeous Sylvania TV set, student activist Mario Savio gave his famous speech against the mechanization and serialization of the university: "There's a time when the operation of the machine becomes so odious, makes you so sick at heart, that you can't take part!" It was the start of a generational rift in a struggle against what was then known as the establishment.

My parents bought an old house in the Kensington section of the Berkeley Hills (250 Cambridge St., telephone no. 524-6447), where we played incessantly. Young professors could still afford those kinds of places back then. We also spent a lot of time on the university campus, because we would often go to pick up my father at his office, and above all because my mother, who had begun her undergraduate studies, brought us at times to the parks for us to play while she read. Three years ago, I gave a lecture at Berkeley, and I strolled through the parks that we had played in: the stream with its cantilever bridge, the dwarfed white oak with its hollow trunk, the shade of the giant redwoods...

Those were years of discovery for me. My brothers and I attended the Kensington Hilltop School. The hill that led to the school was steep, so we would walk our bikes a good portion of the way up there, and we would coast downhill most of the way home, smelling the wet ivy on people's front yards. At home, my parents watched the news with Walter Cronkite, which showed the war in Vietnam. In 1968, my brother Jorge, who was turning fourteen, began to let his hair grow and brought home our first Jefferson Airplane album, *Surrealistic Pillow*.

My father worked in the Department of Geophysics, which shared a building with Paleontology. Its entrance displayed fossils from the Cenozoic and Mesozoic eras, including a few dinosaur bones. All of that fascinated me. As kids, my brother

Jorge had introduced me to obsessive study: a passion for insects, for instance; a fascination with fire, gunpowder, and rockets; for putting together plastic models of planes, cars, and warships with epoxy glue, and a fascination with the heroes of the Iliad, the return of Odysseus, Tintin, Babar, and the Hardy Boys. We built a platform high up in the pine tree behind our house, and Jorge designed a system of cords and pulleys to transmit handwritten messages that, like so many of our inventions, was pretty much useless. But there it was, just in case. We also put together useless collections of stamps...All that.

Cinna in his study in the Berkeley house with a drawing by Alberto of an elephant and a possible femur.

One day my father asked a colleague to recommend a good place to go fossil hunting. He suggested a site that wasn't so very close—the Diablo Foothills beyond Walnut Creek—where they had cut into a hill to make way for a railway line. It was a perfect place to find them, because you could walk along the tracks inspecting the exposed wall of the hill, and start digging wherever you liked. My father chose a narrow cave, and we began to chip away. We would have been happy to have found the fossil remains of a clam, but surprisingly we made a much larger find: the remains of a prehistoric horse. A *Mesohippus*. It took us hours to remove its skull from the hillside, still full of teeth. We also removed a few vertebrae and returned home late in the day, with our treasure stuffed in plastic bags. We spent months cleaning that fossil with toothbrushes. Thanks to Cinna, the paleontological zeal that beat in our childish hearts brought us a true discovery connected to the evolution of the horse.

My generous father died on July 7, 2016. My scientific education was mostly in Jorge's hands, who was also responsible for bringing the counterculture to our home. But the enchanted world in which we grew had my father as both condition and reference. Today I think that his laissez-faire attitude toward our disorganized investigations was influenced by the libertarian spirit of the Mario Savios of Berkeley, and perhaps also by that unforgettable stanza of Dylan's, which reads almost as if it were a blessing from my father:

May God bless and keep you always
May your wishes all come true
May you always do for others
And let others do for you
May you build a ladder to the stars
And climb on every rung
May you stay forever young…

Rainbow scarab

We arrived in Mexico from Berkeley in June 1968. We moved into an old house in the Pedregal, which had originally been a kindergarten and was demolished after we moved out. It was full of empty rooms that we could use for whatever we liked. To keep us entertained, my mother placed Jorge, Alberto, and me in an entomology class at the Museo de Historia Natural.

This was the year of the student movement and the Olympics in Mexico City, and soon after our arrival the army occupied the National University (UNAM), where my father worked. I remember seeing a burning bus one day when we went to get him. I remember also the hazing that was practiced on UNAM students back then, you could see young men with their shaved heads riding the city buses. *Butch Cassidy and the Sundance Kid* played for a full year at the Cine Insurgentes. The horror of Mexican conservatism, after all of the experimentation in Berkeley, was also in full view, and the brutality of its class structure, too. Yes. But above all, I remember marveling at the landscapes and all the towns and villages that we came to know by way of a tireless search for beetles and butterflies.

That was how we first came to know Tepoztlán, too, and we fell in love with the place. We walked all through its valley, which at that time was nothing but cornfields, picking through cow pies with a stick, as we searched for Egyptian emeralds: the rainbow scarab (*Phanaeus vindex*). The entire experience was sublime: the town, all adobe, stone and terra-cotta, the shade of the hog-plum trees in the rainy season, and everything surrounded by the russet-and-green wall of the mountains. Searching for the shiny green scarab in piles of shit. A double pleasure for any young boy.

The rainbow scarab is a dung beetle
abundant in the cornfields
that cover the valley of Tepoztlán.

Final (bar mitzvah)

My grandfather couldn't come to Mexico City because of his heart condition, so it was decided that I would have my bar mitzvah in Caracas. And that's what happened. I went to my grandparents' apartment, in the Plaza de la Estrella, in the San Bernardino neighborhood, and I lived with them for a couple of months before the ceremony.

My grandmother was very involved in planning the event and organizing the banquet, while my grandfather sat down to give me an intensive introduction to Jewish culture. I had that immense fortune. I arrived in Caracas in June, and my bar mitzvah was scheduled for August, so I was able to spend a couple of months shadowing Misha, accompanying him to his clerical job at Lámparas Orly, to Bolívar Park to look for some priests who did linguistic work in the Venezuelan Amazon, or to the supermarket to buy this or that...wherever he went.

Noemí's list for planning my
bar mitzvah banquet, August 1970.

My grandfather taught me a lot that summer. He taught me, for example, how to pretend to pray, so that no one would notice that I didn't know much about what was actually going on in the synagogue. He gave me very precise instructions, although they were only useful for Orthodox services. We talked about Judaism and Christianity. He told me a little about his arrival in Peru, and of the liberation that America had been for him. He spoke of the accomplishments of Jews in science and culture. We spoke of Moses and a bit about the prophets. A little about Jesus, too. Something of Marxism, something of South American history. At the time, I didn't understand his interest in someone like Bolívar (he had several shelves of books on him), or in the independence movements of the various South American countries.

Those were months of great fellowship and love between grandson and grandparents. The bar mitzvah ceremony, in the Unión Israelita in Caracas, directed by an awfully serious rabbi, was exciting despite the gravity. My grandmother Bronis had also come all the way from New York, as well as a great deal of family and friends from Venezuela. After the ceremony, the banquet, and the party, my grandparents invited the family to spend a week on the beach, at the Hotel Marcuto Sheraton. A big expense that they insisted on having. Those were days of intense happiness for my grandfather, who was surrounded by almost his entire family, children and grandchildren, in an event that he and Noemí had organized from start to finish.

I think that plenitude can be a dangerous thing, or, as Misha used to say, "*Mamash* [truly] dangerous!" I have seen that in a couple of other cases. And so it was then that Misha had his second heart attack, with everyone there at the Hotel Marcuto. An ambulance came to take him and Noemí to Caracas, and they spoke during the trip. Misha said goodbye and told her how lucky he had been to share his life with her. He also told her that he did not want to be remembered as a businessman, but as an intellectual.[243]

From his arrival in Peru in 1924 he had struggled for that, in the midst of difficulties that always forced him to do other things — sell clothes with Mr. Sarfaty, found Jewish schools in Cali and Bogotá, teach Hebrew to young people in Israel and in Chile. Contributing through his practical efforts to create a new language for a new national community, and more generally to work for universal emancipation through specific struggles, like the reformation of South American national societies, for instance, or Jewish emancipation and rebirth. Through all of that, Misha had to be attentive to the wants of the real world, to his family survival, surely, but also, for several decades, to the survival of freedom in the world. His work as an intellectual existed and flourished in the midst of those struggles, the way a mountain orchid blooms between the crags. Misha's life was now ebbing like a sigh that had brought a bit of oxygen into a clamped-up world. My grandfather said his loving goodbye to Noemí, who would survive him by only six years, and Misha died before reaching Caracas.

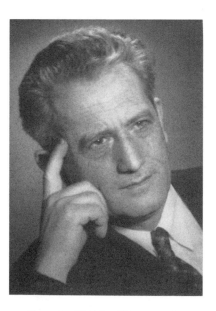

Portrait of Misha. Caracas, 1963.

Having just officially entered religious adulthood, thanks in large measure to Misha, I was able to take part in the prayers of mourning for him. We sat shiva for a week at my grandparents' home. It was then that I said my first kaddish.

Acknowledgments

I had been interested in preserving the history of my family for a while, but I began to conceive of this book in 2012, when a scandal broke out around the hidden Nazi past of a founding figure of Colombian anthropology, Gerardo Reichel-Dolmatoff. When I read the news, I was struck by the fact that Reichel-Dolmatoff's interests in South American Indians in some ways paralleled those of Misha Adler, even though Reichel was an Austrian aristocrat who had for several years been a member of the SS, while my grandfather was born to a Jewish family in the outer reaches of the Austro-Hungarian Empire, and had been a communist. Was there a difference between the motivation of a closeted ex-Nazi and a Jewish communist in their interest in the so-called Indian Question in South America?

That's when I began to think about this book. I became interested in the relationship between the exaltation of "the Indian" and the destruction of Europe. But when I finally started to write, the book took an increasingly more personal turn, and when my father died a few years later, I dropped my academic inquiry altogether and decided to make this book about the origin of my own point of view. This is a demanding subject for anyone, surely, but fortunately I was accompanied by Norma Elizondo throughout this deeply introspective and sometimes personally distressing process. I was nurtured by Norma's love, consideration, and intelligence every step of the way.

And indeed it was a sinuous course, not least because I ended up writing this book twice, first in a Spanish version, and now in this, deeply rewritten, English edition. At first I dreaded the idea of rewriting, and of recalibrating my account for the ear of a different kind of reader, one less familiar with Latin American culture, and maybe more at home in European history. I knew that writing this book in English would be exacting work, even though I was deeply fortunate to have a fine translation of the original Spanish text that I could use as a baseline, done by Vincent Barletta, to whom I am very grateful. I simply could not offer English-language readers quite the same book.

Surprisingly, though, the experience of writing anew proved to be exhilarating: the process provided yet another fascinating bend in this story of constant translations. The effort also opened a new editorial experience for me, thanks to the close and intense dialogue I enjoyed with my editor, Judith Gurewich, whose singular commitment helped me find ideas that had existed only in embrionic form, chapter after chapter. I am deeply grateful to Judith for her passionate intellectual dedication, and for the friendship that she and her family — Victor, Andreas, and Vladimir — have offered Norma and me.

This work is dedicated to my two children, Enrique and Elisa. I hope that it will be instructive for them and for other members of our family. It was important to me that I finish the first version of this book in time for my infirm mother to read it. She has since passed. Larissa was a pillar of our family, and this book is filled with love and gratitude for her incredible vitality.

I am a specialist in almost none of the areas covered in this book. Jewish history, for instance, or German, Colombian, and Peruvian history. Each of those subjects is a world unto itself, so I needed a lot of specialized help. Miraculously I received it at practically every turn, sometimes from unexpected corners. Cristóbal Aljovín and Juan Carlos Lupú found key documents in Lima. José-Carlos Mariátegui kindly facilitated two photos from the archives of his illustrious grandfather. In Colombia, María Victoria Uribe helped me understand the intellectual milieu of the 1940s, and Gustávo Álvarez Gardeazábal dug up new and unsuspected materials out of sheer personal curiosity. It was thanks to his generous spirit that I learned key details of the story of my great-grandparents, Boris and Tania.

My family in Caracas and Bogotá was very supportive of my efforts throughout, and I am especially obliged to my uncles Manuel and Mauricio Adler. Yvonne Adler scanned all of their family papers. On the Lomnitz-Aronsfrau side, Barbara Lomnitz found and sent me invaluable documentation on my grandmother Bronis. I am also grateful to my second cousin, Vivianne Pommier, for her help and advice.

My colleague Naor Ben-Yehoyada helped orient some of my (alas, very limited) reading on the history of Israel, and he put me in touch with Elisheva Shaul, who assisted me with translations from the Yiddish. I am indebted to Elisheva for her fine work. My incursion into Yiddish also found support in Mexico City, from Maia Ajzen and Sara Robbins, who I warmly wish to recognize. In Germany I was overwhelmed by generous help from historian Karen Strobel and her collaborator, Brigitte Zweger. Their painstaking archival research on the assassination of my great-grandfather, Sina Aronsfrau, changed my point of view with regard to my father's story, and so also my own. Karen and Brigitte's commitment to unearthing the history of racism and nationalist violence in their hometown of Mannheim has been an inspiration. I am also indebted to Professor Martin Sabrow, whose work on the Rathenau assassination was critical to discovering the key to Sina Aronsfrau's untimely death. Finally, my friend and former student Xenia Cherkaev translated family correspondence from the Russian, and I am thankful for her careful, helpful clarification of the semantic range of some key words.

A handful of close friends read the Spanish manuscript before it was published and provided invaluable comments. I am deeply thankful to Jesús Rodríguez Velasco, Jorge Aguilar Mora, Beatriz Martínez de Murguía, Fernando Escalante Gonzalbo, and José Ramón Cossío for their close readings and comments. All of these friends, and a few others — Jorge Myers, Adrián Gorelik, Martín Bergel, Erika Pani, Carlos Altamirano — have been generous interlocutors; I hope that I can one day reciprocate their comradery.

From an institutional point of view, this book was written thanks to the support of Columbia University and to the Alexander von Humboldt Foundation of Germany, that granted me its prestigious prize in 2017. This allowed me to write the first (Spanish) version of this book, which I in fact completed in Berlin while affiliated with the Freie Universität. I wish to thank professors Marianne Braig, Stephanie Schütze, and Stefan Rinke for their generous hospitality. I also benefited from time spent as a visiting scholar at the Centro de Investigación y Docencia Económica in Mexico City, and am much obliged to its director, Dr. Sergio López Ayllón, for his invitation.

Finally, I wish to thank the remarkable editorial team at Other Press, especially Yvonne Cárdenas, Alexandra Poreda, Janice Goldklang, Gage Desser, and Walter Havighurst, for their meticulous care.

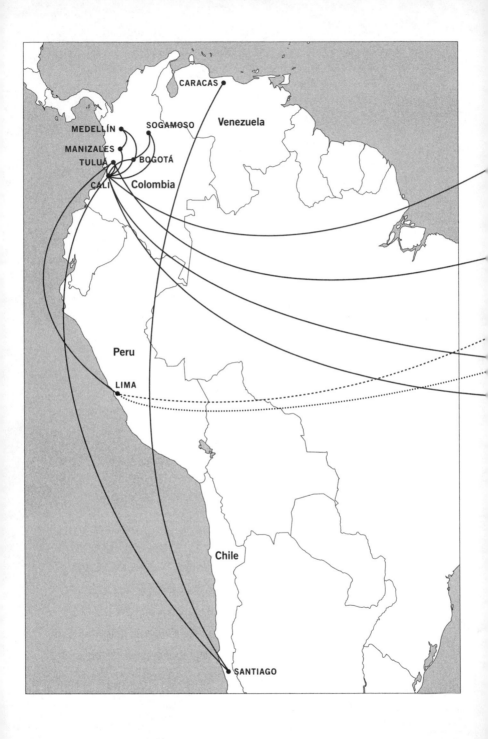

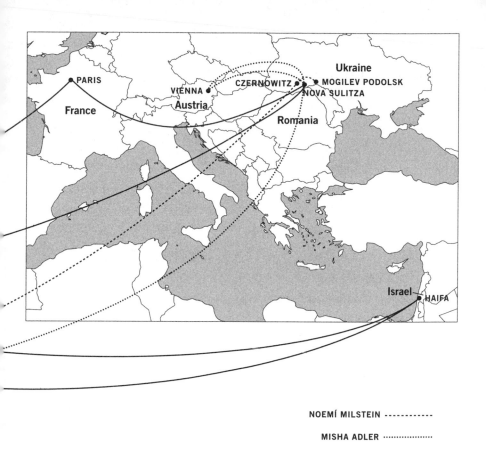

NOEMÍ MILSTEIN ------------

MISHA ADLER ················

TOGETHER ————

Journeys of Noemí Milstein & Misha Adler

Family Tree

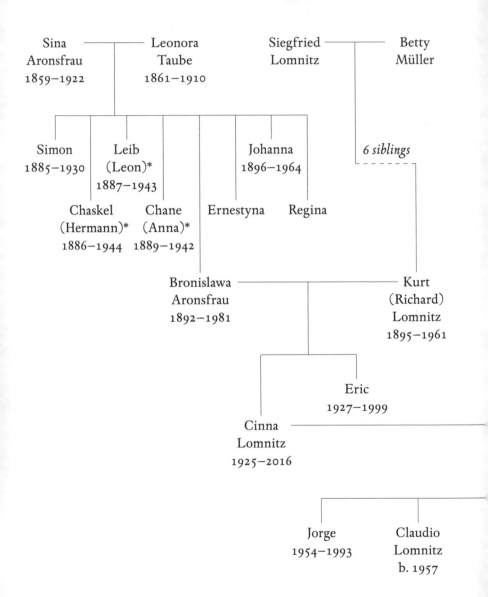

Sina Aronsfrau 1859–1922 —— Leonora Taube 1861–1910

Siegfried Lomnitz —— Betty Müller

Simon 1885–1930

Leib (Leon)* 1887–1943

Chaskel (Hermann)* 1886–1944

Chane (Anna)* 1889–1942

Ernestyna

Regina

Johanna 1896–1964

6 siblings

Bronislawa Aronsfrau 1892–1981 —— Kurt (Richard) Lomnitz 1895–1961

Eric 1927–1999

Cinna Lomnitz 1925–2016

Jorge 1954–1993

Claudio Lomnitz b. 1957

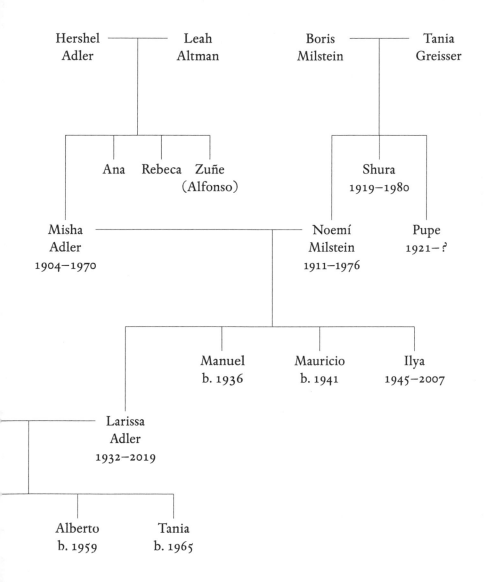

Hershel Adler — Leah Altman

Boris Milstein — Tania Greisser

Ana   Rebeca   Zuñe
                 (Alfonso)

Shura
1919–1980

Misha Adler — Noemí Milstein   Pupe
1904–1970   1911–1976   1921–?

Manuel   Mauricio   Ilya
b. 1936   b. 1941   1945–2007

Larissa Adler
1932–2019

Alberto   Tania
b. 1959   b. 1965

died in the Holocaust along with their spouses and descendants

Notes

INTRODUCTION:
THE LANGUAGE OF PARADISE

1. Umberto Eco, *The Search for the Perfect Language* (Oxford, UK: Blackwell, 1997).

Part One: Citizens of the World

1: UNSTABLE AFFILIATIONS

2. José Carlos Mariátegui, "Israel y Occidente, Israel y el mundo," *Repertorio Hebreo* 1, no. 1 (April–May 1929): 4.

3. For a recent appraisal in English of Mariátegui's work and trajectory, see Lance Selfa, "Mariátegui and Latin American Marxism," *International Socialist Review* 96 (spring 2015), https:// isreview.org/issue/96/mariategui-and-latin-american-marxism. The

English-language anthology that I refer to is Harry E. Vanden and Marc Becker, ed. and trans., *José Carlos Mariátegui: An Anthology* (New York: Monthly Review Press, 2011).

4. "Nacionalismo y vanguardismo," in *Mariátegui total* (Lima: Ediciones Minerva, 1994), 1:308; published originally in *Mundial*, November 27, 1925.

5. Ibid., 1:6 and 4.

6. Osmar Gonzales, *La presencia judía en la izquierda peruana* (Lima: Otramirada, 2014).

7. Pinkas HaKehilot, "'Novoselitsa' (Novoselytsya, Ukraine)," *Encyclopedia of Jewish Communities in Romania* 2 (Jerusalem: Yad Vashem, 1980), 1–8.

8. Great Britain Foreign Office, Historical Section, *Bessarabia* (London: H.M. Stationery Office, 1920), 5.

9. Ibid., 6.

10. Curzio Malaparte, *Kaputt*, English trans. by Cesare Foligno (London: Marlboro, 1982), 208.

11. Josef Govrin, *In the Shadow of Destruction: Recollections of Transnistria and Illegal Immigration to Eretz Israel, 1941–1947* (London: Vallentine Mitchell, 2007), 8.

12. Malaparte, *Kaputt*, 44.

13. Diana Dumitru, *The State, Anti-Semitism, and Collaboration in the Holocaust: The Borderlands of Romania and the Soviet Union* (New York: Cambridge University Press, 2016), 34.

14. Naphtoli Rabinovici, *Ich und Mein Shtetele* (Tel Aviv: Private edition, 1965), English translation for C. Lomnitz by Elisheva Shaul.

15. Great Britain Foreign Office, *Bessarabia*, 21.

2 : WHY MISHA LEFT

16. Marianne Hirsch and Leo Spitzer, *Ghosts of Home: The After-life of Czernowitz in Jewish Memory* (Berkeley: University of California Press, 2010).

17. "Complete equality of rights for all nations; the right of nations to self-determination; the unity of the workers of all nations — such is the national program that Marxism, the experience of the whole world, and the experience of Russia, teach the workers." V. I. Lenin, *The Right of Nations to Self-Determination*, published originally in *Prosvescheniye*, nos. 4–6 (1914), English translation in Lenin Internet Archive, https://wwwmarxists.org/archive/lenin/works/1914/self-det/ch10.htm

18. Quoted in Max J. Kohler and Simon Wolf, *Jewish Disabilities in the Balkan States: American Contributions Toward their Removal, with Particular Reference to the Congress of Berlin* (New York: American Jewish Committee, 1916), 2–3.

19. Ibid., 13.

20. Ibid., 26.

21. Sander Gilman, *The Jew's Body* (New York: Routledge, 1991), 38–47.

22. HaKehilot, "Novoselitsa," 2:5.

3 : EMANCIPATION AND EMIGRATION

23. Moses Mendelssohn, *On Enlightening the Mind* (1784), trans. James Schmidt, https://persistentenlightenment.com/2014/03/18/moses-mendelssohn-on-enlightening-the-mind/, 40.

24. Great Britain Foreign Office, *Bessarabia*, 29.

25. Rabinovici, *Ich und Mein Shtetele*, 3.

26. HaKehilot, "Novoselitsa," 2:3–5.

27. For a history of anti-Semitism in the Austro-Hungarian Empire, see B. E. Pauley, *From Prejudice to Persecution: A History of Austrian Anti-Semitism* (Chapel Hill: University of North Carolina Press, 1992).

28. HaKehilot, "Novoselitsa," 2:7.

29. Rabinovici, *Ich und Mein Shtetele*, 11.

4: THEIR FIRST AMERICA

30. Prefectura de Lima, Inspección General de Investigación y Vigilancia. Mesa de Partes y Archivo, lib. D, fol. 1, núm. 19 (October 7, 1930).

31. HaKehilot, "Novoselitsa," 2:6.

32. For the case of Hungarian migration, see dissertation by Péter Torbágyi, *Magyar Vandormozgalmak Es Szorvanyközøsségek Latin-Amerikában a Második Világháboru Kitöréséig*, PhD thesis, Szegedi Tudományegyetem (Budapest, 2007). I am grateful to Brigitta Cser for translation of relevant passages.

33. Adam McKeown, "Inmigración china al Perú, 1904–1937: exclusión y negociación," *Histórica* 20, no. 1 (1996): 70–71.

34. Salomón Brainski, *Gentes en al noria. Cuentos bogotanos*, Spanish translation by Luis Vidales, 2d ed. (Bogotá: Huecograbajo Litografía, 1973 [1945]), 64.

35. Oscar Terán, "Amauta: vanguardia y revolución," *Prismas* 12 (1984): 174.

36. León Trachtemberg, "Peru," in *Encyclopaedia Judaica*, ed.

Michael Berenbaum and Fred Skolkik, 2d ed. (Detroit: Macmillan, 2007), 15:793–97.

37. "Crisis de maestros y crisis de ideas," *Claridad* 1, no. 2: 3–4., reprinted in *Mariátegui total*, 1:384.

38. Ibid.

39. Carlota Casalino Sen, José Carlos Rivas Harcaya, and Carla Lucía Toche, "La Reforma Universitaria y el movimiento universitario en el Perú de 1919," *Estudios* 40 (2018): 36.

40. For a close study of the connection between voting and literacy in nineteenth-century Peru, see José Ragas, "Leer, escribir, votar. Literacidad y cultura política en el Perú (1810–1900)," *Histórica* 31, no. 1 (2007): 107–34.

41. Casalino Sen, Rivas Harcaya, and Lucía Toche, "La Reforma Universitaria," 36–37.

42. Jorge del Prado Chávez, *Los años cumbres de Mariátegui* (Lima: Ediciones Universidad, 1983), 58.

43. Luis Vidales, "Prólogo a la edición de 1945" (my translation), in Brainski, *Gentes en al noria*.

5: LISA NOEMÍ MILSTEIN

44. Rita Grossman to Claudio Lomnitz, August 14, 2017.

45. Dumitru, *State, Anti-Semitism, and Collaboration*, 56.

46. Ibid., 57.

47. Hirsch and Spitzer, *Ghosts of Home*, 73.

48. Ibid., 70.

49. Del Prado, *Los años cumbres*, 54.

50. José Carlos Mariátegui to Samuel Glusberg, March 9, 1929,

in *José Carlos Mariátegui, Correspondencia (1915–1930)*, ed. Antonio Melís (Lima: Biblioteca Amauta, 1984), 2:525.

6: THE *AMAUTA*

51. Quoted in Del Prado, *Los años cumbres,* 173–74.

52. Alberto Tauro, "Estudio preliminar," in *Mariátegui total,* ed. José Carlos Sandro and Javier Mariátegui Chiappe (Lima: Empresa Editora Amauta, 1994), 2:2018–19.

53. Del Prado, *Los años cumbres,* 40.

54. Oscar Terán, "Amauta: vanguardia y revolución," *Prismas* 12 (1984): 175.

55. For a perceptive review of this period in Mariátegui's life, see Alberto Tauro, "Estudio preliminar," in *Mariátegui total,* vol. 2:2018–2124.

56. Tauro, "Estudio preliminar," 2:2124.

57. Ibid., 39.

58. J. C. Mariátegui, "Heterodoxia de la tradición," *Mundial,* November 25, 1927, in *Mariátegui total,* 1:324.

59. J. C. Mariátegui, "La tradición nacional," *Mundial,* December 2, 1927, in *Mariátegui total,* 1:326.

60. J. C. Mariátegui, "Crisis de maestros y crisis de ideas," *Claridad* 1, no. 2: 3–4, in *Mariátegui total,* 1:384.

61. Quoted in Terán, "Amauta," 183–84.

62. J. C. Mariátegui, "Estudiantes y maestros," *Mundial,* March 9, 1928, in *Mariátegui total,* 1:387.

63. Jorge Aguilar Mora, "Amauta o Vanguardia," in *La cultura de un siglo: América Latina en sus revistas,* ed. Saúl Sosnowski (Madrid: Alianza Editoria, 1999).

64. Del Prado, *Los años cumbres,* 46.

65. Ibid., 176.

66. José Carlos Mariátegui, "El proceso de la literatura," in *Siete ensayos de interpretación de la realidad peruana* (Lima: Biblioteca Amauta, 1968 [1928]), 193.

67. Martín Bergel, "Tentativas sobre Mariátegui y la literatura mundial," unpublished manuscript, 1.

68. José Carlos Mariátegui, "Presentación de 'Amauta,'" *Amauta* 1 (September 1926): 1.

69. Sigmund Freud, "Resistencias al psicoanálisis," *Amauta* 1 (September 1926): 11.

70. Mariátegui, "Israel y Occidente," 4–5.

7: JEWISH AMERICANISM

71. Owing to the effects of guano and, later, nitrate mining booms, Peru was especially slow to industrialize compared to many other Latin American countries. The process began to take off in the 1890s, and industrialization grew at a decent clip of 4–5 percent yearly through the 1920s. See Aurora Gómez Garabatio and Graciela Márquez Colín, "Industrialization and Growth in Peru and Mexico, 1870–2010," in *The Spread of Modern Industry to the Periphery since 1871,* ed. Kevin Hjortshoj O'Rourke and Jeffrey Gale Williamson (New York: Oxford University Press, 2017), 292–93.

72. Quoted in Terán, "Amauta," 182.

73. Del Prado, *Los años cumbres,* 146.

74. José Carlos Maríategui to Sara Hubner, December 27, 1929, in *Mariátegui total,* vol. 2.

75. Mariátegui, "El proceso de la literatura," 256.

76. Miguel Ben-Tzvi Adler, "Presentation," *Repertorio Hebreo* 1, no.1 (April–May 1929): 1.

77. Ibid., 2.

78. Ibid.

79. Ibid.

80. Mariátegui, "Israel y Occidente," 4.

81. Ibid., 5.

82. Ibid., 6.

83. Ibid., 7.

84. Samuel Glusberg to Miguel Adler, June 25, 1929, in *Repertorio Hebreo* 1, no. 3 (1929): 38–40.

85. In the Spanish original: "Americanistica y judaica, sionismo y americanismo han terminado en fundirse y armonizarse en mi íntimo pensar y sentir, hasta constituirse en 'reductio ad unums.'"

86. Jorge C. Muelle, "Zamenhof y el idioma internacional," *Repertorio Hebreo* 1, no. 2 (1929): 30.

87. Mariátegui, "Semitismo y anti-Semitismo," in *La escena contemporánea*, in *Mariátegui total*, 1:1016.

88. Miguel Ben-Tzvi Adler, "Los judíos en la URSS," *Reportorio Hebreo* 1, no. 2: 2.

89. Miguel Ben-Tzvi Adler, "Un estado judío en Palestina," *Repertorio Hebreo* 1, no. 3 (1929): 2.

8: EXPULSION

90. Augusto Leguía, *Yo tirano, yo ladrón* (Lima: Talleres de la Editorial Ahora, 1931), 6.

91. "U.S. Mayor," *Time*, December 7, 1925.

92. "Peru: 'I...Eternal," *Time*, May 5, 1930.

93. Pedro Cieza de León, *The Discovery and Conquest of Peru*, trans. Alexandra Parma Cook and Noble David Cook (Durham, NC: Duke University Press, 1998 [1953]), 37.

94. Richard Halliburton, *New Worlds to Conquer* (Indianapolis: Bobbs-Merrill, 1929), 152.

95. Hans Otto Storm, *Pity the Tyrant* (New York: Longmans, Green, 1937).

96. Luis E. Valcárcel, *Tempestad en los Andes* (Lima, Peru: Populibros Peruanos, 1927), 19.

97. The episode is well narrated by Osmar Gonzales, "José Carlos Mariátegui y los judíos," http://librosperuanos.com/autores/articulo/0000002166/Jose-Carlos-Mariategui-y-los-judios.

98. Quoted in Gonzales, *La presencia judía*, 3.

99. Correspondence between Mariátegui and Vallejo can be read at https://socialismoperuanoamauta.blogspot.de/2009/03/dos-cartas-de-mariategui-cesar-vallejo.html.

100. Quoted in Gonzales, *La presencia judía*, 8.

101. Carlos Aguirre, *The Criminals of Lima and Their Worlds: The Prison Experience, 1850–1935* (Durham, NC: Duke University Press, 2005), 104–09.

102. Cited ibid., 106.

103. Cited ibid.

104. Alberto Flores Galindo, *La agonía de Mariátegui: la polémica con el Komintern* (Lima: Centro de Estudios y Promoción del Desarrollo, 1980), 68.

105. Del Prado, *Los años cumbres*, 93.

106. Mariátegui to Glusberg, November 21, 1929, in *José Carlos*

Mariátegui, Correspondencia (1915–1930), vol. 2, ed. Antonio Melis (Lima: Biblioteca Amauta, 1984).

107. Mariátegui to Adler, July 13, 1929, collection of Manuel Adler.

108. Manuel Adler to Claudio Lomnitz, February 26, 2017.

109. Leguía, *Yo tirano*, 32.

Part Two: The Debacle

9: ADULTHOOD

110. Porfirio Díaz del Castillo, *El Valle del Cauca, historia y realidades de sus municipios* (Cali: Imprenta de Márquez, 1937), 194–95.

111. Miguel Adler to Paul Rivet, July 7, 1953, Correspondence of Paul Rivet, ZAP1C1A, Musée de L'Homme.

112. James Clifford, "On Ethnographic Surrealism," *Comparative Studies in Society and History* 23, no. 14 (1981): 539–64.

113. Christine Laurière has written the standard work of reference on the life and work of Paul Rivet: *Paul Rivet, le savant et le politique* (Paris: Publications Scientifiques du Musée National d'Histoire Naturelle, 2008).

114. Laurière summarizes these events and their strong effect on Paul Rivet and the ethnologists of the Institut d'Ethnologie (ibid.. 487).

115. Curzio Malaparte, *Kaputt*, English trans. Cesare Foligno (Marlboro, UK: Marlboro Press, 1982), 39.

10: GENOCIDE

116. Naphtoli Rabinovici, *Ich und mein Shtetele* (Tel Aviv: private edition, 1965), ch. 12, translated for the author by Elisheva Shaul.

117. Ibid., ch. 13.

118. Ibid., ch. 18.

119. Ibid., ch. 25.

120. Jean Ancel, *Transnistria, 1941–1942: The Romanian Mass Murder Campaigns*, 3 vols. (Tel Aviv: Tel Aviv University Press, 2003), 17.

121. Ibid., 24.

122. Matatias Carp, *The Black Book: The Sufferings of the Jews from Romania, 1940–1944*, vol. 1: *The Legionary Movement and the Rebellion*, trans. Gerda Tanner (Bucharest: Socec & Co. S.A.R. Publishing, 1946), 8.

123. Ibid.

124. Ibid., 9.

125. Carp (*The Black Book*, 15) calculates the number of dead in the Nova Sulitza pogrom at around 800; the number 975 is from Pinkas HaKehilot, "'Novoselitsa' (Novoselytsya, Ukraine)," *Encyclopedia of Jewish Communities in Romania* (Jerusalem: Yad Vashem, 1980), 2:7, and it is based on facts that were not available at the time of Carp's meticulous treatise.

126. Rabinovici, *Ich und mein Shtetele*, ch. 44.

127. Carp, *The Black Book*, 16.

128. Ibid.

129. Malaparte, *Kaputt*, 144–45.

130. Josef Govrin, *In the Shadow of Destruction: Recollections of Transnistria and Illegal Immigration to Eretz Israel, 1941–1947* (London: Vallentine Mitchell, 2007), 23.

131. Malaparte, *Kaputt,* 143.

132. HaKehilot, "Novoselitsa," 7.

133. Manuel Adler to Claudio Lomnitz, September 29, 2016.

134. This account—minus the portions that tell directly about my family—comes from HaKehilot, "Novoselitsa," whose source was one of Nova Sulitza's deportees, who signs with the initials S.A.G.

135. Rabinovici, *Ich und mein Shtetele,* ch. 53.

136. Ibid., 8.

11: THE NATIONAL DISEASE

137. Hannah Arendt, *Eichmann in Jerusalem: A Report on the Banality of Evil* (New York: Penguin Classics, 2006 [1963]), chs. 4–6.

138. Ibid., 252.

139. Ibid., 43.

140. Matei Calinescu, "Ionesco and *Rhinoceros*: Personal and Political Backgrounds," *East European Politics and Societies* 9, no.3 (1995): 417.

141. A French translation was published in 1998, an English translation in 2001. See Mihail Sebastian, *Journal, 1935–1944* (London: Pimlico, 2003).

142. Eugène Ionesco, *Present Past, Past Present*, trans. Helen R. Lane (New York: Grove Press, 1971), 78–79.

143. Sebastian, *Journal*, 370.

144. Ibid., 382.

145. Ibid., 385.

146. Mircea Eliade, *The Portugal Journal (1941–1945)*, trans. Mac Linscott Ricketts (Albany: SUNY Press), 8.

147. Ibid., 9.

148. Ibid., 65.

149. Cristiano Grottanelli, "Fruitful Death: Mircea Eliade and Ernst Jünger on Human Sacrifice, 1937–1945," *Numen* 52, no. 1 (2005): 119.

150. Mircea Eliade, *Journal I, 1945–1955*, trans. Mac Liscott Ricketts (Chicago: University of Chicago Press, 1990 [1973]), entry for 11 October 1946.

151. Ionesco, *Present Past*, 116–18.

CODA: SHURA

152. Rita Grossman to Claudio Lomnitz, August 14, 2017.

153. Rabinovici, *Ich und Mein Shtetele*, chs. 57 and 58.

154. Ilana Shtar to Claudio Lomnitz, December 12, 2016.

Part Three: Colombian Refuge

12: FAMILY LIFE

155. J. M. Eguren, "María," *Repertorio Hebreo* 1, no. 1 (April–May 1929): 8.

156. Gustavo Alvarez Gardeazábal to Claudio Lomnitz, June 16, 2017.

157. Lina María Leal Villamizar, *Colombia frente al anti-Semitismo y la inmigración de judíos polacos y alemanes, 1933–1948*, master's thesis, History Department, Universidad Nacional de Colombia (2011), 4.

158. Ibid., 5.

159. Ibid., 58.

160. "Nota editorial," *Nuestra Tribuna* 4, no. 43 (1937): 1.

161. Quoted in Leal Villamizar, *Colombia frente al antisemitismo,* 25.

162. Ibid., 30.

163. Prefectura de Lima, Inspección de Investigación y Vigilancia, Mesa de Partes y Archivo, lib. D, fol. 1, núm. 19 (October 7, 1930).

164. Simón Guberek, "El problema de la educación entre nosotros," trans. from the Yiddish by Miguel Adler. *Nuestra Tribuna* 4, no. 43 (1937): 26–28.

165. Ibid., 26.

166. Ibid., 27.

167. Ibid., 28.

168. Simón Guberek, *A yid in Colombie* (Buenos Aires, 1973), chapter "Los Idelmans," trans. from Yiddish by Elisheva Shaul.

169. Senator Armando Solano, in *Nuevo Mundo,* December 1, 1938.

170. For the rich history of Jewish publishing in Buenos Aires, see Alejandro Dujovne, *Una historia del libro judío: la cultura judía argentina a través de sus editores, libreros, traductores, imprentas y bibliotecas* (Buenos Aires: Siglo XXI, 2014).

171. Manuel Adler to Claudio Lomnitz, June 20, 2017.

172. Guberek, "El problema de la educación," 26.

13: THE NEED FOR A NEW WORLD

173. "Normas y propósitos," *Nuevo Mundo* 1, no. 1 (April 1943): 1.

174. "Nuestra portada," *Nuevo Mundo* 1, no. 1 (April 1943): 1.

175. Miguel Adler, "El destino del nuevo continente," *Nuevo Mundo* 1, no. 1 (April 1943): 3.

176. Miguel Adler, "El caso de Agustín Tisoy," *Nuevo Mundo* 1, no. 1 (April 1943): 57.

177. Agustín Tisoy, "Lo que me contó mi abuelita," *Nuevo Mundo* 1, no. 1 (April 1943): 57.

14: THE LIMITS OF ADAPTATION

178. Larissa Adler to Claudio Lomnitz, February 6, 2016.

179. Alberto Flores Galindo, *La agonía de Mariátegui: la polémica con el Komintern* (Lima: Centro de Estudios y Promoción del Desarrollo, 1980), 194–97.

180. "Trotski reconoce la necesidad de una patria hebrea," *Nuestra Tribuna* 4, no. 43 (April 1937): 35.

181. Lazar Jeifets and Víctor Jeifets to Claudio Lomnitz, August 29, 2017. See also Lazar Jeifets and Víctor Jeifets, "América latina en la Internacional Comunista, 1919–1943," *Diccionario biográfico* (Santiago de Chile: Adriadna Ediciones, 2004).

182. Terry Martin, *The Affirmative Action Empire: Nations and Nationalism in the Soviet Union, 1923–1939* (Ithaca, NY: Cornell University Press, 2001).

183. Ibid., 9.

184. Diana Dumitru, *The State, Anti-Semitism, and Collaboration in the Holocaust: The Borderlands of Romania and the Soviet Union* (New York: Cambridge University Press, 2016), 97.

185. See Marianne Hirsch and Leo Spitzer, *Ghosts of Home: The*

Afterlife of Czernowitz in Jewish Memory (Berkeley: University of California Press, 2010), 105.

186. Miguel Adler, "Los judíos en la URSS," *Repertorio Hebreo* 1, no. 2 (June 1929): 2.

187. Dumitru, *State, Anti-Semitism, and Collaboration*, 95.

188. Ibid.., 57.

189. Ibid., 90–92.

190. Ibid., 181.

191. Robert Weinberg, *Stalin's Forgotten Zion: Birobidzhan and the Making of a Soviet Jewish Homeland: An Illustrated History, 1928–1996* (Berkeley: University of California Press, 1998).

192. Ibid., 67–71 and 82–85. See also Masha Gessen, *Where the Jews Aren't: The Sad and Absurd Story of Birobidzhan, Russia's Jewish Autonomous Region* (New York: Schocken, 2016).

193. Miguel Ben-Tzvi Adler, "Grancolombia del mundo judío," *Grancolombia* 1, no. 1 (July 25, 1947): 11.

194. Ibid.

195. Ibid., 3.

196. María Victoria Uribe to Claudio Lomnitz, August 14, 2017.

197. Adler, "Grancolombia del mundo judío," 11.

198. Thomas Williford, *Armando los Espíritus: Political Rhetoric in Colombia on the Eve of La Violencia, 1930–1945*, PhD thesis, Department of History, Vanderbilt University (2005), 149 and passim.

199. Daría Betancourt Echeverry, "El 9 de abril en Cali y en el Valle," www.bdigital.unal.edu.co/35700/1/36113-149818-1-PB.pdf.

200. Miguel Adler to Paul Rivet, July 7, 1953, Correspondance de Paul Rivet, 2A1C1A_Adler, Biblioteque Musée de l'Homme.

15: THE LIMITS OF TRANSLATION

201. Manuel Adler to Claudio Lomnitz, June 20, 2017.

202. Gustavo Alvarez Gardeazábal, *Cóndores no entierran todos los días* (Barcelona: Ediciones Destino, 1972), 57.

203. Ibid., 60.

204. Ibid., 135.

205. Manuel Adler to Claudio Lomnitz, June 20, 2017.

206. Gustavo Alvarez Gardeazábal to Claudio Lomnitz, June 19, 2017.

16: DIALECTIC OF SILENCE

207. Ilana Shtar to Claudio Lomnitz, August 15, 2017.

Part Four: National Liberation

208. Miguel Adler to Paul Rivet, July 7, 1953.

209. Bronislawa Aronsfrau Lomnitz, "Autobiographie," unpublished ms., in English (c. 1963), Barbara Lomnitz Collection.

210. Ibid.

211. Cinna Lomnitz, "Mi vida," unpublished ms. (1987), 100–01.

212. Ibid., 101.

213. Ibid.

214. Ibid.

215. Ibid.

216. Miguel Adler to Paul Rivet, July 7, 1953.

217. Victor Perlman to Claudio Lomnitz, August 9, 2017.

Part Five: *Childhood as a Collective Achievement*

218. My translation, with apologies to Neruda and my readers.

219. Cinna Lomnitz, "Mi vida," unpublished ms. (1987).

220. Ibid.

221. Alfred Brehm, *Brehms Tierleben* (1863–69) (Berlin: Safari-Verlag, 1950 [1863]).

222. Cinna Lomnitz to Claudio Lomnitz, October 18, 2009.

223. Bronislawa Aronsfrau Lomnitz, "Autobiographie," unpublished ms., in English (c. 1963), Barbara Lomnitz Collection.

224. Cinna Lomnitz to Claudio Lomnitz, October 20, 2009.

225. Robert G. Waite, *Vanguard of Nazism: The Free Corps Movement in Post-War Germany, 1918–1923* (New York: Norton, 1952), 214.

226. The source for this Wikipedia entry is Martin Sabrow, *Der Rathenaumord. Rekonstruktion einer Verschworun gegen die Republik von Weimar* (Munich: Oldenbourg, 1994).

227. Ernst von Salomon, *Fragebogen*, trans. Constantine Fitzgibbon (New York: Doubleday, 1955), 56.

228. Quoted in Martin Sabrow to Claudio Lomnitz, October 31, 2017.

229. Salomon, *Fragebogen.*

230. Bronislawa Aronsfrau Lomnitz, "Autobiographie."

231. Ibid.

232. Karen Strobel with the cooperation of Brigitte Zwerger, "From Hatred to Violence: The Early Völkish Movement and NSDAP until 1922 in Mannheim," unpublished ms. (2020).

233. Paul Lerner, *The Consuming Temple: Jews, Department Stores, and the Consumer Revolution in Germany, 1880–1940* (Ithaca, NY: Cornell University Press, 2015).

234. Bronislawa Aronsfrau Lomnitz, "Autobiographie."

235. See Vinkash Pandey and Sverre Holm, "Linking the Fractional Derivative and the Lomnitz Creep Law to Non-Newtonian Time-Varying Viscosity," *Physical Review* E94, 032606 (2016).

236. Cinna Lomnitz, "Mi vida."

237. Ibid., cuaderno 1, 12–13.

238. Ibid., 16–17.

239. Ibid., 17.

240. Ibid., 13.

241. *Frankfürter Zeitung*, May 25, 1922, cited in Sabrow, *Der Rathenaumord*, note 26. Translation by Stephan Rinke.

242. Quoted in Waite, *Vanguard of Nazism*.

243. Larissa Adler to Claudio Lomnitz, February 6, 2016.

Illustration Credits

72: From María Leal Villamizar, "Columbia frente al antisemitismo y la inmigración de judíos polacos y alemanes 1933–1948," master's thesis, Department of History, Universidad Nacional de Colombia (2011).

75: Collection of Victor Perlman.

79: Reproduction of a nineteenth-century photograph, Biblioteca Nacional del Perú, Archivo Courret. Reproduced from Wikimedia Commons.

81 (*left*): Reproduction of a 1920 photograph, Centro de Estudios Histórico Militares del Perú. Reproduced from Wikimedia Commons.

81 (*right*): Reproduction of a photograph by Harris & Ewing, Library of Congress Prints and Photographs Division, Detroit Publishing Company Collection.

100: From *Mariátegui total*.

102, 169 (*bottom*): From Jorge del Prado Chávez, *En los años cumbres de Mariátegui* (Lima: Unidad, 1983).

138: *Repertorio Hebreo* 1:26.

139: *Repertorio Hebreo* 1:30.

154: From Halliburton, *New Worlds to Conquer* (1929).

171: Collection of Tania Lomnitz. Photograph by Emiliano Landa.

172 (*right*): Courtesy of Cristóbal Aljovín and Juan Carlos Lupú.

208: *Grancolombia* 1, no. 1 (July 23, 1947): 1.

226, 228, 234, 255, 257 (*left*): Collection of Rita Grossman.

235: Courtesy of Gustavo Álvarez Gardeazábal.

241: *Anacleto*, December 4, 1938, in María Leal Villamizar, "Columbia frente al antisemitismo y la inmigración de judíos polacos y alemanes 1933–1948," master's thesis, Department of History, Universidad Nacional de Colombia (2011).

252: *El Tiempo*, December 2, 1942, 1.

257 (*right*): Courtesy of Roberto Esquenazi.

277: From Dumitru, *State, Anti-Semitism, and Collaboration*, 134.

287: *Grancolombia* 1, no. 1 (July, 1947): 15.

295: *Grancolombia* 1, no. 1 (July 25, 1947): 10.

368: Courtesy of Professor Martin Sabrow.

373, 377: Collection of Barbara Lomnitz.

381: Courtesy of Mannheim City Archives.

383, 385: Courtesy of Karen Strobel.

386: Courtesy of Karen Strobel and Mannheim City Archives.

408: https://www.inaturalist.org/taxa/83930-Phanaeus.

409: Collection of Mauricio Adler.

CLAUDIO LOMNITZ is an anthropologist, historian, and critic who works broadly on Latin American culture and politics. He is Professor of Anthropology at Columbia University. Lomnitz's books include *Death and the Idea of Mexico* and *The Return of Comrade Ricardo Flores Magón*, among many others. As a regular columnist for the Mexico City paper *La Jornada* and an award-winning dramaturgist, he is committed to bringing historical and anthropological understanding into public debate.